Praise for *Creative Strategy Generation*

"Mixing traditional marketing acumen and understanding with the creative process of songwriting, Bob encapsulates how the two worlds of business and music can provide the storytelling tools that help shape a solid business strategy. This book is incredibly informational and entertaining to see the parallels between art and the fundamentals of business."

Bill Richards, VP Marketing, Sony Music Entertainment

"Caporale effectively invokes the mindset and language of the artist—the canvas, melodies, and story arcs—to create a highly practical toolkit that will be especially useful for practitioners looking to compose product and business unit-level strategy."

Sean Gallagher, Chief Strategy Officer,
Northeastern University Global Network

"*Creative Strategy Generation* provides a fresh new look at the topic of strategy. Using his passion for music as the starting point, Bob Caporale provides us with a step-by-step guide for infusing much-needed creativity into the strategic planning process. A must-read for anyone seeking to add more value to their products or brands!"

John Gerzema, *New York Times* bestselling author,
social strategist, and leadership consultant

"Bob Caporale composes a book on strategy that is influenced by and extends classic strategic frameworks by infusing his own passion to create an easily accessible read that will be sure to have you singing along!"

Kevin D. Rooney, former Chief Strategy Officer,
American Access Casualty Co.

"I worked in Product Management and Strategy for most of my career, and I wish I had this book to revert back to during annual planning meetings and product launches. Bob has laid out strategy planning in a very easy to follow storybook. I know I will share this methodology with my colleagues and can't wait to use it for my next strategy plan!"

Cheryl Nash, President, Fiserv Investment Services

"Mr. Caporale presents a compelling model, blending the expressiveness of art with the objectivity of strategy. A thought-provoking approach, keeping the customer perspective in the forefront and providing a dose of reality throughout."

Steve Thompson, VP Business Strategy, National Oilwell Varco

"As a founder of a high-growth start-up with no preexisting roadmap to follow, I appreciate the way that Bob demystifies the strategy process and gives us specific and practical tools for creating our own unique product and market strategies. Most strategy books point to high-profile success stories and try to extract common themes for us to follow. But every success story contains a complex mix of ingredients that are hard to "bottle" for others to repeat. Bob's process doesn't rely upon the past but, rather, gives business practitioners real tools for building their own paths to success."

Aaron Gowell, Chief Conductor, SilverRail Tech

CREATIVE STRATEGY GENERATION

USING PASSION AND CREATIVITY TO COMPOSE BUSINESS STRATEGIES THAT INSPIRE ACTION AND GROWTH

BOB CAPORALE

New York   Chicago   San Francisco   Athens   London
Madrid   Mexico City   Milan   New Delhi
Singapore   Sydney   Toronto

1 2 3 4 5 6 7 8 9 0   DOC/DOC   1 2 1 0 9 8 7 6 5

ISBN   978–0–07–185011–7
MHID   0–07–185011–2

e-ISBN   978–0–07–185012–4
e-MHID   0–07–185012–0

Library of Congress Cataloging-in-Publication Data

Caporale, Bob.
   Creative strategy generation : using passion and creativity to compose business strategies that inspire action and growth / Bob Caporale.—1 Edition.
      pages cm
   ISBN 978-0-07-185011-7 (hardback : alk. paper)—ISBN 0-07-185011-2 (alk. paper)
1. Strategic planning.   2. Creative ability in business.   I. Title.
   HD30.28.C3764 2015
   658.4'012—dc23   2015016487

McGraw-Hill Education books are available at special quantity discounts to use as premiums and sales promotions or for use in corporate training programs. To contact a representative, please visit the Contact Us pages at www.mhprofessional.com.

This book is dedicated to every mentor that I have ever had, including bosses, colleagues, family, friends, team members, suppliers, customers, and even a few passing acquaintances. I have learned something from each one of you and continue to do so every day of my life.

I would also like to dedicate this book to my brother, Anthony, who taught me not to be afraid to "drop the bike."

CONTENTS

FOREWORD

It's an honor and a privilege to write this Foreword. My goal for this is to inspire you to embrace this book and its content. My hope is that it will be a faithful companion and resource for business practitioners, strategists, product managers, and others who will craft various strategies in their careers.

Bob and I have worked together for about five years. He started out as a client at Sequent Learning Networks and now serves as the company's president. When he first started at Sequent, I couldn't help notice what he was up to. First, he purposefully connected with everyone to understand what they did, how, and with whom. Next, he carefully looked at what we did as a company: operations, sales, marketing, finance, and so on. He examined the financials and evaluated our competitors. His hunger for information seemed insatiable. In a nutshell, Bob was listening to the drumbeat of our business. He wanted to get his mind around where we were and where we were going. While my vision was clear to me, it needed some fine-tuning. What we have now is a greatly unified vision for our company, a clear strategy, and the wherewithal to execute.

I worked in the corporate world for decades, in finance, operations, and product management. I started Sequent Learning Networks in 2002 to help companies organize more effectively so they could produce the products that customers would clamor for. Over the years, I've benchmarked hundreds of large, complex firms. One of the consistent findings from this research reveals that a large number of people who work in these firms, who should be able to articulate the strategy for the firms in which they work, cannot. This dissonance is reinforced in findings from the diagnostics I carry out. In these evaluations, I often seek to learn how product people and other business professionals defend their investments. To do this, I ask, "What do you do to ensure that your investments are strategically important?" In more cases than not, people (regardless of function) cannot answer this question. This is quite troubling.

Given the number of great strategy books and other resources available, one would think that strategy formulation should be a cinch. With this, shouldn't everyone in the organization be able to march to the beat of the same drummer? It's logical, but not the reality.

In his genes Bob Caporale is a business strategist. He's also a musician and composer. His successes in all aspects of his life are directly attributable to this uncanny ability to tie together his creative self and his rational self. In that bridge between those two worlds, he's discovered how to connect disparate pieces of what is often a complex puzzle. These could be parts of a musical composition or parts of an organization. The main idea is that he seeks to create harmony. In a business, it's a hard thing to do. Yet he does so with aplomb.

What he's done with this book is to extend this gift to business practitioners who can learn by example. When they do, they can then teach other people, and by association, become better leaders.

The chapters in the book relate directly to what's done to compose music. I can safely say now that I "get it," because when I started I knew nothing about musical composition. As I studied the content and how things were connected, I was able to see things more holistically. It was then that I realized that strategic planning and strategy formulation can be made much easier when they are broken down into easy-to-digest pieces, and then reassembled to put the big picture back into perspective! Then I realized that what Bob did in the book is what he did with Sequent Learning Networks and what he's done with the numerous clients, leadership teams, and individuals he's taught.

Bob Caporale, in *Creative Strategy Generation*, has created a work of art that business practitioners and organizational leaders can use to demystify and simplify their approach to strategic planning. The benefits will be apparent: clear vision to the future and the ability to harmonize resources that ultimately produce optimal outcomes and the encores you strive for.

Steven Haines
Author of *The Product Manager's Desk Reference*

INTRODUCTION

I am a business strategist. I'm not sure if such a thing officially exists, but I do know that this is exactly what I have spent most of my career doing. I am not a professor or a well-studied scholar or the CEO of a large corporation. I develop strategies for products, portfolios, and business units, and I have done so for over 20 years, many times over. These days, I spend most of my time advising and training other practitioners about how to develop these types of strategies. And it is exactly from this position that I felt I needed to write this book.

There are plenty of resources available for corporate-level strategists. There are, however, far fewer resources available for the thousands of product managers, marketing professionals, and other business unit–level strategists who are tasked with developing and implementing strategies, while being continually reminded that they may not have the training, knowledge, tools, or time to do so. Ironically, this is where the majority of business strategies reside. Yet this is also where the biggest gap seems to exist between strategic theory and strategic practice.

Most of the books I've read about business strategy seem to approach the topic from one of two main directions. In the first corner is the academic approach. Here, the reader is usually presented with a series of observational case studies of companies that have successfully developed and implemented strategies. From these case studies authors attempt to deconstruct the thought process behind the strategies, and from these analyses they develop frameworks that can be followed by others.

In the second corner is the consultative approach. This is usually undertaken by a person or group of people who have served as consultants for companies and who have actually helped those companies develop and implement their strategies. Books written from this perspective usually start out by putting down the academic approach as being too theoretical or not practical enough. And so they march forward drawing from their very specific experiences with a handful of very specific companies, to derive theories that may or may not apply on a broader scale.

And maybe there's a third corner somewhere in between the first two in which a high-level business executive (usually a CEO of a big corporation) writes about his or her own experiences with developing

xii   Introduction

and implementing a strategy for a very large enterprise. This approach is usually very interesting and insightful to anyone who is familiar with the company in question. But it may not be applicable to someone who sits below the highest levels of his or her own company and who is tasked with developing strategies for a product line, portfolio, or another functional area of a business.

Please understand that I am not putting down any of these approaches, because I truly believe that they all have merit in that they can inspire new ways to think, feel, and act. So how can that be a bad thing? But I do feel that there's a fourth, perhaps as of yet untapped, corner that can still be explored.

All of the aforementioned three approaches seem to be directed at senior-level leaders who are tasked with applying broad strategic concepts across complex organizations. The examples and cases that are presented are usually of large companies that overcame major macro-level obstacles to arrive at whatever level of success they ultimately achieved, and the resulting strategies are usually backed by deep pockets and very high levels of authority. It is for this reason, I believe, that practitioners of what I'll call the more "functional" strategies within an organization might have trouble relating to these approaches. And so the lessons that they teach may fall somewhat short of connecting with a broader audience of strategic practitioners.

The other problem with these strategic approaches is that they often rely heavily on showing people how to imitate what another company already successfully executed. And although the execution of these strategies is often analyzed (and perhaps overanalyzed) in depth, the reader is usually still left asking questions about how they were conceived in the first place. What were people at these companies thinking? How did they come up with their strategic ideas? What exactly was going on in their heads, not in hindsight, but at the moment their strategies were conceived? These are difficult questions to address, and so they are often left unanswered.

Ironically, the answer to these questions lies at the very heart of how we should be teaching strategy to the people who are actually responsible for creating it. When we instruct people how to imitate, we get a collection of mediocre plans, developed by semi-interested strategists who fill in required templates on an annual basis just because their bosses told them to. Unfortunately the strategic results follow in kind.

If this sounds anything like what you or your teams are experiencing, then this "fourth-corner" book is for you.

If you want to understand what drives a person to develop and execute a truly great strategy, you have to first see that the process of building a strategy is not an academic or imitative endeavor—it is a creative one. The difference, in my mind at least, is that an academic endeavor is undertaken for a "grade," which is largely based on your ability to re-create or regurgitate that which is already known or has already been done. A creative endeavor, on the other hand, is aimed at producing something truly unique and different, and that is based largely on the creator's passion to change the world, even if in some small way.

When you're developing a strategy because you've been told you have to and, worse, you've been told that it needs to look like something that has already been done before, that's just another form of a "grade." But if you develop a strategy because you truly love the journey, you passionately care about the result, and you're willing to break a few of the established rules to achieve your goal, then you've entered the realm of creativity. That's where most successful strategies reside, and that's where the teaching needs to begin.

I indicated earlier that I've been developing successful strategies for most of my career. What I didn't tell you is that I have also been writing music for a good part of my life and that I consider myself to be both a composer and a songwriter. Although this is by no means my full-time job, I do have five independently released albums, several corporate video soundtracks, and even a full-length musical to my name. I write music because I love to do so. I love sitting down at the piano and turning my emotion into a musical idea; I love capturing that idea into a recording; I love adding different musical parts and instruments to turn the idea into a song; I love listening to the finished piece and reliving the emotion I felt when I wrote it; I love sharing that song with others; and I love the effect it has when it is being listened to and enjoyed. I love the entire journey—and that's why I do it.

Believe it or not, I feel exactly the same way about developing strategies. And the success I've had with both developing strategies and teaching others how to do the same has come from applying the same creative process that I use to write music. In this way, I like to say that I *compose* my strategies rather than develop them. It might sound like a subtle semantic difference, but as you'll see throughout this book, it's an important one, if only to continually remind myself of the parallels.

So this book is about correlating the very creative process of writing music with the equally creative process of composing strategies. It is a highly personal account, and you will undoubtedly see that throughout. But to focus on *my* process would be missing the point. What I am really hoping to do by using this metaphor is to encourage you to find and apply *your own* creative process to the art of strategic planning. All of us are creative beings, whether that creativity displays itself through music, art, writing, performance, business, or science. The trick is to find whatever it is that you are passionate about creating and apply that same process to your business strategies. I'll show you how to do it using my passion, but if in so doing I inspire you to find your own creative metaphor, I'll be just about the happiest author on the planet!

It's at this point that I want to set expectations about what this book is, and what it isn't, as well as who I am and who I am not.

First of all, although I was a fairly good student, I tend to be a much more tactile learner. That is to say, I learn by doing and practicing and feeling my way through things. As a result, I have taken the same intuitive approach to writing this book. The process that I will share with you has been validated many times over; some through my own strategic successes, some through the successes of the hundreds of managers and marketers to whom I have taught these techniques throughout my career, and some through the training and advisory company that I run with my esteemed colleague Steven Haines, the well-known author of *The Product Manager's Desk Reference*. If you are expecting to find dozens of case studies and examples of large companies that have used this process for their corporate strategies, however, then you've come to the wrong place. See Corners 1 or 2 for that type of approach.

I think my 13-year-old son summed it up best. When I told him that I was doing research for my new book, he replied, "If you're writing a book about Abraham Lincoln, do research. If you're writing a book about strategy, make it up!" Of course, his position was partially based on the fact that he wanted me to take him to the movies that day instead of working on my book. Still, there was a lot of simple truth in his statement. And, although I don't intend to make anything up, I will definitely be sharing more perspective than research because, at least in my opinion, that's where I believe successful strategy comes from.

Second, since much of what I will write about is based on my own experiences and observations, I have tried to include as many examples as I can of everyday practitioners applying this creative process to the business of developing functional strategies. Some of these examples are hypothetical, others are accounts of real companies or situations that I have encountered or observed, and still others are a hybrid between the two. In all cases, I have attempted to ground the concepts that I am presenting in real-life scenarios so that you will be better able to relate to and apply them into your own particular situations.

Finally I want to say that I am not writing a book just for the sake of seeing my name in print; in fact, quite the opposite. Quite frankly, I am terrified at the thought of putting myself "out there" for all to criticize.

But the reason I'm fighting through that fear is because I really feel there is a need, and I also feel that I can help. The fact is, I currently spend most of my time going into large international corporations and teaching these techniques to highly skilled, very experienced, very intelligent individuals who simply do not know how to put together a strategy. They've read all the books, and many have graduated with honors from highly acclaimed MBA programs from around the globe. Even so, they seem to struggle with really being able to get their hands around this subject. Many of these individuals are in marketing or product management positions within their companies, and because of that they are expected to be able to develop clear and actionable strategies for the businesses that they support. Many more are business unit leaders or general managers who, although they may have a harder time admitting it, struggle with exactly the same thing. I help them, and lights go on. And I want to try to share this with you as well.

One more little qualifier before we get started: if, by way of my Introduction, you're expecting a book that ignores all of the previous strategic theories and encourages radical free thought, you may be sorely disappointed. One of the reasons that I like the songwriting analogy so much is that music is based on hundreds of years of standardized theory, frameworks, and styles that every great songwriter must have in his or her toolbox. The creativity doesn't come from ignoring these things but rather from using and applying them in unique and different ways. This is also true of strategic theory. Throughout this book, not only will I be referring to many of these standardized strategic tools, I will also be letting you know about their origins, why they came to be, and how they are most commonly applied. My hope in doing this is to give you the most comprehensive toolbox possible that you can utilize in your creative strategic process. Again, we do not want to ignore hundreds of years of theory; we simply want to apply it in new and different ways.

With all of that said, I cannot teach you how to be creative. What I can do is teach you how to tap into the creativity that you are innately born with but perhaps didn't know you had. I can teach you how to find your passion in the strategic process by correlating it to something you truly care about and believe in and love. As much as it's been written about, the subject of strategy still seems to elude so many people. But it's not in the theory; it's in the application. And I intend to help bridge that gap through this book.

So please join me as we explore the wonderful, fascinating art of creative strategy generation.

There are not more than five musical notes, yet the combinations of these five give rise to more melodies than can ever be heard.

—Sun Tzu, *The Art of War*

PART

1

PROFICIENCIES

INTRODUCTION

Everything we create, no matter the genre or application, will contain two basic elements: inputs and outputs. In the simplest of terms, you take some amount of raw material (the input) and then you apply some process or processes to that material in order to create something different from what you started with (the output).

Strategy is no different. There will be inputs to your strategy, and there will be outputs. The inputs will generally be where you are now and where you've been before; the outputs will generally be where you're going and how you want to get there. Classic strategic theory has challenged us with these very questions:

- Where are we now?
- Where have we been?
- Where do we want to go?
- How are we going to get there?

Four simple questions to answer, the culmination of which will form your strategic plan. That sounds simple enough. So what's the catch?

1

The first catch is that, although developing a strategic plan is a process, you will need to be able to think creatively in order to get an output from this process that is truly unique. I'll tackle this subject in depth in Part 2 of this book as I step through the process of creative strategy generation.

Before I address this first catch, however, I need to address the second, which is that you're going to have to take a bit of time to build your strategic skills before you just jump into the business of developing a strategic plan. Few people can simply walk up to a piano and start writing a song. Before you jump right in, you need to take a little time to study music theory, find out how the instrument works, and learn to develop your "ear" for how certain feelings can be expressed through sound and music. The same can be said for developing a strategy, although it seems that far fewer people actually take the time to build their critical strategic skills before attempting, right out of the gate, to put together a strategic plan.

You might be thinking that the skills I'm talking about stem from classic strategic theory: the kind that people are often taught about in business school. In my view, that's only one part of the puzzle.

The academic part of strategy is all about looking at the past: seeing what other companies have done and trying to capture the successes into a framework that can be reapplied by others. This is useful and necessary, but only one of what I believe are four broad sets of skills that you need to have. Because these are broader areas within which several more specific skills will be required, I am going to refer to these four groupings as "proficiencies," which implies not only that you possess certain skills within each grouping but also that you master them to some degree.

To capture these four proficiencies, I tend to think of everything in terms of relative time. Back to our four questions, we are really asking about the past, the present, the future, and how those three dimensions will all come together to determine the ultimate path. It's really that simple, and it's a formula that has been used successfully time and time again. In fact, many of us watch this formula play out multiple times every year when we view the thousandth or so replay of Charles Dickens's classic story *A Christmas Carol*. Every December we sit glued to our television sets to watch remake after remake and spin-off after spin-off of this classic tale in which the main character visits his past, present, and future and uses that information to affect some strategic change. The formula works, and we relate to it because, by and large, this is the way we all live out our own lives.

So that covers three of the proficiencies: the ability to understand the past, the present, and the future. So what is the fourth?

The fourth ingredient might just be the most important one of all. The past, present, and future are just about information: where we are now, where we have been, and where we want to go. These are just data points. And although you will need certain skills to collect and understand these data points, our fourth proficiency gives us the wherewithal to do something with all of this information and process it into an actionable plan: How are we going to get there?

Ebenezer Scrooge could have awoken from his final visitation and decided not to do anything with the information that he had gathered. But that's not what happened. Instead, he was driven to put all of those pieces together, process them, and then take action upon them. That's the final proficiency I want to try and capture.

Many things can motivate this fourth proficiency. In the case of Ebenezer Scrooge, he was motivated by fear, which, by the way, has also driven many a great strategy throughout the years. Sometimes the motivation is greed, other times it's compassion, and still other times the call to action might be motivated by the desire to build or create something or to leave a legacy of some type. Whatever the driving force, the fourth set of skills has to do with having both the desire and the drive to do something about whatever you have learned. And the action you take will ultimately become your chosen path.

So those are areas around which we must develop our proficiencies:

- Past
- Present
- Future
- Path

The problem is, these are conditions, not proficiencies. So what are the proficiencies that correspond with each of these areas?

Here's the way I see it: What do you do when you reflect on the past? In general, you are recalling a situation, and using your memory of what happened to ignite some emotion that will ultimately bring you to action. The proficiency required for this is *Recollection*.

Looking at the present, we can immediately think in terms of classic strategic theory where we are taught to observe and understand key elements of our surroundings such as our environment, our enemies, and our own comparative strengths and weaknesses. What we are doing is scanning and analyzing our current situation. That proficiency is *Analysis*.

For the future component, we are looking toward what will likely occur but which cannot be currently proven. Our ability to see the future more accurately than anyone else is one of the most important ingredients to a winning strategy. The proficiency that will get us there is the ability to use our "gut instinct" more effectively than anyone else. That proficiency is *Intuition*.

The last proficiency is perhaps the most difficult to capture and also the most difficult to teach. But it is also the proficiency that is perhaps the most critical to bringing a strategy to life. This last proficiency is that unseen force that drives people not only to act but also to *act differently*—from their past, from their present, from their otherwise predestined future. The differentiation is the key. And that doesn't just require action; it requires creativity. The proficiency that best enables this drive to both create and to perform is *Artistry*. And from this proficiency will arise a person's strategic path.

So now we have our four broad proficiencies:

Present = **A**nalysis
   Past = **R**ecollection
Future = **I**ntuition
   Path = **A**rtistry

In keeping with my musical analogy, these four proficiencies come together, as luck would have it, to form the mnemonic ARIA. And the order, although a bit different than *A Christmas Carol*, has significance as well, because for most strategies you start with where you are, then visit where you've been, then think about where you're going, and finally process it all creatively to determine how you want to forge your path into the future.

In Part 1 of this book, we'll explore each of these four proficiencies and discuss some of the key steps you can take to help build each one. This will be critical, if only to put you in the right frame of mind to build your strategic plan.

FIGURE P1.1

ARIA Inputs and Outputs

ANALYSIS	RECOLLECTION	INTUITION	ARTISTRY
Present	Past	Future	Path
Company/Capabilities	Influences	Vision	Strategy
Competitors	History	Goals	Story
Customers	Performance	Objectives	Resources
Industry	Experience	Target Market	Execution

← ——————— INPUTS ——————— →←——————— OUTPUTS ——————— →

As I mentioned earlier, strategy will consist of both inputs and outputs. Therefore, the proficiencies you build in Chapter 1 will correlate to the inputs and outputs shown in Figure P1.1.

I will discuss these inputs and outputs in much greater detail throughout Part 2 of this book, when I take you through the step-by-step process of building your strategic plan. But first we need to work on building the four proficiencies that will allow you to take an otherwise linear process and use it to create a dynamic work of art.

CHAPTER 1

ARIA

ANALYSIS

ANALYSIS	RECOLLECTION	INTUITION	ARTISTRY
Present	Past	Future	Path
Company/Capabilities	Influences	Vision	Strategy
Competitors	History	Goals	Story
Customers	Performance	Objectives	Resources
Industry	Experience	Target Market	Execution

Certainly you've heard of people having analytical skills. This usually conjures images of highly organized individuals with a penchant for numbers, data, and a black-and-white approach to getting things done. Being an engineer, I've carried this stigma, oftentimes negatively, throughout my career. And being labeled as "highly analytical" always appeared to be in contrast with being "highly strategic" when in fact these two characteristics are not in opposition.

The first step in dispelling this myth is in realizing that *analysis* is not synonymous with *data*. Instead, analysis involves taking large amounts of data and processing it with the intention of drawing additional information or a conclusion out of that data. In this way I like to think of analysis as a present-state condition, because the processing happens in real time and the conclusions we draw are fixed at the point in time that the analysis occurs. When we consider analysis to be a past-state condition, we are ignoring the critical aspect of actually processing that information. Even if we analyze what happened, we are doing so in the present and through a present-day lens. So analysis is about the processing of data just as much as it is about the data itself. Because of that, being good at analysis will require a careful balance between being data driven and being driven to do something with that data.

I have seen many strategists who do not consider themselves to be analytical. Usually that's because they don't have the time or the patience to sort through the vast amounts of data that they feel they need to analyze. The fallacy in this conclusion is the assumption that lack of analytical proficiency is due to a lack of patience when in fact what it is really due to is a lack of organizational skills.

Think about your basement (or your attic, as the case may be). If you have a whole lot of stuff in your basement and can't fit anything else in, you're going to need to throw a few things away and organize the rest so that you can make room for some new stuff to be stored there in the future. If you don't do this, you will never allow yourself to collect anything new for fear that it will be too overwhelming or that you'll have no place to put it.

Although this isn't a book about how to keep yourself organized, I'd like to give you a few tips about how you might be able to clear some of your own mental space so that the process of analysis won't be so overwhelming to you:

Tip 1: Keep everything organized on the way in. Keep information organized as it is being collected. This will make it easier to access when you most need it, and it will also prevent unneeded data from piling up and cluttering your thought process.

Watch any cooking show and you'll always see a countertop filled with prepared ingredients neatly placed in the exact order in which they will be used, premeasured to save as much time as possible, and presliced, crushed, or puréed so that the chef can focus on the cooking process rather than on the preparation of various ingredients.

Strategy preparation is no different. You start with a lot of data—of that there is no doubt. But if you don't spend any time sorting and processing that data as you collect it, the task will be too overwhelming to handle in an effective way once you begin developing your strategy. It would be akin to turning on the pan, putting in a tablespoon of olive oil, and then going to chop up your garlic. By the time you finish chopping, your oil has already caught fire. Then you have to think about putting out that fire instead of sautéing your garlic to just the right shade of golden brown. If you keep going through your entire recipe like that, I guarantee the end product will be ruined.

Tip 2: Don't be afraid to throw things away. Some people believe that there is no such thing as too much data. I completely disagree, and so will your executives when they have to sit through an hour-long presentation of you highlighting each and every bit of data that you collected because you don't want to waste any of it.

Think of a whiteboard. Those of us who work in an office environment on a regular basis know that the whiteboard is our conference room friend. The only problem is that the space a whiteboard gives you is finite. Many people who use the whiteboard are afraid to erase it at the end of their session because it might contain information that has to be formally captured, remembered, and utilized at some point. To protect this sacred domain, some whiteboard artists choose to scare off would-be trespassers by scrawling the famous DO NOT ERASE phrase across the top of their brain dump (usually written in all caps and encircled for added effect). And there the masterpiece sits, virtually untouched, for weeks at a time as other conference room users are forced to wonder who exactly issued such a dire warning and why this coveted information is so important that it would earn such a position of permanence.

Eventually some daring soul takes it upon himself to decide that the warning has overstayed its welcome, and in so doing he quickly erases the board, almost as if pulling a bandage off an open wound. But the ritual usually isn't quite as simple as all that. Heeding at least a little bit of caution, most people who are bold enough to take back this important bit of corporate real estate won't do so all at once. Instead, they scan the board and erase only those portions that they feel are less meaningful than others. This leaves a limited amount of space upon which they can write only their most essential points. This process may repeat itself one or even several more times until only the most salient point of each meeting remains—all of which can now be put to better use.

There are two points to this story: First, retaining too much information usually equates to it never being used. Second, if you distill your information to only the most relevant points, you can make room for more data, in summarized form, that can then be processed much more effectively. In the case of strategic development, this idea of space-clearing not only will make the information you have appear to be less intimidating and burdensome, it will also free up some room for additional data that you may have otherwise left out of your strategic thought process.

Tip 3: Don't confuse written data with valid data. Another fallacy about supposedly analytical people is that every piece of information they collect and analyze is tangible—that is, it is formally written down and documented. Although written documentation will be required for at least some part of the data that you will be gathering, it is not necessary for every piece of information to be collected in this way.

Many great strategists have the ability to process information in real time. They observe, collect, analyze, process, and plan all in nearly one step. Of course, in most business situations, this level of intuitive analysis can be somewhat dangerous, because more than one person will likely be contributing to the strategic process. So having everything reside in one person's head can be limiting (and risky if that person ever decides to leave the company). That said, you also shouldn't feel that *everything* will need to be captured on paper or in a database, because doing so may limit both your creativity and the speed with which you can put your data to use. The key in this situation is to maintain a healthy balance.

Similarly, you should not feel as though the analytical part of your strategy will not be valid unless you have X amount of data or unless it took you Y amount of time to collect that data. There are no formal rules here. So, yes, give yourself an ample amount of time to go about collecting and analyzing data, and give yourself some minimums as to what critical data you will need to support your future plan, but don't feel like every box has to be checked on your checklist for every single strategy that you wish to pursue. More than likely your analysis will have gaps, and more than likely you'll be able to fill in those gaps with some of the other proficiencies that we'll discuss next.

There you have it: three tips on how to approach analysis, even if you consider yourself to be nonanalytical. Remember that being analytical is not a bad thing or something that should be relegated to data crunchers. The only reason I can see for the (sometimes) negative connotation around this term is that so few people have the discipline to actually collect and analyze information in an organized way. If you want to build a successful strategy, this is a proficiency you must develop within yourself. Don't be afraid of it. Instead, you should embrace it and, in so doing, join the ranks of successful strategists who can analyze their present situation in an organized, efficient, and nearly real-time manner and who can use that information to help determine where they want to go in the future.

RECOLLECTION

ANALYSIS	RECOLLECTION	INTUITION	ARTISTRY
Present	Past	Future	Path
Company/Capabilities	Influences	Vision	Strategy
Competitors	History	Goals	Story
Customers	Performance	Objectives	Resources
Industry	Experience	Target Market	Execution

Our second proficiency, Recollection, is all about drawing upon our influences, experiences, and understandings of what has worked before. It is all about what's happened in the past and roughly translates into whatever formal training you choose to receive, as well as whatever personal history you choose to draw upon.

For my songwriting analogy, this equates to whatever skills I was taught, whatever tools I was given, and whatever influential musical styles I am equipped to work within. For example, there are many times that I have wanted to write a song in a certain style—for some reason, boogie-woogie comes to mind (perhaps because it's a style that has somehow always eluded me). There are many resources available to me if I want to learn to play or write in this style. If I choose to pursue those resources, I would probably go online and do some homework first. Then I would likely read, watch, listen, and practice—and all of this time would be spent learning from people who have a firm understanding of this style and can distill it down into parts and pieces that can be taught back to someone like me. After I had learned that style to whatever degree I felt suited my purpose, I would make those learnings a part of my personal toolbox and use them going forward. The same could be said of any other musical style, influence, theory, or practice that I might wish to pursue. Musicians all grow up in their crafts by learning the styles of players who came before them. No one style was ever invented by any one person. Instead, styles are cumulative and evolve over time from previous styles and the many others that came before them.

The same exact line of thinking can be applied to our topic of strategy. A big part of your Recollection proficiency will come from learning about the many companies that have successfully pursued one type of strategy or another. It will also come from the many strategic thought leaders who have captured these experiences and added their own insights into what may or may not have worked in the past.

Later, when we examine creating our strategic plans, I am going to refer to three common frameworks that I have found to be useful tools, particularly with respect to the process that I am outlining. I have also provided references to additional books, articles, and other interesting information in the Resources section at the back of this book. But these are only a sampling among the literally hundreds of other frameworks, articles, books, and methodologies that have been written about, rewritten about, and presented to would-be strategists in some form or another. The important thing is to understand what your influences are and to know how to supplement, enhance, or grow your knowledge and training based on the type of strategy that you are trying to put in place.

In addition to what others have written, your own observations will be equally important to consider when preparing your strategy. Companies are executing strategies every day right in front of your eyes. As a consumer, you experience the results of those strategies—both good and bad—and can draw your own conclusions about how effective they are. By studying what others have done, you can use those influences to help drive what you ultimately want to achieve yourself, and to help guide how you might, or might not, go about getting there.

In music, this equates to the hundreds of songs and artists that will serve as influences for any given songwriter at any given time, depending on the type of song that is being written. And although songwriters will use their influences as a guide, the best songwriters will be careful never to copy any one of those influences outright.

This lesson translates directly into the business world as well. The public rewards originality and generally condemns outright copycats. It is absolutely necessary to use what other companies have done as part of the toolbox from which you draw inspiration; however, it is important that you remember to put these lessons into their proper context. For example, you may be inclined to want to do things exactly as Company X or Company Y did them, when in fact, just like copying someone else's song, doing so would likely not yield the same results because that strategy has already been written, implemented, performed, and rewarded, and that pattern is unlikely to repeat itself unless you add your own twist to it.

Another key part of recollection will involve drawing upon your own history, experiences, and observations. The key is all about keeping your eyes and mind open and watching what's going on around you.

Remember that we are looking back in the past with the intention of ultimately determining where we want to go in the future. If we think about the game of chess (which is arguably considered to be one of the most strategic games in existence), being able to win the game is completely dependent on your ability to outthink your opponent. You do that by assessing your current situation and using that situation to try to predict what your opponent will likely do in response to any number of moves that you might be considering. And the way you will be able to predict those future responses will be based on all of the moves you've seen all of your various opponents make in response to all of your various moves in the past. So the chess player's brain becomes a database of cause and effect, and the person with the most complete and effective database usually wins.

It is important that you learn to build your own internal database of the moves that you (or your company) have made in the past and the effects that those moves may or may not have had. To do this, you will need to know as much as you can about all of the conditions that existed at the time those moves were taken. In this way, you will begin to set up that same type of cause-and-effect database that a chess player constantly keeps inside his or her head at any given time. This database of past events will then be used when you analyze that information to begin determining what might happen in the future. So you can see how all your proficiencies will begin to merge around your strategic process.

In using your own experiences to guide you, it is important not only to remember those experiences but also to learn from them. In a society where erasing our facial lines is becoming more of a norm, I am constantly left wondering why we are so eager to hide the very symbol of our own age and experience. Our facial lines are formed as a result of years upon years of repetitive expression, which itself is an indicator of all of the range of emotions that we've experienced and all of the challenges that we've overcome. This is not something that should be forgotten and discarded. Instead, these experiences should be worn with pride.

Companies are no different. I am constantly amazed at how many companies choose to ignore their own experiences. It is almost comical how many times some companies choose to reorganize themselves, often going back to iterations that have already been tried and discarded many times over. It's almost as if companies don't trust their own histories, which attests to a collective corporate self-confidence that appears to be fairly low.

Perhaps it is for this reason that many companies decide to erase their own facial lines and hide, or ignore altogether, the many different expressions that they have made over their long and storied histories. Good or bad, companies need to remember their experiences, learn from them, and weave them back into the fabric of their future strategic plans. Yes, it is important to know and learn from what others have done. Just don't leave yourself out of that equation.

In short, remember that strategy came long before schooling. You can learn to do something more effectively with formal training, but chances are, even in lieu of that, your company has been executing strategies for years. So always remember to balance your formal training with real-life experiences and, in so doing, you will round out the skills needed for effective recollection.

INTUITION

ANALYSIS	RECOLLECTION	INTUITION	ARTISTRY
Present	Past	**Future**	Path
Company/Capabilities	Influences	Vision	Strategy
Competitors	History	Goals	Story
Customers	Performance	Objectives	Resources
Industry	Experience	Target Market	Execution

We've looked at the present, we've drawn from the past, and now we have to focus our third proficiency squarely on the future. To do this, let's explore this magical, mystical, highly misunderstood proficiency we call Intuition.

I once worked for a leader who had a keen sense of intuition. Most people described him as street smart, and he was wildly successful as a result. The reason is because he followed his instincts. He didn't overanalyze things, he didn't try to make things more complex than they needed to be, and he didn't follow any prewritten book of business rules. He just knew what needed to be done and he did it. When I used to present my strategies to him, he would usually tell me, "Bob, just tell me what you want to do." In other words, he wanted me to stop trying to fit my strategies into some preconceived formula and instead just tell the story from my gut. And every time I followed this advice, my strategies ended up being more successful.

Irving Berlin, one of the most prolific and influential songwriters of modern times, never formally learned to read or write music. And it is in this simplicity that some of his most famous songs were written. When he asked one of his collaborators, Victor Herbert, who was a traditionally schooled composer, whether or not he should study music composition, Mr. Herbert was quoted as saying, "You have a natural gift for words and music. Learning theory might help you a little, but it could cramp your style."[1] That must have been pretty good advice because the Berlin-composed song "White Christmas" was listed in *Guinness World Records 2015* as having sold an estimated 50 million copies throughout its existence.[2]

It's hard to deny that some people just seem to have a better innate ability to see the future than others. The same can be said for musicians and composers. Some of them seem to have a knack for developing a melody that connects with people. But should we attribute this capability to some sort of genetic disposition, or is it something that can be developed and taught?

Traditional methods of learning tend to rely on recollection— that is, in mastering theories that have already been established. And although I believe this is an important component of learning, if you do not leave some room for new feelings, insights, and observations, then you will spend all of your time trying to imitate the past and not enough time applying that past to the future.

Such are the concert pianists who work their entire lives to master the works of the great composers who have come before them. In return, they are able to play each piece with a level of precision, accuracy, and feeling that can hardly be matched by the casual student. But this is *not* the same skill that will be required to compose an original piece of music. For that, our experts need to let go of a little of what they were taught and make some room for their own observations and instincts.

The same can be said of highly schooled business leaders. They may spend a lot of time learning what other people have done but not enough time coming up with their own original ideas. In my observation, I believe this is one of the main shortcomings of many businesses today. They chase one another. They compete and chase and compete and chase; while too few are actually opening their minds to seeing a future that no one else has yet envisioned.

It seems clear that we are all born with some level of empathetic instincts: a keen sense of what other people are feeling and, to some extent, what they're about to do next. The problem with rational creatures such as ourselves is that we can easily suppress some of these natural instincts in favor of the many billions of other inputs that we receive on a constant basis. This means that in order to tap into some of our more innate abilities we may need to learn to shut down a few of our acquired learnings—even if temporarily.

It is thought that if you take away any one of our senses, the others will become that much more heightened. One interesting example of this can be observed in certain individuals who have lost their sight and then learn to navigate by making a series of noises and listening for how the resulting sound waves are absorbed or reflected by the surrounding environment. It is suggested that this ability to echolocate is processed using the same part of the brain that would otherwise have been used to process visual information.[3] Using this sense of sonar that most of us couldn't even dream of tapping into, these unique individuals navigate in certain circumstances with nearly as much accuracy as somebody with full sight. This suggests that we may, in fact, be able to tap into otherwise unrealized abilities when some of the inputs that we are normally exposed to are not present.

All of this culminates in two main suggestions to help build your own intuitive proficiencies:

1. You must believe that you have a creative, visionary energy source that can be tapped into. Erase the notion that some people are born with vision and others are not. The ability exists in all of us to varying degrees. So assume it exists in you as well and that it just needs to be cultivated.

2. You must open your mind to the possibility that this energy source can only truly be tapped into if you learn to put aside a few things that you may have been taught in school. You don't have to erase them from your memory; you just need to move them out of the category of things you *need* to do and into the category of things that might *inspire* you to be more aware. And then you can use those inputs later when you begin to develop your strategies.

When you master this intuitive proficiency, you will be able to foresee a future that others could not. And this will give you perhaps the most important strategic advantage you could ever hope to acquire: the element of surprise.

Good strategy—I mean *really* good strategy—needs to have an element of surprise. In war, this can be demonstrated, quite literally, by the fact that if your enemies can predict exactly what you will do next, they will very likely be able to outsmart you and prevent you from achieving your overall objective. One of the first things your enemies are likely to do in fact is balance what they know about the past with what they believe will happen in the future. This combination of learning and feeling will give them certain insights as to your next anticipated move.

If you do as they predict, you will lose. If, on the other hand, you are always staying one step ahead of your enemies—anticipating not only what they're likely to do but also what they're likely to think that *you're* likely to do—then you'll win. The point is that your gut needs to guide you past what you know, past what you observe, and well into what you anticipate might happen based on both of those inputs. That's where your intuition will live, and that's the proficiency you have to develop in order for your strategy to succeed.

ARTISTRY

ANALYSIS	RECOLLECTION	INTUITION	ARTISTRY
Present	Past	Future	**Path**
Company/Capabilities	Influences	Vision	Strategy
Competitors	History	Goals	Story
Customers	Performance	Objectives	Resources
Industry	Experience	Target Market	Execution

There's one last proficiency that you'll need to master before setting out to build your strategic masterpiece. In many ways, it brings the other three proficiencies together in a way that allows them to be fully utilized and harvested. This is the proficiency that will enable you to be an "artist."

When I think of an artist, the first image that usually comes to mind is of a person in a beret and a smock, dipping his brush into a multicolored palette of various paints that he holds in one hand, while alternately stroking upon a semi-blank canvas with the other. I'm not sure why I put a beret on the poor fellow, but somehow that's what I picture! In any event, in so many words, I first think of an artist as someone who paints or draws, or, more accurately stated, someone who can translate what's in his or her mind into something that can be shared with others.

If I expand upon this a bit, I might say:

- An artist has an important feeling or idea that she or he wants to share with others.
- An artist expresses that important feeling or idea so that others can also experience it.

Following this line of thinking, it's not hard to see how art and artistry expand far beyond drawing or painting. An artist can express his or her ideas or feelings through any number of different mediums, including acting, filmmaking, comedy, music, writing, or even (you guessed it) a business strategy. The key to being an artist is that you have to care enough about something to want to express it, and then you have to translate what you care about in a way that will allow people to experience it.

This really all boils down to two main characteristics that comprise the Artistry proficiency: passion and expression. Let's explore both a little further.

Passion

There are many surveys that have been done with respect to job satisfaction, with satisfaction rates ranging from just under 50 percent to just over 80 percent, depending on which slice of the workforce is being polled and at which point in time. More interesting, however, is the correlation between job satisfaction and compensation: as higher-paid workers generally indicate a higher rate of job satisfaction than lower-paid workers.[4] So this begs the question: Are they more satisfied because they're being paid more, or are they being paid more because they're more satisfied? It's an interesting question, to be sure.

There may not be a definitive answer to that question, but my experience tells me that satisfaction comes before reward, not the other way around. I have personally given large bonuses, raises, or other financial rewards to people who were clearly unhappy with their jobs, and the resulting job satisfaction was very temporary—only to be replaced by another gripe or complaint about another aspect of the job several months, or even mere weeks, down the road. On the other hand, I have observed that people who are truly passionate about what they do don't care as much about what they get paid. They do what they do because they love to do it. The result is better performance, and the result of *that* is almost always greater long-term financial reward.

Mind you, I'm not talking about rewarding people who work *harder*. I'm talking about rewarding people who are easy to work *with* because they absolutely love what they do. That holds a lot of weight in the business world, oftentimes to the chagrin of workers who believe they should be measured only on the number of hours they work or the number of brain cells they utilize in any given day. Passion is what is rewarded, because passion oftentimes leads to far greater and far longer-term success.

Week after week, I go into large companies and work with their product managers, marketing teams, and strategy experts, and I watch so many of them try to apply a strategic formula to a product that they simply do not care about. They may say they care, and superficially it may even appear that they do. But if the caring doesn't go much deeper than the paycheck and job security, it simply isn't enough. And the only way that I can help those strategies to be successful is if I can build excitement and passion in their strategic owners.

Almost without fail, the strategies that end up being the most effective and that end up having the most profitable results are also the ones that are driven by the most passionate strategic owners. That's not to say that passion is the only differentiator, but it certainly is one of them. The reason, I believe, is simple: *passion is infectious*. Passionate people care about their products, which in turn causes them to care about their strategies. And their strategies usually involve solving problems that they care about, with products that they care about, for customers whom they care about. And that, in turn, almost inevitably leads to greater profitability. I've seen the pattern enough times to recognize it, and that pattern holds far more weight than the person who works 80 hours a week and hates every minute of it.

So you have to have passion. Of that I am certain. But passion isn't a skill. If it were, our acronym would be ARIP! In fact, in business, as in life, caring will have little impact without sharing. So it is in the expression of your passion where the true skill resides.

Expression

Passion, like most emotional responses, is difficult to measure tangibly, so we can only judge its magnitude based on the effect it has on others. If I think that I'm passionate about something, but nobody else sees it, then my passion will serve little purpose. It doesn't mean that my passion is nonexistent. It just means that it will be inconsequential. That is the same as the age-old question about the tree falling in the forest. If nobody is around to hear it, does it make a sound? Yes, sound waves are actually generated. But if no ears are around to actually receive those sound waves, then it is the same as if they never existed in the first place.

Expression allows your passion to be shared and felt. People can express themselves in any number of different ways. To try to organize this a little, let's turn to the receiver instead of to the sender. Expression is a method of communicating from one human being to another. We communicate based on how a person will receive the messages that we are trying to send. So if I want someone to hear something, I use audio communication. If I want someone to see something, I use visual communication. You get the idea. The important point here is that effective communication is based on the *receiver* because, if I send a message and it isn't received, then the communication fails.

This is no small point because if I, as the communicator, do not pay attention to the way my audience is not only *able*, but also *willing*, to receive my message, then sending it might have no effect.

So how exactly do we receive messages? This happens through some combination of our five senses:

- Sight
- Hearing
- Taste
- Smell
- Touch

Artists can, and often do, draw upon each of these senses in order to transmit their messages. But here's the trick: the more senses that are touched, the more effectively your message will be received. The reason for this is simple: you are attacking on all fronts, leaving no room for the receiver to be distracted by anything other than your message. In short, you are totally immersing the user in your experience.

This is the same concept that I discussed with respect to enabling your intuition, only viewed from the other side of the equation. If all of your senses are being fully utilized, there may be little room for additional information. As a sender of information, this is exactly the effect you are trying to have on your receivers.

Artists have long understood this concept, at least on a subconscious level. For example, when silent films were first introduced, producers must have instinctively known that the more immersed a moviegoer was in the experience, the more effective that experience would ultimately be. Although technology did not yet allow for synchronized sound, it was commonplace for silent movies to feature live musical "soundtracks" that would complement the story and help set the mood for critical emotional cues within the film. This, of course, eventually evolved into the use of fully synchronized audio tracks that, interestingly, continued to feature some type of musical soundtrack to help focus the audience's auditory senses on the story that was being told. With modern sound systems, this has been taken to such an extreme that when you walk into a movie theater, you literally can't hear anything other than what's happening on the screen.

Businesspeople could do well to take a few cues from this immersive approach. Most business presentations contain some combination of sight and sound, but often there's very little coordination between the two. Usually there is some form of slide show carrying on as the backdrop for what seems like an endless monologue, nervously delivered by a not-very-interesting presenter who may be more concerned with showing people how much he or she knows than with actually communicating that knowledge to an entirely distracted and utterly disinterested audience. I've been there several times myself, and I've witnessed it even more often. The focus is usually on jamming as much information as possible into as little time as possible, all of which seems like a lifetime for the audience because not enough attention is being paid to actually trying to engage people. And usually this approach, although the accepted norm, completely fails.

Perhaps this is a slight exaggeration, but the point is that any presentation delivered without consideration for the receiver will ultimately miss the mark. And any presentation delivered without any passion behind it will have no chance of succeeding at all, because there is really nothing to express.

Most artists are so passionate about the message they are trying to convey that they absolutely couldn't fathom *not* expressing that message through whatever means are available to them. In business, if you are passionate about your strategy, it will not end with the presentation, with the first sign of resistance, with a battle of functional egos, or even with your paycheck. If you are truly passionate about your strategy, you will drive it right through implementation, no matter the obstacles, and holding everyone's attention along every step of the way. In so doing you will be touching all five senses of your receivers and truly expressing your passion just as an artist would.

So what does it mean to be an artist? In this case, it's about connecting the passionate desire to express something with the skill to actually express it.

Later in this book, I'll cover the expression part of this equation in depth. I'll teach you how to present your strategy, how to implement your strategy, and how to lead the teams that will help you to drive your strategy. But passion is something that I cannot teach you directly. What I *can* do is to encourage you to *find* your passion. And if the product that you are currently managing isn't it, then find something about that product that you can get excited about, or go develop a different strategy that *will* make you excited about your product. Because if you get excited, chances are your customers will get excited too. And, more important, if you're not excited, nobody else will be either.

In short, you have to connect your strategy to something you care about. Usually this can be found in the problem you are trying to solve—not for your company, but for your customer. Focus on this, and the passion will find you. And if it doesn't, then you may just need to find another problem to solve.

MIXING THE INGREDIENTS

You will need to balance the four proficiencies of Analysis, Recollection, Intuition, and Artistry in order to successfully compose and implement your strategic plan. From a musician's standpoint, I am always thinking in terms of the "mix," meaning: Are all of these proficiencies required in equal parts, or should one be more prominently featured than the others?

To help answer this question, let's look at two scenarios that, as luck would have it, just happen to support our songwriting analogy!

1. A professional songwriter who writes music for a living.
2. A newly formed rock band that is still trying to find its sound.

In the first example, the songwriter has a job to do. She may have been hired by a publishing company that pitches new songs to music labels and recording artists. In this case, the songwriter will have been contracted to work in a certain style, within a certain time frame, and perhaps even in relation to a certain subject. To do this, she might need to rely much more heavily on her Analysis or Recollection proficiencies, drawing more upon her knowledge of how to compose within a given musical style, and basing her songs heavily on what has worked for other successful artists in the recent past. That's not to say that the more creative aspects of Intuition and Artistry will be completely ignored. On the contrary, these too are essential ingredients to getting just the right sound that is inspired by, but does not mimic, other songs that are already on the market. Still, this scenario is bound by parameters that will require a heavier weighting on one or both of our first two proficiencies.

In the second scenario, the newly formed rock band is working, more or less, without limits. Certainly they have training and influences that they are drawing upon, and, in hopes of one day being signed to a record label, they may have even done research into various aspects of their potential audience, competing local bands, and current musical trends. But for this group the sky is pretty much the limit and, because of that, they have the ability at this point to work without the financial restrictions that a record label might have otherwise placed upon them. This group can now rely more heavily on their Intuition and Artistry proficiencies, possibly even defining a new musical genre that doesn't sound or feel like any other band that has ever existed before them. Not that every start-up band chooses to go this route, but they certainly can, and many have.

In business, the same basic principles will apply. Weighting your recipe toward one proficiency or another will result in different strategic outcomes. The more you rely on your Analysis or Recollection, the more conservative your plan is likely to be. The more you lean on your Intuition or Artistry, the better chance you will have at developing a breakthrough strategy.

To help guide you along this path, I have created a quick reference chart, as shown in Figure1.1, that defines this relationship in a bit more detail. The idea here is to help balance the proficiencies that you apply and utilize for your strategy based on the strategic result you are trying to achieve.

FIGURE 1.1

Strategic Proficiency Mix

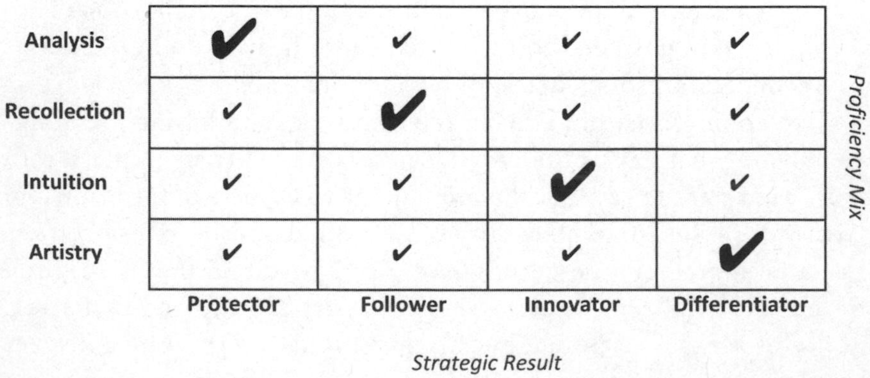

	Protector	Follower	Innovator	Differentiator
Analysis	✔ (large)	✔	✔	✔
Recollection	✔	✔ (large)	✔	✔
Intuition	✔	✔	✔ (large)	✔
Artistry	✔	✔	✔	✔ (large)

Proficiency Mix

Strategic Result

In my experience, if you balance your recipe toward any one of your four proficiencies, your strategy will be more likely to have one of the following outcomes:

- **Protector.** If you tend to use more Analysis in your strategic formula, you will be focused mostly on the present. The result will be a strategy that leans toward protecting your current position, standing your ground, or defending your territory.

- **Follower.** Strategies that use more Recollection in their creation will tend to be more focused on the past. The result will be a strategy that uses many elements of other strategies that have been implemented before or that uses frameworks or models that are largely based on activities that have already been (usually successfully) utilized. This could result in more of a "me too" or "fast follower" outcome, which, contrary to some beliefs, is not always a bad thing.

- **Innovator.** Leaning more on your Intuition will give you a natural tendency toward looking at the future and anticipating what is likely to happen next, usually over the long term. This will most likely lead to innovation, which itself is focused on using your gut instinct to constantly improve above and beyond your own current state.

- **Differentiator.** If you draw from your Artistry—that is, your passion and relative expression of that passion—your strategy will likely become focused not just on improving what you have today, but improving it in a unique or creative way that nobody else has thought of before.

As I mentioned, your strategic plan will have inputs and outputs. The inputs will be based on the past and present, and the outputs will be based on the future and your chosen path. If you draw more heavily on the proficiencies that are focused on your inputs (Analysis and Recollection), then your resulting plan will be more focused on the past and present. If, on the other hand, you draw more heavily on the proficiencies that are focused on your outputs (Intuition and Artistry), then your plan is more likely to be focused on the future and, perhaps even a future that nobody else has yet envisioned.

I often hear people at companies say that they want to be more innovative or differentiated. Yet at the same time these companies may be overemphasizing past or present-day concerns, such as working capital restrictions, mandatory short-term revenue and profitability goals, or the most recent competitive or industry performance reports. Not that these are invalid parameters to pay attention to, but a heavier weighting on these types of concerns will inevitably cause people to lean more on their Analysis or Recollection proficiencies and less on their Intuition or Artistry proficiencies. This will yield strategies that are more focused on protecting or following rather than on innovating or differentiating.

Of course, this tendency is understandable. Companies naturally want to protect what they have, and in fact they have a fiduciary responsibility to their investors to do just that. The problem is, if large companies truly want to innovate to the same degree as their smaller start-up counterparts, they're going to need to embrace some of the proficiencies that are focused on the future, not just on the past or present. And this must be done not only through words but also by truly investing in the right resources with the right risk profiles to enable this type of long-term strategic outcome.

The point of all this is that you (and your company) need to decide what type of strategy you want to end up with, and then focus your mix of proficiencies in order to achieve that end result. If you want protection, focus on Analysis. If you want to follow your competitors, focus on Recollection. If you want to innovate, focus on Intuition. And if you want to differentiate, focus on Artistry. Don't ignore the other proficiencies; just lean a little more heavily on those that will get you closest to your desired end state.

So we have our proficiencies all laid out in front of us, we know which proficiencies we want to focus on, and we've measured everything relative to the end result that we're looking for.

Now we're ready to begin composing our strategies.

P A R T

PROCESS

INTRODUCTION

Now that we have our proficiencies firmly in place, it's time to apply them to our strategy. The process that I am going to take you through is the same one that I use to write music, the same one that I use to create a piece of art, and the same one that I used to write this very book. All of these pursuits involve building something from a thought into a tangible piece of art that someone else can enjoy. Whether this is applied to music, painting, sculpture, architecture, poetry, theater, film, or just about any other creative pursuit, you can follow the same basic steps to creatively bring an idea out of your mind and into the real world.

The trick is that we don't often think of the strategic planning process in these terms. Instead, you might be inclined to view it as more of a corporate exercise, something that needs to be done on an annual basis because your company requires it for long-term planning purposes. In this way, strategic planning is often relegated to a fill-in-the-template financial exercise, accompanied by a semibelievable story to support whatever growth numbers your company demands to see.

Personally, I never viewed the strategic process this way. I always approached strategy as something that I was going to build from an idea in my head into something that could be implemented, shared, and celebrated, not because I had to, but because I wanted to. There was a passion that I needed to express, and strategy was the business canvas upon which I could express it. In short, I always saw my strategies as creative works of art. Because of this (and as I mentioned earlier), I prefer to think about "composing" my strategies rather than developing them. So that's how I will refer to this process from this point forward.

So what exactly is the difference between a creative process and a systematic exercise? The only way I can describe it is to compare the process of painting by numbers to drawing freehand. Using a paint-by-numbers process, if you follow certain steps you will always get the same results. You don't have to think, you don't have to stray from the formula, you just plug and chug. A creative process, on the other hand, enables you to work outside the lines. There are still some basic rules that you need to apply and some basic steps that you need to follow. These steps, however, tend to serve more as layers, with each one building fluidly upon the next, but without rigidly defining exactly how you move from one step to the other or what exactly the result of each step needs to be. In this way, a creative process teaches you *how* to build rather than *what* to build. And that I believe is what makes it so exciting.

What I will do through these next chapters is to provide you with that creative process using the music composition analogy to help guide you. Through this process, you will be using the four proficiencies of Analysis, Recollection, Intuition, and Artistry to create the inputs and outputs that I introduced in Part 1 by following seven distinct steps:

1. Preparation
2. Inspiration
3. Genre
4. Ideation
5. Arrangement
6. Orchestration
7. Production

FIGURE P2.1

Creative Strategy Generation Model

ANALYSIS	RECOLLECTION	INTUITION	ARTISTRY
Present	Past	Future	Path
Company/Capabilities	Influences	Vision	Strategy
Competitors	History	Goals	Story
Customers	Performance	Objectives	Resources
Industry	Experience	Target Market	Execution

←————————— INPUTS —————————→←————————— OUTPUTS —————————→

PREPARATION	PREPARATION	INSPIRATION	IDEATION
		GENRE	ARRANGEMENT
			ORCHESTRATION
			PRODUCTION

| I | II | III | IV |

This is reflected in the model shown in Figure P2.1, which we will use as a guidepost along the way.

As you can see in Figure P2.1, much of your creative energy will be spent on the outputs—that is, looking toward the future and deciding how you are going to affect that future. That said, before you can determine where you're going, you need to understand where you are and where you've been. These are critical inputs that will be required to help define your strategy. And these are the inputs that will begin our journey.

CHAPTER 2

PREPARATION

ANALYSIS	RECOLLECTION	INTUITION	ARTISTRY
Present	Past	Future	Path
Company/Capabilities	Influences	Vision	Strategy
Competitors	History	Goals	Story
Customers	Performance	Objectives	Resources
Industry	Experience	Target Market	Execution

◄────── INPUTS ──────►◄────── OUTPUTS ──────►

PREPARATION	PREPARATION	INSPIRATION	IDEATION
		GENRE	ARRANGEMENT
			ORCHESTRATION
			PRODUCTION
I	II	III	IV

What You Will Do

- Prepare your strategic baseline analysis

In preparing myself to write a new song, I am both consciously and subconsciously drawing from more than 35 years of musical training, influences, history, performance, and experiences, all of which are somehow expected to culminate in some new and original expression of my art. And the way this generally happens is by overlaying all of these past experiences onto whatever present-day situation is driving me to write that song. This combination of past and present dimensions results in a future path, which ultimately becomes my new song.

In business, the collection of information may or may not be a bit more formal, but the general idea is exactly the same. Something in the present is driving you to want to determine a future path. To determine that path, you analyze your current situation, recall what has happened in the past, and use all of that information to help determine your future. That's about as basic as it gets, but it also happens to be the very foundation of strategic theory. I call this exploration of present and past dimensions the *preparation stage*.

Since the purpose of this book is not to try to reinvent strategic theory but to show you how to put that theory to better use, I will attempt, in this chapter at least, not to stray too far from the same basic elements that have been taught for literally thousands of years. Yet as many times as this topic has been explored, tweaked, and reimagined, I am amazed at how often I go into classrooms full of business professionals from different companies in different countries with a multitude of different backgrounds and university pedigrees, and I still see light bulbs illuminate over people's heads when I break strategic theory down into its most basic parts. It is here, then, that we will begin our journey.

The term *strategy* is roughly derived from the Greek word *stratēgia*, which itself is derived from the word *stratēgos*, which is a combination of *stratos*, meaning "multitude, army, expedition," and *agos*, meaning "leader." More succinctly, the word *strategy* was used to represent the "art of a general."[1] This is an interesting choice of words to be sure. So now we have to examine exactly what kind of art a general would want to create.

Today military generals surely have to perform any number of administrative tasks, in addition to what they would have also needed to do hundreds of years ago, which primarily was to lead their troops into battle. So we get a visual of a highly decorated commander, with the daunting, but I imagine rather necessary, task of leading an army into a pending conflict of some sort. Sometimes the general would be advancing his troops. Other times, he would stand his ground and wait for another army to descend upon his own. The choices that any given general might make in any given situation would be based on the knowledge that he possessed, while the "art," I suppose, would be in how effective and creative those choices were.

The general is in charge, and everyone is looking to that person to choose what moves to make. So what kinds of things might a general need to consider before making such critical decisions? From a practical standpoint, the general's knowledge can be separated into five main categories:

1. Motivation
2. Enemy
3. Capabilities
4. Environment
5. Plan

Out of interest for the origin of the word *strategy*, I will explore each one of these areas using this analogy of a general leading his respective army into war. Granted, I am not an expert in military strategy, nor am I a particular fan of two or more groups of people trying to kill one another. But it is a necessary subject to explore, if only to fully understand why the concept of strategy is so often applied to business and also why it is not always the easiest connection to make.

MOTIVATION

Before we ever get into vision statements, goals, or objectives, there has to be a driving force that motivates us to want to take action. Many people believe that strategy begins with a vision. While this is an important part of a strategy, your vision is usually derived from a base motivation or an overarching reason for wanting to make something happen in the first place. This base motivation is where your strategy ultimately begins. It is your backstory, in a way, and it must be identified before your vision can be developed.

Sometimes these elements are confused. For example, if you are going into battle, clearly your vision will be to win the war. But after you get over that knee-jerk statement, you'll probably find that there is something else, something deeper, that is actually causing the war to happen in the first place. Perhaps you want to acquire land. Or maybe you are trying to defend the land you already have. You might want to weaken your enemies so they can't attack you in the future. Or you might want to spread your beliefs or your particular point of view. You might just want to get from one point on the map to another. Or you might even be fighting over a relationship of some kind. The point is, many different motivating factors could exist. The key is to understand the true motivation behind your strategy before you go about the business of putting one together.

Relating this to a business scenario, starting with a vision like "we want to be the number-one provider of widgets" is strikingly familiar to saying, "we want to win the war." Growing and winning are valid aspirations, but there is usually some underlying reason why those things are actually important. For example, a professional American football team more than likely has a goal to win all of their games, so they will very likely put a strategy in place to do that every week. But the *reason* they want to win every week is so that they can win enough games to vie for a playoff spot at the end of the season. And the *reason* for that is so that they can play in the championship game. And the *reason* they want to win the championship game is so that they can have bragging rights and more endorsements and better television contracts and better merchandise sales and ultimately more money. So there are many more underlying motivations behind the goal of winning.

So why is all of this important? Many a business war has been fought in which the troops understand only the vision but not the real motivation that drives that vision. And many of those wars have been lost. A truly great leader will tell his or her troops not only *what* they are fighting for but also *why* they are fighting. Sharing, or at least translating, this crucial component of your thought process will be one of the keys to your strategic success.

In the next chapter, I will talk about finding your inspiration, which will be at least partially derived from your motivation. So at this point it will be important to know what your true motivation is.

ENEMY

What else might a general need to know before leading his or her troops into battle? Understanding a thing or two about the enemy might be a good place to start. Whatever is motivating your strategy, one thing is for certain: your enemy is standing in your way. So before you decide how to deal with this obstacle, you probably want to take a little time to understand what it's all about.

So what kinds of things might you need to know about your enemy? It's easy to rattle off the usual list of suspects: strengths, weaknesses, capabilities, and so on. But before we get there let's just think in terms of our own personal survival because, as with most things, our natural instincts usually serve as our best guide. To help illustrate this point, I'd like to share a personal story that I believe sums up this sentiment quite nicely.

When I was about 14 years old—right around the time when boys are just beginning to flex their muscles and mark their new-found territories—I remember the tougher kids starting to emerge out of the group of people whom I used to call my friends. And there was one young man in particular who seemed to be just a little bit tougher than the rest. To protect the innocent, let's just call him Joe. One day, I went into my social studies class and sat down at the same desk that I had always sat in, which was also the same desk that was shared by an unknown number of other students who occupied this same classroom during other classes throughout the day. As I began to take out my single piece of lined paper and jot down the assignment for the afternoon, I noticed that my pencil wasn't gliding quite as smoothly across the page as it had in the past. Looking underneath, as the curious among us are inclined to do from time to time, I found that the culprit was a freshly carved, rather unflattering phrase about good ol' Joe. I chuckled to myself, moved the paper, and went on about my day.

The next day, thinking nothing more about that silly little carving, just as I was heading to my last class of the day, one of my friends hurriedly approached me with a demeanor that was one part panic and three parts "I'm sure glad I'm not you!" Before I could even say hello, he was blurting out the words, "Did you hear that Joe is looking for you?" *This can't be good*, I thought in a flash. But before I could respond, my friend blurted out the sentence that no 14-year-old passive-aggressive young teenager wants to hear: "He said he wants to call you out!"

At least in my neighborhood, people didn't just fight one another; they fought each other in a public arena. "Calling someone out" was the modern-day equivalent of challenging someone to a duel. In our case, the chosen battlefield was the other side of a hill just across from our middle school. This put the whole spectacle just out of view of the faculty parking lot, but still close enough to the school so as to draw a full-capacity crowd of student spectators. The only thing worse than being called out was being told to meet someone "over the hill." Once that location was named, there was no turning back. Thankfully, things hadn't progressed to this point just yet, but all signs were pointing in that direction. And, as you can imagine, the person doing the calling usually had a far better chance of winning than the person being called!

Trying to ignore the fact that my so-called friend seemed a little too happy about all of this, and that I was, quite frankly, scared out of my wits, I asked for an explanation. As you may have guessed, I had been accused of publicly dishonoring Joe's good name by way of a certain desk carving. And Joe apparently was none too happy about it.

Like most young boys growing up in the suburbs, I went through my phase of thinking that I was tougher than I actually was. Unfortunately for me, that phase had come and gone about a year prior to this little situation. Joe, on the other hand, didn't appear to be growing out of his phase. In fact, he was growing quite nicely right into it! All things considered, things weren't trending in my favor. He was bigger and stronger, had more to prove and less to lose, and appeared to be highly motivated to damage me in some way. My motivation, on the other hand, was just to stay alive. All of this analysis happened in about 10 seconds, after which time I had devised the first part of my strategy: get the heck out of Dodge! Thank goodness it was a Friday, so I had all weekend to devise the next part of my plan.

Joe was stronger than I was. He was a better fighter. He was less afraid. I, on the other hand, was probably a better talker. Maybe I could use that to my advantage. There was also the little reality that I didn't actually carve anything into anyone's desk in the first place.

So I stood wrongly accused. That had to account for something, didn't it? There was also the fact that Joe and I used to be friends at one time—or at least friendly acquaintances. If I combined all of that together, maybe, if given the chance, I could talk my way out of this whole thing. I was pretty sure that that would be my strategy, but my analysis didn't end there.

Next I started playing out different scenarios in my head. What if we did get into a fight? What specifically would he do? I knew he wasn't a killer—or at least I didn't think he was. He had no history of ever wielding any weapons of any sort. So I was pretty certain that, although technically possible, he probably wasn't going to do any real harm to me.

Then I began to think about what might be motivating him. Why did he want to fight me in the first place? Obviously he had something to prove. He wanted to make everyone very well aware of the fact that he was the boss and that nobody should ever use the boss's name in vain. So if there was another way of him achieving that same end result without resorting to violence, knowing what I knew about him, did I think he might take that other option? Yes I did. All of this had to be contemplated.

What if we fought and he lost? Even though I was afraid of Joe, I wasn't exactly the smallest kid in the class. And the last time Joe and I interacted, I was in fact, going through that tough phase that I mentioned. Maybe he didn't know that I had grown out of it. So if his motivation was to show the school who was boss, would he really be willing to risk fighting me and losing? It was an interesting thought.

The point I'm trying to make is that sizing up your enemy is not just about looking at what's happening on the surface; it's also about knowing their strengths and weaknesses, knowing how they have used those advantages and disadvantages in the past, and then thinking about how all of that will translate into what they might do in the future.

In business we sometimes try to isolate these factors. For example, if I worked for a soft-drink company, I would probably look at Coca-Cola as a competitor. So I might be inclined to learn as much as possible as I could about Coca-Cola and start listing all of that company's strengths, weaknesses, market share numbers, product portfolios, financials, geographies, and so on. Then I might do the same thing for PepsiCo, and Dr Pepper Snapple Group, and any other number of similar companies. Then I would probably put all that vast amount of data into a strategic presentation and feel as if I had completed my competitive analysis. I've seen it happen too many times: large amounts of competitive data presented in a static way without any critical analysis of how all that data will react and interact under given situations.

The root cause of this problem is that we may have moved too far away from our basic instincts. If you were confronted with a fight, what would you need to look for in your enemy? Yes, strengths; yes, weaknesses. But, perhaps more important, you must anticipate what that person will do with those strengths and weaknesses under any number of different circumstances, which you may very well help to create. That's how you need to look at your enemy, and that's why I want you to think about what you would do if you were facing "Joe" rather than simply running through a list of what you need to know about your competitors. You'll have the opportunity to run through your list, but not before examining your gut instincts first.

There's one more thing you ought to consider about your enemy. It's fairly straightforward to know whom you're fighting today, but it's not so easy to know whom you may be fighting tomorrow. Stated more simply, you need to think about the enemy who may be waiting in the wings to attack you or your market but whom you aren't confronting currently. I doubt many computer services or telecommunications companies were viewing an online bookseller as much of a competitor at the beginning of our current century. Looking back, maybe they should have seen it coming. Amazon .com had the infrastructure, the customer base, and, perhaps most important, the desire. All it needed to do was put all of those things together, and suddenly an enviable online cloud storage business was born. The point is, it's not always easy to see a sneak attack, but you'll have a much better chance of doing so if you have a few spotters constantly posted in the turrets or, in business terms, if you always have at least one eye looking outside your own company at all times.

Now you know who your enemies are, who they aren't, and who they might just be. In case you hadn't guessed it, your enemies in business will translate into your competitors, which is how I will refer to them from this point forward.

CAPABILITIES

The phrase "know thyself" goes back to the time of the Ancient Greeks[2] and has been used as a directive for self-awareness ever since. My personal take on this saying is that most people do know themselves fairly well. The harder part may actually be admitting it.

When you are standing close to the edge of that battlefield and getting ready to lead your troops into battle (whether metaphorically or not), you absolutely must take a realistic and candid view of your own strengths and weaknesses so that you can overlay them against all of your other analyzed variables and formulate a plan of action. The biggest challenge in this situation will be allowing yourself to truly see what you are good at and what you are not, despite any of the beliefs that you may have (or want to have) about yourself.

Coming back to my story with Joe, I knew that I was weaker than him, and I knew that I would more than likely lose that fight. I also knew that I was smart enough to talk my way out of things if I only had the chance to face him for a few minutes alone. And although I had no problem admitting those things to myself, what would happen if the rest of the world knew them as well? Then what? It's not like I walked around school telling everyone how weak and afraid I was. At age 14 that wasn't exactly the image I was trying to portray. Sure, I knew myself, but nobody else knew who I really was. So one of my biggest challenges was that this little inner conflict might just be revealed to the world.

Companies are no different. In an attempt to continuously sell themselves to their investors, executive team members are always trying to make their companies look more attractive; it's one of their main jobs. This isn't a bad thing, because nobody wants to invest in, or work for, an organization that is always pointing out its own faults. That said, when it comes to developing strategy, you have to learn to break through that very thick, seemingly impenetrable facade and truly know thyself. Again, you probably already do. The challenge will be to admit it.

I am reminded of the story told many times before: about the 1980 U.S. Olympic hockey team led by coach Herb Brooks. Facing teams that were stronger, more experienced, and better positioned to win, Brooks was able to take a true inventory of his own team's weaknesses and devise a strategy that would ultimately allow them to win the gold medal. He bonded the team around a common enemy—himself—while, at the same time, helping them build the stamina and strength they would need if they were to have even the slightest chance of winning on the global stage.[3] I'm sure it wasn't easy for Brooks or his team to admit that they weren't as strong or as capable out of the gate as their country expected them to be. However, by admitting just that and by painting a truly accurate picture of who they were and what they could and could not do, they were able to build on their strengths, overcome their weaknesses, and go on to both surprise and amaze the entire world by winning against the favored Soviet Union team and going on to ultimately earn the gold medal.

When I work with companies on their strategies, I spend some time up front getting everyone to talk about the company that they really work for. One of those catchy little phrases that I've heard many times but can't seem to attribute to anyone in particular is "breathing your own exhaust." Roughly speaking, it means that you are so busy inhaling whatever comes out of your own mouth, that you forget to breathe in some fresh, untainted air every once in a while. Unfortunately, it happens to companies all the time.

If you work for a company that is constantly telling the world how much people love its products, then, as an employee, you'll be likely to believe it too. Taking that statement at face value, you may put it in your "strength" column. You know you should validate whether or not customers really feel that way about your products, but admitting that fact would require that you take extra time (that you probably don't have) to actually do that validation—not to mention having to tell an executive that the slightly exaggerated claim that he or she has been spewing to investors and employees for the last however many years is downright wrong. I can't possibly see what could go wrong with that plan! It's probably easier to go on living with the illusion that customers really do love your products and building your strategy on the hope that there may be some ray of truth to even some part of that statement.

Those who work in the real world know that this happens every single minute of every day. We may know ourselves; we just don't always want to admit it.

What, then, can we do about it?

When preparing for your strategic analysis, you absolutely have to allow yourself to take an honest look at your company and admit your own strengths and weaknesses. Sometimes, the best way to do that is to obtain some level of outside validation, usually from customers.

I once worked with an organization that sold long legacy, high-quality industrial products. This company had a flagship product that it had both invented and successfully brought into the marketplace over 50 years ago, and although the product had since been copied many times over, this brand still held a very respectable share of the market. The president of the company had grown up within the company and started his career selling this particular product—with much success. This was both a blessing and a curse: a blessing because the president knew the product and the marketplace so well, and a curse because the president knew the product and the marketplace so well. In fact, his version of the marketplace was now approximately 20 years old and, because of that, what he believed customers liked about this product nobody really cared about anymore. When I was brought in to help with this strategy, it was, by and large, because the product manager was literally petrified to go in and tell the president the truth, and he felt that a little outside support might be required.

What I suggested was hardly earth shattering. It was simply to contract an unbiased third-party company to talk with the company's customers and put it all in a report. With that important piece of evidence in hand, the president was forced to admit to some of the product's shortcomings and open his eyes to the new reality that existed in the marketplace. The one thing I have yet to see any company leader turn his or her head away from is true customer validation.

Another way to validate your own capabilities is to see how those capabilities have translated into performance results over time. There are two main performance-related dimensions that you will likely be tracking. The first is how your key metrics (sometimes called *key performance indicators*, or *KPIs*) have been tracking your results against overall expectations. These may include the following:

- Revenues
- Profitability
- Costs
- Prices

- Market share data
- Market growth data
- Customer satisfaction metrics

Preferably, this information will be presented in the form of a simple chart that culminates in the current performance of the business.

The second performance dimension that you should focus on is where your product or company is in its life cycle. Every product or company will follow a life-cycle curve—that is, it will be born, it will grow, it will mature, it will decline, and it will die. In general, that curve looks like the one shown in Figure 2.1.

For products, we generally replace the words *birth* and *death* with softer terms like *introduction* and *exit*, but the meanings are the same. The reason I prefer to use more realistic terminology is because, as harsh as it may sound, it is called a *life* cycle for a reason; not only does every product go through this curve, pretty much everything on earth goes through this curve—including us! When we talk about a product being introduced, it feels as though it was already existing and just waiting for us to announce its presence. But that's not really how it happens. Products are instead born out of a laborious process of observation, insight gathering, strategizing, ideation, development, and launch. Their introduction to the world is the culmination of a very long gestation period. Saying that products are *born* seems, in my mind, to capture that process much more adequately.

FIGURE 2.1

The Product Life-Cycle Curve

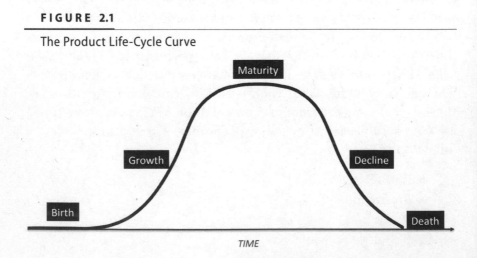

Similarly, when we say that we exit products, it implies a choice that is completely within our control. Although this is certainly the preferred route, it does not always reflect the reality that many companies face. If products aren't consciously exited after they have lived out their useful lives, they will inevitably die on their own—without a plan, without a replacement, and without a proper send-off. The truth is, products die, sometimes slowly and painfully if we do not take care of them, and sometimes in a much more dignified fashion if we can properly plan for their demise. I know that may sound morbid, but we have to state things as they truly are, lest we fool ourselves into believing that the process is somehow different than it really is.

You might have noticed that the Y axis on the life-cycle curve in Figure 2.1 has no definition. Oftentimes, you will see this axis labeled as "Sales Volume" or another pinpointed measurement. Unfortunately, real-life experience will poke holes in just about any variable that you want to put on this axis. For example, I can have a 50-year-old product that has had increasing sales volume every year due to continued market growth. But if my relative market share has remained constant over the past 40 years, I would be hard pressed to define that product as still being in its growth stage.

The problem comes when you try to view the life-cycle curve as a technical graph rather than a visual representation of a product's life. Like any form of life, everything ages differently. I can't really say that a 70-year-old person is in the decline phase of his or her life if the dimension I'm measuring is knowledge. If, on the other hand, I am measuring body function, then I could probably say that this person is indeed in decline. The measurement is relative to whatever function is important to you, whether that is sales or share—or anything else for that matter. And for most businesses (and most of life as we know it) it is some combination of all of these things, not necessarily measured, but felt. So the curve becomes a visual representation of what typically happens between the life and death of a product. Knowing where you are between these two points at any given time will allow you to develop strategies that take advantage of this position and help bring you smoothly to the next.

So know thyself—or, more accurately, allow yourself to admit what you already know about thyself. And then validate that with the people who know you best. Then you will be ready to use that information to develop your strategy.

This idea of knowing your own capabilities will translate, in business, into understanding your company's strengths, weaknesses, abilities, desires, performance, and culture. I will collectively refer to this, through the rest of our analysis as "company/capabilities."

ENVIRONMENT

The last of the inputs that a general needs to know about is the environment that he will be working within. So if you were a general, you might think about things like the terrain, the weather, or the critters and creatures that you may encounter as you carry out your plan. And like all of your other elements, you can't think of this one element separately from the others. It's not enough to know if you have poisonous snakes to contend with. What you really need to know is how well your troops are prepared to deal with those snakes and, just as important, how well your enemy is prepared to deal with them. Many a battle has been won or lost based on which team is most familiar with or equipped to deal with the battlefield elements.

Sometimes, your environment includes the tools and resources you have at your disposal as well. Again using a traditional battle as an example, most people will think about weapons as being a part of either side's strengths or weaknesses. But what about other resources such as food, water, and shelter? An army's ability to find and harness those things, particularly in a long, drawn-out battle, could certainly mean the difference between life and death.

In 1795 the French military offered a reward to anyone who could find a way to keep food from spoiling. We take it for granted today, but in those times, armies on lengthy campaigns simply couldn't sustain themselves because there didn't yet exist a way to preserve large quantities of food for long periods of time. If an army could solve this problem, it could gain a significant advantage over its enemies. Some years later, the problem was solved by brewer and confectioner Nicolas Appert, who discovered that food cooked inside sealed glass jars remained free of spoilage until the seals were broken.[4] This became the basis for modern-day canning and is a perfect example of how a strategy can be devised around an observed environmental factor.

In business, our environment is actually split into two main areas. The first is the environment in which similar competitors gather. We will refer to this as our "industry." The second is the environment in which similar customers gather. We will refer to this as our "market."

Analyzing either environment will involve understanding the factors that will have the greatest impact on each. For your *industry* environment, this will include any **P**olitical, **E**conomic, **S**ocial, or **T**echnological factors that will influence the arena in which you will compete. This is often referred to as a *PEST analysis*, which, by most accounts, seems to have been derived from a suggestion made by Harvard Business School professor Francis Aguilar in his 1967 book, *Scanning the Business Environment.* In this book, Aguilar makes reference to understanding the "social, political, scientific, and economic" environments within which a given industry operates.[5] The PEST analysis covers these same four basic categories, which allow companies to effectively evaluate the outside influences that may be affecting their respective industries at any given time (past, present, or future). Some examples of typical PEST influences that might affect an industry are shown in Table 2.1.

Other factors have been added to the PEST analysis over time, including regulatory, legal, environmental, demographic, and even the ambiguous category of "other." Generally, though, most of these factors can be considered in one of the original four PEST categories just to keep things simple.

Analyzing your *market* environment will involve understanding the needs and behaviors of the customers that gather there. Because of this, the term *market* has come to be defined as "a group of similar customers," which is generally the convention that I will follow throughout the rest of this book.

In a sense, the market is equivalent, in military terms, to the land you are trying to acquire or the territory you are trying to protect. If you have any hope of obtaining or holding on to that territory,

TABLE 2.1

PEST Analysis

Political	Economic	Social	Technological
Government Policies	Economic Growth	Cultural Trends	Consumer Technology
Laws	Interest Rates	Preferences	Business Technology
Regulations	Exchange Rates	Population	Research Trends
	Unemployment	Health Factors	Information Systems

you need to know where it is, what its value is, and, if any part of that territory happens to involve living breathing entities, how they think, feel, and act. It may be uncomfortable to think that you might be fighting for the right to have access to a person or group of people, but in business that's exactly what we're talking about.

When analyzing customers, you need to understand two main things:

1. What motivates customers to buy something?
2. How will customers behave under certain conditions?

To better understand these things, we need only look at ourselves because, as it turns out, we are all customers of someone. So let's think about what drives us to take up that coveted title.

It all starts with a need or a desire. Yes, needs and desires are different, and, yes, they are also the same. Needs are easy: I have a problem and I *need* something or someone to help me solve it. Desires are a bit more optional: I have a problem and I *want* something or someone to help me. On the surface, this appears to be a subtle, yet significant, difference. But if we go one level deeper, we may see it another way.

The difference between a need and a want is purely subjective. One might conclude that a need is something that you absolutely cannot live without. But who really decides what that is? Let's say I have a leaky gas pipe in my home. You might conclude that I, as the resident of that home, *need* to have that gas pipe fixed. But in reality that need only arises from the fact that I *want* to live there or, more correctly, that I want to live there without dying. So a need implies that there are no other alternatives when in reality this situation almost never exists.

In my view, then, every need is a desire. That just helps to remind me of the fact that customers almost always have options. Rather than try to clearly define the difference between needs and desires, it is probably more appropriate to consider needs on a hierarchical basis, with some needs being more critical to our basic survival than others. Thankfully, this has already been very conveniently laid out for us by A. H. Maslow in his groundbreaking article "A Theory of Human Motivation," published in 1943 in *Psychological Review*.

Commonly referred to as *Maslow's hierarchy of needs*, this framework conveniently organizes human needs into five hierarchical groups, beginning with the things we need for our core survival, and ranging to the things we need to realize our greatest potential as human beings. In the terminology I introduced previously, this might be interpreted as basic human *needs* on the bottom (or foundation) of the hierarchy and aspirational human *desires* at the top of the hierarchy.

The needs that Maslow outlined, starting with the core needs and working our way up the hierarchical pyramid, are (in summary):

- **Physiology.** The need to survive as human beings
- **Safety.** The need to remain intact and able-bodied
- **Love.** The need to belong and feel attention from others
- **Esteem.** The need to feel valued and recognized by others
- **Self-actualization.** The need to realize our ultimate potential as human beings[6]

Using this hierarchy, you can begin to identify, characterize, and categorize customer motivations and include them in your customer and market analysis. Of course, just knowing what motivates customers isn't enough. You also have to *do* something with this information. To drive toward that, you'll need to focus on the second aspect of customer analysis, which is to understand how customers are likely to behave under certain circumstances. This will allow you to prioritize customer needs and ultimately key in on the ones that matter the most in any given situation.

The best way to understand your customers is simply to observe them in action. But as obvious as this may sound, it is unfortunately not practiced as frequently as you might think. During every product management and strategy workshop that I facilitate, I poll the audience to inquire what percentage of time each person spends analyzing and understanding customer needs. Incredibly, through this informal sampling of what now numbers thousands of participants, the average percentage of time spent *truly* understanding customer needs is less than 10 percent. When polled further and asked why they spend so little time in this area, the answer inevitably comes down to two main factors: (1) they don't have time, and (2) they don't know how.

My solution to this is to make the process as simple as possible. Like everything else, if you overthink this task, it will become too overwhelming to tackle. So I propose that you distill it down to three simple steps:

Step 1: Review direct customer feedback. Every business receives customer feedback of one type or another. Whether this is in the form of unsolicited customer complaints, social media interaction, formal survey responses, or even transactional anecdotes, direct feedback provides important touchpoints that must be considered when understanding market needs, trends, and behaviors. It is important to note, however, that customers will rarely volunteer feedback unless they are incredibly oversatisfied or incredibly frustrated; even so, they will only volunteer whatever information is most immediately on their minds. Therefore, this is not the only type of market analysis that you should rely upon.

Step 2: Observe your customers in action. Now that you have an idea of what's on your customers' minds, you have to take some time to observe them in their natural habitats. Depending on your industry, there is any number of different ways to do this. I come mostly from a heavy industrial business-to-business background. In that world, I would spend a lot of time in the field, watching customers handle and install the products that I managed. Consumer-based companies, on the other hand, will often hire firms to either watch customers within their natural environments or to observe customer reactions and interactions within controlled focus groups. Whatever your method of actual observation, this is a critical step since it will help you to fill in any gaps that may exist in the information you gathered during step 1.

Step 3: Talk to your customers. The final step is to validate what you've observed with targeted, solicited customer feedback. To do this, you need to talk to your customers and find out what they're thinking, what they're feeling, and how they view your company and your products. You can use the information gathered in steps 1 and 2 as a guideline to have these conversations, and you can use the conversations to help validate the information that you gathered. When speaking with customers, you must be clear in your objectives. If your intention is simply to meet with customers, that meeting may well turn into a sales call (which may not be a bad thing, but will not satisfy the true purpose of your visit). Prepare yourself with specific questions that you want to ask or specific points that you want to validate, and make your customers aware that their voices will be represented in your future strategy. In return, you will receive valuable information about not only what your customers are feeling but also what they're seeing with regard to market, industry, and even your own company's trends.

To summarize, your business environment will include two main elements:

- Industry environment
- Market environment

From this point forward, I will refer to these two areas separately as "Industry" and "Customers."

I've spent a lot of time here, and for good reason, because the environment in business strategy includes something that even the best military generals rarely had to contend with: customers. If you get that wrong, it will be just as catastrophic as not knowing your battlefield. In business, customers are a big part of the arena in which you play, and the companies that know them best will have a clear advantage over their competitors. I've spent a lot of time on this input because you need to as well. Your strategy will be all the better for it.

PLAN

The last piece of our military analogy is the plan. The plan, quite simply, is what you intend to do with all of this baseline information in order to satisfy your motivation. Essentially, the plan is your strategy, which, of course, we will be covering throughout the remainder of this book. That said, I do want to plant one fundamental idea with respect to how you might use all of this newly analyzed data to develop your plan, and it is an idea that is very often overlooked or, at the very least, not consistently practiced.

In a military sense, it may seem obvious that generals need to understand their motivation, their enemy, their capabilities, and their environment in order to develop a strategy. But it's not enough to just know all that information. You also have to use that information to *anticipate* what all of those elements are likely to do in the future. It is in this anticipation that strategies are developed. And it is in these strategies that battles are won or lost.

In case you're wondering whatever happened between Joe and me, here's the plan I came up with:

Since I was on the defensive, I thought it would be best to wait for him to make the first move. I figured that if I confronted him, even with the hope of talking my way out of a fight, I was likely to swat the hornet's nest and force him into action. So my short-term plan was to lay low. In the meantime, I would start a rumor that I was *also* trying to find the person who carved that saying into my desk. This would position me as a partner with Joe and also as a guy who wasn't afraid to start a little bit of trouble myself. So I put myself on the offensive, but with some unknown person. Of course, there was a risk to this as well, because I really didn't know who carved that saying into the desk, and that person could well have been even tougher than Joe. But at that point I would have Joe on my side, so it was a chance I was willing to take.

Following this plan, I laid low, planted my rumor, and, sooner than anticipated, Joe sought me out as a partner rather than an enemy. It worked. I was off the hook. We never did find out who carved that unflattering phrase about Joe and, to be honest, despite self-perpetuated rumors to the contrary, I really didn't care. The important thing is that I lived to tell this little tale, and I had taken my first unknown step into the world of strategic planning.

BASELINE ANALYSIS

Now that you have all of your information, you'll want to capture it in a convenient format so that it can be easily referenced throughout the rest of your strategic process. We're going to call this our *baseline analysis*.

The purpose of a baseline analysis is to give a quick and accurate snapshot of where you are today. This will include all of the same elements that I've been talking about for our military analogy using slightly modified business terminology as follows:

- Motivation
- Company/Capabilities
- Competitors
- Customers
- Industry

FIGURE 2.2

Baseline Analysis

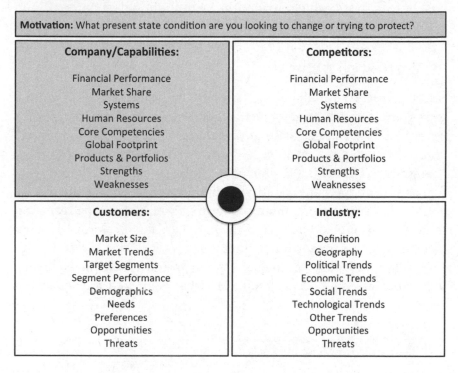

Motivation: What present state condition are you looking to change or trying to protect?

Company/Capabilities:	Competitors:
Financial Performance	Financial Performance
Market Share	Market Share
Systems	Systems
Human Resources	Human Resources
Core Competencies	Core Competencies
Global Footprint	Global Footprint
Products & Portfolios	Products & Portfolios
Strengths	Strengths
Weaknesses	Weaknesses

Customers:	Industry:
Market Size	Definition
Market Trends	Geography
Target Segments	Political Trends
Segment Performance	Economic Trends
Demographics	Social Trends
Needs	Technological Trends
Preferences	Other Trends
Opportunities	Opportunities
Threats	Threats

There is nearly an infinite amount of detailed information that can be analyzed in any one of these categories. However, to get you started, and so as not to challenge the law of diminishing returns, I have listed some of the most important baseline data in Figure 2.2.

To complete the analysis, you should gather as much information as possible, as long as that information is relevant to your strategic motivation. It is not necessary to try to squeeze all of this data into a slide with four quadrants as shown in Figure 2.2. Instead, this baseline analysis template is designed to be more of a tool, or a checklist, for gathering information in support of your plan.

It may also be helpful, as you begin to process this information, to think of these baseline categories in terms of internal and external dimensions. Doing so will help you compare and contrast what's happening outside your company to what's happening inside your company, thereby giving you a more balanced view of your entire current-state situation. The motivation and company/capabilities dimensions will therefore become your internal baseline analysis, whereas the other three dimensions will form your external baseline analysis, which is why they are highlighted differently in the baseline analysis template.

REFLECTING ON THE PAST

As you proceed through your baseline analysis exercise, it will be important not only to understand where you are today but also to reflect on how you may have gotten there. This will give you critical clues as to what may happen in the future if similar patterns repeat themselves. To enable this line of thinking, I encourage you to perform a second (perhaps less formal) baseline analysis that will inspire you to ask key questions about the future based on what patterns you may have been able to observe in the past. This backward-looking baseline analysis is shown in Figure 2.3.

When reflecting on the past trends of these baseline elements, it is important not only that you note what happened previously but

FIGURE 2.3

Backward-Looking Baseline Analysis

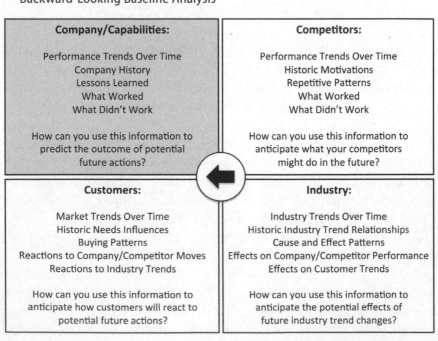

Company/Capabilities:

Performance Trends Over Time
Company History
Lessons Learned
What Worked
What Didn't Work

How can you use this information to predict the outcome of potential future actions?

Competitors:

Performance Trends Over Time
Historic Motivations
Repetitive Patterns
What Worked
What Didn't Work

How can you use this information to anticipate what your competitors might do in the future?

Customers:

Market Trends Over Time
Historic Needs Influences
Buying Patterns
Reactions to Company/Competitor Moves
Reactions to Industry Trends

How can you use this information to anticipate how customers will react to potential future actions?

Industry:

Industry Trends Over Time
Historic Industry Trend Relationships
Cause and Effect Patterns
Effects on Company/Competitor Performance
Effects on Customer Trends

How can you use this information to anticipate the potential effects of future industry trend changes?

also that you process this information in such a way that will allow you later to develop strategies that take these patterns into consideration. In this way, you will be building the same cause-and-effect database that I referred to in the chess analogy in Chapter 1.

DRAWING UPON YOUR INFLUENCES

Just as a songwriter has years of training and influences that she can draw upon when she sits down to write a new song, so do you, as a business strategist, have a plethora of resources that you can draw upon to help you develop your strategic masterpiece. There are many excellent books that have been written about strategic theory, some of which are listed in the Resources section at the back of this book. Whether based upon what successful companies have already accomplished or the personal observations of great strategic minds, these resources, along with your own experiences, will collectively make up the unique and personal repertoire of influences from which you will draw both inspiration and knowledge to devise your strategies.

Although it would be impossible to introduce you to all of these theories within the context of this book, there are several influences that I would like to share that you may find useful as you proceed through the process of composing your own strategy.

The first of these theories comes to us from Dr. Michael E. Porter, one of the preeminent strategic thinkers of our time. It would be difficult to write a book on strategy without making a reference, either directly or indirectly, to at least one of Porter's many prominent works on the subject of business strategy. In his hallmark book *Competitive Strategy*, first published in 1980, Porter outlines three generic strategies that companies can use to help categorize and guide their business strategies. These three strategies are devised around two dimensions: (1) how narrow or wide your strategic target is, and (2) what type of advantage your company or product brings to the marketplace. The outputs from this model enable companies to categorize their strategies into three overarching "buckets" as follows:

- **Cost Leadership.** Maintaining a cost advantage on an industrywide basis
- **Differentiation.** Maintaining a differentiated product or business advantage on an industrywide basis

- **Focus.** Focusing on the specific needs of a narrow target market, whether those needs are satisfied through cost or differentiation[7]

The idea behind this model is that a company must choose to focus primarily on *one* of these approaches: cost leadership, differentiation, or the needs of a particular market. Companies that try to master two or more of these areas may be strategically ineffective.

Another widely used strategic model is H. Igor Ansoff's product-market growth matrix. Ansoff's matrix was presented in an article that he wrote for the *Harvard Business Review* in 1957 entitled "Strategies for Diversification," and that was later expanded upon in his book *Corporate Strategy* in 1965. This matrix essentially gives companies four ways to categorize their growth strategies based upon the relative newness of the products they intend to produce and the relative newness of markets they wish to serve. This results in four product-market growth strategies as follows:

- **Market Penetration.** Growing with existing products within existing markets
- **Market Development.** Growing with existing products in new markets
- **Product Development.** Growing with new products within existing markets
- **Diversification.** Growing with new products in new markets[8]

These strategies all generally relate to how a business wants to grow, and so this model tends to be a bit more internally focused than some of the others. Still it is an excellent way to categorize how a company will approach the marketplace and which resources they might need to invest in to do so.

Another perhaps less commonly known model was given to us by strategy consultant Kenichi Ohmae. In his book *The Mind of the Strategist*, published in 1982, Ohmae gives us his "four routes to strategic advantage," which, like Ansoff's model, utilizes the relative newness of a product or business as one of its inputs. On the other side of his 2 × 2 matrix is a choice of whether to face competition wisely or to avoid it altogether. Intersecting these inputs provides guidance on how a company might approach the marketplace in one of the following ways:

- **Facing competition with existing products** by focusing on the key factors that drive success in the industry
- **Facing competition with new products** by redefining the products, processes, or services that are currently being supplied
- **Avoiding competition with existing products** by utilizing internal strengths in ways that competitors cannot match
- **Avoiding competition with new products** by defining new and previously unexplored ways to maximize user benefit[9]

On the surface, Ohmae's model looks similar to Ansoff's, although the focus on the newness of the market has been updated with a focus on the competition that will (or will not) be faced in those markets. In this way, Ohmae's approach tends to be more directly focused on competitors than any of the previous models that we have discussed.

Another approach to at least part of Ohmae's framework can be found in the book *Blue Ocean Strategy*, by W. Chan Kim and Renée Mauborgne. Published in 2005, this model expands upon the concept of avoiding competition by asking strategists to define new "Blue Ocean" market spaces—as opposed to the "Red Oceans," where competitors typically fight their "bloody" battles on similar terms. Using this clever analogy, the Blue Ocean model encourages companies to occupy these previously uncharted market spaces in order to gain a competitive advantage that nobody has thought of before.[10]

Of course, there are many more models to choose from, depending on which aspects you wish to consider when developing your strategies. Personally, I tend not to use any of these models directly; instead, I use them to help spark my thought process around three strategic perspectives that I discuss in Chapter 5:

- The Customer Perspective
- The Company Perspective
- The Competitor Perspective

I tend to use Porter's model to help me see through the customers' eyes, Ansoff's model to help me see through the company's eyes, and Ohmae's model to help me see through competitors' eyes. I will talk about exactly how to do this later in the process when we begin to develop our actual strategies.

For now, these models, and any other strategic theories, influences, and experiences that you may wish to utilize, should serve as a foundation for the critical piece of your preparation step that is focused on the past.

At this point in the process, you have explored your present and past elements using your Analysis and Recollection proficiencies. Now you have all the inputs you need to begin thinking about the future and to determine the ultimate path you will take to get there. Armed with a fully prepared baseline analysis and a strong foundation of knowledge, it is now time to tap into your Intuition and begin thinking about where all of this might be headed.

Finding Your Creativity

It may seem as though the preparation stage is all work and no play, but, in fact, this couldn't be further from the truth! Here are some tips to help you find your inner creativity during this step:

- A large part of the preparation stage will involve your Analysis proficiency. Try to remember our discussion in Part 1 regarding "space-clearing" and using only the data that will be absolutely necessary for your plan. Sorting through your baseline information with this higher-level view will not only save valuable time, but will also help you develop a more visionary and strategic focus.

- Think back to what you learned about Recollection in Part 1. Try to view all of your foundational learning as an opportunity to gain new insights, experiences, and influences rather than attempting to memorize concepts simply for the purpose of regurgitating them later.

- Take every opportunity to connect your baseline information with something you are passionate about. Whether it is your product, your market, or simply your competitive drive to win— your passion will help shape your strategy in exciting and interesting new ways.

- Always remember to keep the bigger picture in mind. As you sort through data and details, remember that all of these individual "notes" will eventually come together to form a symphony of sorts. As you read through the rest of this book, you will learn how all of these pieces fit together, and then you will be better equipped to put your baseline information into its proper context with respect to the overall plan you are trying to create.

CHAPTER 3

INSPIRATION

ANALYSIS	RECOLLECTION	INTUITION	ARTISTRY
Present	Past	Future	Path
Company/Capabilities	Influences	Vision	Strategy
Competitors	History	Goals	Story
Customers	Performance	Objectives	Resources
Industry	Experience	Target Market	Execution

←———— INPUTS ————→←———— OUTPUTS ————→

PREPARATION	PREPARATION	INSPIRATION	IDEATION
		GENRE	ARRANGEMENT
			ORCHESTRATION
			PRODUCTION

I II III IV

What You Will Do

- Establish your vision
- Establish your goals
- Establish your strategic objectives

Some of the best songs haven't actually been written; they've been inspired. I say this because when songwriters are asked the question about where their songs come from, one of the more typical responses is, "I really don't know." When probed more deeply, they may be more likely to tell you about *why* the song was written rather than *how* the song was written. In short, they are talking about what inspired them.

When people are inspired, it usually means that an external force has pulled on their emotions and caused them to see or feel something that they may not have been seeing or feeling previously. In this way, inspiration is often driven by the same unseen force that drives our intuition. In fact, the very origin of the word *inspiration* comes from the same root as the word *spirit*, implying some divine or unexplained intervention.[1]

Often, inspiration leaves a person feeling compelled to take some action in response to this newly discovered feeling. We usually think of inspiration as being a good thing, but it's not always that way. It simply represents some new insight that causes us to feel something and want to do something about it. Tying back to our discussion on Artistry, an inspiration usually taps into a passion that you already had but that just needed to be brought to the surface. What we do in response to this inspiration can be seen through our expression. So in many ways you can think of inspiration as being the spark between passion and expression, which will ultimately allow a person to create art.

When I teach people about business or strategy or product management, I am not telling them exactly what to do. What I am doing is providing them with new insights and new ways of thinking about things that, I hope, will inspire them to take action and improve their work practices in some way. Very few people will ever take everything that I say and implement it exactly. If they did, the world, I fear, would never progress. Instead, most students take what they learn (assuming it has been taught in an effective way), they interpret it, they modify it to suit their needs, and then they apply it in a way that is uniquely their own. In short, my words help spark emotions that compel people to take action.

When we speak about inspiration in music, the meaning is clear: somebody felt something and they wrote a song about it. And the mood and tone of that song usually reflects the way the composer felt at the time he or she was inspired to write it. Easy. But how do we translate that to the world of business? What can be so compelling as to inspire us to create a business strategy?

You may be inclined to say that the inspiration for your business strategy will come from a basic need. If your business is in decline, you need to turn it around. If your business is stagnant, you need to kick it in the pants. If your business is growing, you need to keep it on the right path so that you can continue to invest in it. These are some common origins of many business strategies. But these are hardly inspirational ideas.

The reason is that most of these needs are truly one-dimensional, meaning they are all internally focused. In the previous chapter, I referred to this as *motivation*, which itself is a far different driver than *inspiration* and therefore could yield very different results.

I believe that we are motivated by internal drivers and inspired by external drivers. You may be motivated to be a better person, but you will be inspired to change the world. This is a subtle but, in my mind, important difference because many strategies are in fact motivated rather than inspired, meaning that they are focused mostly on what the result will be for the company rather than what the result will be for the customer. That's not to say that one is better than the other, but it *is* to say that both will yield very different results.

I usually get called into large, established, healthy companies to help them develop their product strategies. Many times those strategies are motivated, quite rightly, by those companies wanting to ensure sustainable and continuous growth. The problem is, those same companies often say that they want to be more innovative or develop products that will change the world, not because they really want to change the world, but because they want to grow. That's not inspiration. That's motivation. And the result, almost inevitably, is that those companies don't change the world because in reality they don't really want to. Why? Because the world in its current state is pretty darned comfortable for those companies. So their motivation to grow and remain stable may actually outweigh their inspiration to do something to improve the lives of their customers, particularly if that improvement carries any significant amount of risk with it.

Smaller start-up companies, on the other hand, tend to be more focused, or inspired, by external needs, perhaps because their own internal motivations haven't yet been fully developed. That's not to say that these companies don't have any selfish motivations, but they are usually better positioned to be driven by somebody's passion to make a difference in the world, with the internal reward serving as a result rather than as a primary driver.

Strategies of nonprofit organizations may have similar characteristics. The purpose of these organizations is usually to provide a charitable service. They exist because an external need has inspired them to, and their strategic drivers usually reflect that inspiration. Again, that's not to say that there isn't a self-serving motivation that may exist as well. Having sat on the board of directors for several nonprofit companies, I can tell you that there is certainly a motivation to keep the organization solvent and to keep its employees employed. But the core reason for the organization to exist is so that it can continue to satisfy the external need that it has been chartered to address. So the inspiration outweighs the motivation, and the strategic result follows in kind.

My feeling is this: you can only change the world if you are willing to change your own world with it. In other words, if a company is truly inspired to help its customers, it will do whatever it takes to do that, confident in the fact that it will eventually be rewarded for it. On the other hand, if a company is only motivated to make more money and is not willing to take any internal risk to satisfy an external need, then the world is unlikely to be changed as a result. Again, both are valid approaches. You just need to know which one you are pursuing and develop a strategy that is aligned with your true intention.

Here's where I'll draw the comparison to songwriting to help further illustrate this point. Some songs are written solely to make money. Songs built on this foundation alone, however, may not resonate with their audiences, and therefore they are less likely to be hits. The only proof I have of this is the many less than stellar follow-up albums that I have in my collection that were recorded solely because the first album was a hit and the record company wanted to make more money. I can also think of quite a few "Part 2" movies that were produced solely on the coattails of their much more successful, much more inspired original installments. We see it in books, we see it in product design, and we even see it in our own careers. Inspiration drives success. And when that inspiration turns into us just going through the motions, that success begins to fade away. I know this is hardly researched proof, but remember, we're using our intuition now, so just observing the world around us is perfectly fair game.

None of this discussion suggests that you will need to choose between motivation and inspiration. In reality, a successful strategy will have a healthy dose of both. I also don't want to imply that basing your strategy solely on an internal motivation will yield a poor result. Part 2 movies continue to be produced, so they must be making money, even if all of them are not totally inspired!

Instead, what I am suggesting is that you should understand the balance between motivation and inspiration and, perhaps more important, that you should understand the consequences of developing a strategy that is weighted toward one or the other. In my experience, inspired strategies tend to have greater risk, but they also tend to lead to greater reward.

Whichever way you decide to balance your strategy, you should have the tools at your disposal to find and identify both your motivations and your inspirations and then to turn those, in whatever ratios, into a vision that will help guide your strategy. You'll do so by processing the information in your baseline analysis through one of the most commonly applied tools in the strategic repertoire: the *SWOT analysis.*

SWOT ANALYSIS

While the SWOT analysis is indeed a common tool in the arsenal of most strategic planners, I feel that there are some shortcomings in the way it is typically applied. Oftentimes, a SWOT analysis is performed by a group of businesspeople huddled around a whiteboard, calling off bullet points to place in each of four quadrants, labeled as follows:

Strengths
Weaknesses
Opportunities
Threats

At the conclusion of the exercise, this so-called analysis is put into a presentation, thereby allowing the planners to check off another box on the obligatory strategic to-do list. Meanwhile the real purpose of the tool—which is to help define strategic initiatives—is all too often lost.

The origins of the SWOT analysis are not completely known, but most sources seem to credit a consultant named Albert Humphrey who worked at the Stanford Research Institute in the 1960s and 1970s. His work there led to something called a *SOFT analysis* (which stood for Satisfactory, Opportunity, Fault, Threat), and this, either directly or indirectly, seems to have led to the development of the SWOT analysis that we all know today.[2] Whatever the roots, it is clear that just about every strategic consultant and business leader has at one time or another embraced this tool or some derivative thereof.

The way that a SWOT analysis is *supposed* to work begins with that same group of people huddled around a whiteboard. A matrix is drawn like the one shown in Figure 3.1.

The strengths and weaknesses are normally identified as internal or controllable factors, whereas the opportunities and threats are identified as external, or noncontrollable, factors. The idea is that your attack strategies generally will be derived from your strengths and opportunities, whereas your defense strategies generally will be derived from your weaknesses and threats. So if there is something you want that you don't currently have, you can capitalize on your strengths and develop attack strategies to go out and seize those opportunities. On the other hand, if you currently have something you don't want to lose, you will need to address your vulnerabilities and develop defense strategies to address any threats that may exist.

FIGURE 3.1

SWOT Analysis

Strengths (S)	Weaknesses (W)
Opportunities (O)	Threats (T)

Although all of this makes sense on paper, there are a few deficiencies in the actual practice that I've observed more times than I care to count.

The first problem is that the SWOT analysis typically looks at only one dimension of time: the current state. Of course, anyone can also perform a SWOT analysis that looks in the past or in the future. But without specific direction the SWOT analysis is at risk of being inconsistently applied with respect to which point in time is actually being analyzed. Interestingly, the SOFT analysis, from which the SWOT analysis seems to have been derived, takes a slightly different approach. This analysis has a time-based element to it, with good and bad *present* factors being listed, respectively, as Satisfactory and Faults, and good and bad *future* factors being listed as Opportunities and Threats.[3] As a strategic planning tool, this just makes more intuitive sense to me.

The second problem I see is that the internal part of the SWOT analysis (strengths and weaknesses) is only valid if you know what you're comparing yourself to. So let's say that I'm a manufacturer of laptop computers. If I'm comparing my product to a desktop computer, *portability* will most likely end up in the Strengths quadrant. On the other hand, if I'm comparing myself to a manufacturer of tablets, *portability* will most certainly be listed in the Weaknesses quadrant. In this way, strengths and weaknesses must be measured relative to some baseline; otherwise these terms are at risk of becoming meaningless.

The third problem that I often witness is that, although the exercise is supposed to lead to the development of strategies, I find that this is not always the result. Instead, as mentioned, the SWOT analysis often leads to a collection of static bullet points that serve to bring information to the surface that might not otherwise have been readily observed. The listing of this information alone does not fulfill the true goal of the SWOT analysis, which is to develop strategies that actually deal with all of these conditions. This may be due to a methodology that encourages list making over critical thinking, which, of course, is in direct conflict with the intended purpose of the exercise.

In fairness, there has been an attempt to rectify this last issue with the introduction of what is known as a *TOWS matrix*, a term coined by its creator, Heinz Weihrich in his 1982 paper entitled

"The TOWS Matrix: A Tool for Situational Analysis." What this approach attempts to do is plot the SWOT analysis on a 2 × 2 matrix, with each intersecting quadrant resulting in some strategic direction. This results in the identification of several strategic opportunities as follows:

- **S-O Strategies.** Utilize strengths to maximize opportunities.
- **W-O Strategies.** Overcome weaknesses to maximize opportunities.
- **S-T Strategies.** Utilize strengths to minimize threats.
- **W-T Strategies.** Overcome weaknesses to minimize threats.[4]

The TOWS matrix encourages its users to make the link between SWOT analysis and strategy. It can, however, be a bit formulaic in its approach. Because of that, I believe there is still another way to use the SWOT analysis that does not lead directly to developing strategies but rather leads to the identification of opportunities that can be used as the *foundation* for strategies.

Toward this end, I use the SWOT analysis as a tool to brainstorm opportunities. I then filter these opportunities through my vision, goals, and objectives, and later develop strategies to address whichever opportunities I have chosen through this process.

To perform a SWOT analysis in this way, you will proceed through the task of identifying strengths, weaknesses, and threats, and then list all of the possible opportunities that arise from those three parameters, making sure to follow a few general rules to help you overcome some of the shortcomings of the SWOT analysis that I discussed previously:

1. To address the element of time that is normally missing from the SWOT analysis, I prefer to break the SWOT analysis into present and future rows, with strengths and weaknesses being analyzed with respect to the present state, and threats and opportunities being analyzed with respect to the future. In this way, I am reinforcing the time element that was intended with the original SOFT analysis, and that will be so critical when translating opportunities into future strategic actions. This will also encourage you to introduce your intuition into a tool that traditionally has been much more focused on analysis.

2. Next, we need to address the lack of relative comparison for strengths and weaknesses. To do that, we must also challenge the notion that strengths and weaknesses are internal parameters and opportunities and threats are external parameters. I have had much more success with the SWOT exercise when applying internal and external elements to all four SWOT dimensions. For the Strengths and Weaknesses side of the equation, this involves viewing your product or company through the eyes of your customers (external) and then comparing that to your own perceived strengths and weaknesses. Not only does this approach help reveal critical gaps between internal and external perceptions, but it also solves the problem of not knowing to which companies or products your strengths and weaknesses are being compared. Now, you will be listing your externally perceived strengths and weaknesses relative to whomever or whatever your customers are most likely to compare you. Revisiting our laptop computer example, if your customers are mainly tablet users, you will list your strengths and weaknesses relative to tablets. If they are desktop users, then that will be your comparison. Either way, it will be important to state this up front so that the target of your analysis is clear, and so that additional SWOT analyses can be performed, if required, with respect to different target markets. On the Opportunities and Threats side of the equation, I equally believe that these are not purely external factors. In fact, there are many threats that can be internally generated. Pending structural changes, looming employee morale issues, upcoming management changes, planned mergers, acquisitions, or divestitures, and potential labor issues are all examples of threats that can be internally attributed. Similarly, on the Opportunities side we might gain access to new skills, knowledge, technology, or suppliers that could generate opportunities from within our own organization. All of these internal factors must be considered in addition to any external opportunities and threats that you perceive.

3. Finally, we need to address the typical bullet-point approach that most people take when doing a SWOT analysis. The remedy for this can be found by approaching the SWOT analysis in a particular order. The key is to go through all

of your present strengths and weaknesses, which will mostly be derived from your capabilities; then work through your threats, which will mostly be derived from your competitors, the environment, and, in some cases, your company as well; finally you will list your opportunities, which will mostly be derived from your customer and market needs, as well as any gaps you found between the internal and external parameters of your strengths, weaknesses, and threats. When doing the SWOT analysis in this way, it is important that you list as many opportunities as possible, whether or not you intend to pursue them. At this point, you should resist the urge to filter out any potential opportunities based on your own strategic biases. Instead, you should list all possible opportunities, no matter how unrealistic they may appear. Later, you will be filtering these opportunities through the vision, goals, and objectives that you will create in the next step of our process. When performed in this way, your SWOT analysis will take on the form of a story rather than a haphazardly generated list.

When all is said and done, your modified SWOT analysis should look like the one shown in Figure 3.2.

As you work through the modified SWOT analysis, it is important to note that your subject can be a tangible good, a service, or even your entire company. Which one you choose will depend largely on the motivation that you determined during your baseline analysis and the type of strategy you want to compose. The important thing to keep in mind is that your SWOT analysis should always be performed with respect to whatever product you are trying to sell to the marketplace. So if you are developing an overall corporate strategy, the product is your company, and, accordingly, you should perform a SWOT analysis for your business as a whole. If, on the other hand, you are developing a strategy for a particular good or service, then you should focus your SWOT analysis on whatever specific product or service you will ultimately be selling in relation to your strategy.

Let's run through a quick example of exactly how this modified SWOT analysis might be used. Keeping with the laptop example, let's

FIGURE 3.2

Modified SWOT Analysis

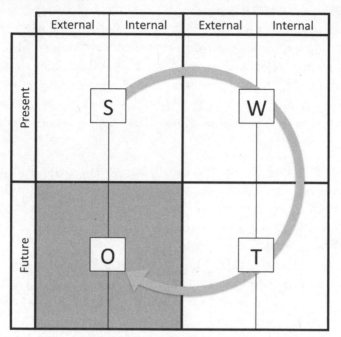

say that we are a manufacturer of laptop computers. Let's also say that our baseline analysis shows the following, at a high level:

- **Motivation.** Our shareholder value is decreasing due to competing technologies taking our market share.
- **Customers.** Our customers are moving over to those competing technologies such as tablets and smartphones. They value speed, ease of use, portability, and the "cool factor" over performance and versatility.
- **Competitors.** Most of our competitors have moved into specialty laptop markets such as gaming or power business users. Some have also decided to manufacture tablets.
- **Industry.** Socially, everyone wants information and connectivity at their fingertips 24/7, without long boot times, awkward interfaces, or any degree of complexity. As

technology continues to advance, devices that can meet these needs are becoming smaller, lighter, more powerful, and more secure.

- **Company/Capabilities.** We have significant design and electronics resources within our company. We also have strong supplier relationships and even stronger channel relationships. That said, our current product portfolio is in decline, our financial performance has been steadily decreasing with respect to expectations, and we are losing share to competing technologies.

Now it's time to run through our SWOT analysis in order to come up with some possible future opportunities. Beginning with our strengths, we can brainstorm through our first three SWOT parameters, focusing on present strengths and weaknesses, and future threats, as shown in Table 3.1.

Next, we begin to think about all of the different strategic opportunities that might come from these first three parameters, referring back to our baseline analysis at each step along the way. Thinking about external opportunities that could lead to potential market strategies, and internal opportunities that could lead to potential product strategies (more on this later), we can begin to brainstorm all of the possibilities, as shown in Table 3.2.

Notice that these opportunities are not strategies, because we are not yet talking about how we will go about *doing* any of these things. Instead these are simply opportunities that we might ultimately develop strategies to pursue.

Also notice that we are not yet choosing exactly which opportunities we will pursue. Instead, we are simply listing all of our possible opportunities. Everything is fair game at this point, because all of these opportunities are based collectively upon our own capabilities, the needs of our customers, and any external industry or competitive factors that will serve to either threaten or fortify those dynamics. Admittedly, this is a slightly different approach to a standard SWOT analysis, but it is one that allows you to consider all of your strategic options without prefiltering them through a paradigm that hasn't yet been fully vetted. These opportunities will now serve as your inspiration so that you can develop a balanced vision based upon both what customers want to buy and what your company wants to pursue.

TABLE 3.1

S-W-T Analysis

STRENGTHS	
External	**Internal**

Versus Other Laptops:
  Superior customer support
  Easy to use
  High quality/reliability
  Known brand
  Low price
 	
Versus Tablets:
  Large screen size
  Component connectivity
  Long battery life
  Keyboard input
  More powerful software
  Enhanced security
  Large storage capacity
	Abundant technical resources
	Strong supplier base
	Strong channel partner relationships
	Strong customer support and service functions

WEAKNESSES	
External	**Internal**

Versus Other Laptops:
  Consumer brand only
  Mid-range speed
 	
Versus Tablets:
  Slow boot time
  No touch screen
  Lack of "cool" factor
  More complex to use
  Lack of fun apps
	Limited expertise outside of laptops
	Weak channels outside of laptops
	Reluctance to change
	Low risk tolerance

THREATS	
External	**Internal**
More advanced laptop/tablet hybrids Tablet apps meeting laptop functionality Increased tablet security solutions Cloud storage New technologies surpassing tablets	Financial performance limits investment Employees leaving for tablet companies Increasing internal costs Risk of divestiture

TABLE 3.2

Opportunity Analysis

OPPORTUNITIES	
External (Market)	**Internal (Product)**
Identify new user markets for laptops - Specialty businesses - Education - Power users - Desktop users Identify new geographic markets for laptops - Emerging markets - Internet and mail-order Pursue new markets with new technologies - Tablet users - Premium/Breakthrough device users Dominate existing channels - Lower cost products - New laptop models Exit the market altogether	Develop a competing tablet product Develop a hybrid laptop/tablet Develop specialty application laptops Develop a new breakthrough technology Develop a lower-cost laptop

DEVELOPING YOUR VISION, GOALS, AND OBJECTIVES

Before we discuss vision, goals, and objectives, we need to spend a little time defining exactly what these things are. To begin with, all of these terms represent the future, and that is certainly what your strategy needs to be guided by. You may also notice that I have left the term *mission* off of this list. In general, a mission statement defines how a company behaves in the current state; therefore, whatever it contains should already be reflected in your baseline analysis. I want your strategy to be focused on the future, and so I prefer that you keep all of your strategic drivers pointed firmly in that direction.

Toward that end, here is my one-sentence definition for each of the future-looking parameters that will help guide your strategy:

- **Vision** describes who you want to be in the future and how you want to affect the world.
- **Goals** describes the aspirational steps you will take to achieve your vision.
- **Objectives** describes the measurable results of each of those steps.

If prepared properly, your objectives will allow you to validate that you've reached your goals, which collectively will enable you to achieve your vision.

Let's look at a quick example:

Vision

- I want to affect a radical change in the way people view philosophy, making it more accessible and more applicable to a modern world.

Goals

1. To obtain a doctorate in philosophy from a top-tier university.
2. To become a highly regarded philosophy professor at an Ivy League university.
3. To become a world-renowned author, speaker, and advocate for modern-day philosophical principles.

Objectives

1. To graduate in the top 1 percent of my class and obtain a position with an Ivy League university upon graduation.
2. To publish three internationally recognized papers on the topic of modern-day philosophy in top journals within three years of receiving my doctorate.
3. To publish a book on modern-day philosophy with an internationally recognized publishing house within six years of graduation and sell at least 50,000 copies in the first two years of publication.
4. To have at least four speaking engagements per year, to audiences of at least 250 people, after the book has been published.

As you can see, the vision is very broad. It captures who I want to be at some point in my future and the overall effect that I want to have on the world. My goals provide specific milestone achievements, each of which, cumulatively, should allow me to realize my vision. The objectives, then, give me specific and measurable targets that will serve to guide the actual performance of my goals.

One way to approach your objectives is to use what is commonly referred to as the *SMART method*. First popularized in a 1981 *Management Review* article entitled "There's a S.M.A.R.T. Way to Write Management's Goals and Objectives," by George T. Doran, this method says that objectives should have these five characteristics:

Specific
Measurable

Attainable

Realistic

Time-bound[5]

Although contrary to what the article title may imply, it is typical (as shown in our example) to set goals on a broader, more general scale and then set objectives using the SMART method to help achieve those broader goals.

The relationship between vision, goals, and objectives can be visualized as shown in Figure 3.3, with an overarching vision supported by goals and objectives that complement one another in the form of milestone steps and relative measurements.

There does not necessarily have to exist a 1:1 relationship between goals and objectives, as some goals may encompass multiple objectives. It is also important to realize that your objectives are likely to be revised over time, particularly as you approach

FIGURE 3.3

Vision-Goals-Objectives Pyramid

VISION

GOALS

OBJECTIVES

- Milestone
- Milestone
- Milestone
- Milestone

- Measurement
- Measurement
- Measurement
- Measurement

any one of your milestone goals. One of the benefits of taking this three-tier approach is that you can modify your objectives as conditions require without drastically varying your goals. Likewise, you can modify your goals (albeit to a lesser extent) without having to constantly change your overall vision.

Now that we've defined these three terms, let's see if we can put them to work.

The first thing you need to do is establish your vision. You will do this by going back to your strategic motivation and connecting it with how you want to help your customers, which you will have discovered, at least partially, through the opportunities that you identified in your SWOT analysis. In this way your vision should provide a healthy balance between your own motivation and whatever external factors are inspiring you to move forward.

Your vision will also take into consideration the strengths, weaknesses, and threats that you identified, but it should not be limited by these factors. Ultimately, your vision will serve as a filter to help you decide which opportunities you want to pursue. Your resulting strategy will then tell you how to best pursue those opportunities by addressing whatever strengths, weaknesses, or threats need to be leveraged or overcome in order to attain your vision.

To better understand how this works, let's look at a hypothetical example.

Let's say that you are a product manager for a software company that serves the music industry, and you are putting together a strategy for your portfolio over the next three years. Your main product has a leadership position in the market and because of that, your market share in your current market is saturated. Let's also say that the market growth is currently flat and is expected to decline steadily over the next 10 years.

Based on this scenario, the main motivation that is driving your strategy might be stated as follows:

> **Motivation.** We have saturated our market share with our existing software solution, which is currently stalling our growth. We need to look for opportunities to gain additional share and drive additional profitability to our bottom line.

Although this may be a strong motivation, it is unfortunately not very inspirational.

After going through your SWOT analysis, you uncovered some very real and very unmet customer needs. In short, you found that musicians would like to have faster, simpler software solutions for music notation and recording that would allow them to increase their output without sacrificing quality. Combining your motivation with your newfound inspiration, you might develop a vision statement that reads as follows:

Vision Statement. We want to be the provider of choice of breakthrough, innovative software for musicians in need of faster, simpler notation and recording solutions that will help them earn more revenue from their music and in turn will deliver more profitable margins to our company.

Had you tried to develop your vision before getting your inspiration, it might have looked something like this:

Vision Statement. We want to be the number-one manufacturer of music software by providing innovative solutions that will deliver profitable margins.

Both of these vision statements are valid, but which is more inspiring? The first is all about the customers, with your company's health being stated as a result. The second is all about your company, with the customer need being stated as a necessary means to that end.

Think back to the example of a songwriter who writes songs for the sole purpose of making money. It might be fun at first, but it would rather quickly become a chore. The same can be said about developing business strategies. Removing the inspiration and focusing only on the bottom line takes all the fun out of it. It's no wonder why so many businesspeople aren't exactly in love with their annual strategic planning processes!

So if we agree that an inspired vision is the way to go, now we can begin looking at our goals and objectives. Being that they are both on the same plane in our vision-goals-objectives pyramid, I usually approach goals and objectives as one step, meaning that I establish both my goals and my measurements at the same time.

The important thing to remember is that your goals and objectives have to collectively represent the measurable results and outcomes that you want to achieve by implementing your strategy. This will not only allow you to validate your vision but will also allow you to measure the success of your strategy when you are in the implementation stages.

Continuing on with our music software example, some of the goals and objectives that might apply are shown in the completed vision-goals-objectives pyramid illustrated in Figure 3.4.

Of course, there can be many more goals and objectives, but this is a good start. Notice how everything is aligned with our vision. Also note how the goals and objectives align with one another and, as such, could easily be stated as one common phrase. Again, the choice of how exactly to present this step is a stylistic one and will ultimately be up to you.

It will also be important to align the vision, goals, and objectives related to your strategy with your overall company or corporate vision. Using the software example above, if the vision for your strategy is to provide breakthrough innovative software, but your overall company vision is to provide low-cost software solutions, these two visions may well be at odds. Perhaps there is a way to provide an innovative low-cost solution, but that opportunity must certainly

FIGURE 3.4

Vision-Goals-Objectives Pyramid Example

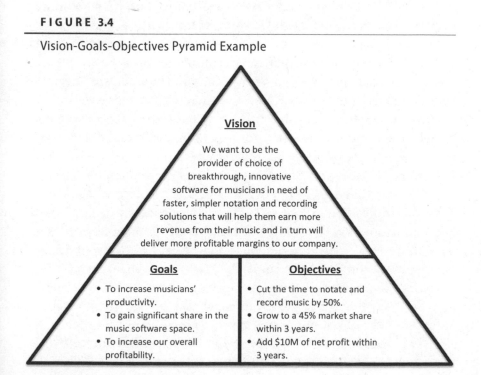

Vision

We want to be the provider of choice of breakthrough, innovative software for musicians in need of faster, simpler notation and recording solutions that will help them earn more revenue from their music and in turn will deliver more profitable margins to our company.

Goals

- To increase musicians' productivity.
- To gain significant share in the music software space.
- To increase our overall profitability.

Objectives

- Cut the time to notate and record music by 50%.
- Grow to a 45% market share within 3 years.
- Add $10M of net profit within 3 years.

be explored, or at least reconciled, before your strategic vision is finalized.

Of course, this type of alignment will require that you first understand what your overall corporate or company vision actually is! One of the most interesting parts of almost every strategy workshop that I conduct is when I pose the very logical, not-at-all trick question of "What is your company's vision?" The almost instinctive response is for a large percentage of class participants to jump on their smartphones and punch up the company website. As the network is churning, I implore them to lay down their weapons and just tell me, in their own words, what they believe their company wants to be in the future.

As half the class participants try to work through this exercise with me, the other half are still buried in their smartphones, determined to dig up the vision statement that they know they've seen and were probably even told to memorize at some point. Inevitably somebody produces a laminated card from his wallet that was given to him several years ago and contains the very vision statement he was neither remembering nor following.

Overall company goals and objectives tend to be more clearly understood, but only because they are often tied back, in some way, to employee performance reviews or compensation incentives. As such, these goals and objectives may be overly focused on internal financial performance, which can certainly be motivating, but may not always be inspiring. So if they exist, you should always seek out your company's customer-related goals and objectives as well.

Most people believe that it is incumbent upon their companies to clearly communicate the corporate vision, goals, and objectives to all of its employees. In concept, I generally agree with this sentiment. However, I am also a realist; being a realist, I know that communicating to large numbers of employees with any amount of "stickiness" will require no less effort than advertising products to large numbers of customers. The message has to be transmitted many times, on many different levels, in a language that is easy to understand, and on an almost continuous basis so that people never forget what you are telling them. It takes time, money, and resources that companies may not be willing to spend on internal messaging. And so it is not always done—at least not as effectively as it could be.

The solution that I present for your consideration is that you shouldn't wait for your company to tell you what its vision is.

Instead, you should seek it out yourself. That means sitting with your managers—and your managers' managers, if necessary—and talking through what the vision is. And if they aren't sure, or if it's not written down somewhere, then you need to spend some time discussing it and agreeing upon it and drawing some conclusions with your management team. Then you need to spend some time aligning others around those conclusions. In short, you need to take matters into your own hands.

While you're at this stage, now is a good time to understand your corporate strategy as well. This may be more difficult to define, and it may not even be written down in a formal way. Later in the process, we will find out how to deduce a company's strategy based on its actions, and you might have to do the same for your company. If you work for a publicly traded company, you should review your company's Form 10-K filing, or equivalent annual report, where a version of the strategy (albeit sanitized for public consumption) will provide at least some high-level guidance about how your company wishes to represent its strategy to investors and shareholders. You should also get comfortable with the fact that corporate visions, goals, objectives, and even strategies are broad, ambiguous, and often loosely defined. This means that *your* strategy will ultimately help to define the corporate strategy as much as the corporate strategy will help to define yours. So not only will you play a key role in understanding the corporate strategy, you will also play a significant role in helping to create it. This is what true strategic alignment is all about.

When all is said and done, you will end up with a strategic vision that has been derived from your motivation, balanced by inspired opportunities, and aligned with your corporate vision. You will also have clear goals and objectives that, if achieved, will allow you to realize your vision in a way that is aligned with your corporate strategy. At this point, you are ready to start sorting through your opportunities and using them to guide your strategies.

FILTERING OPPORTUNITIES

Now that you have your inspired vision, along with goals and objectives to support it, you'll need to filter your opportunities so that you will only be focusing on the ones you wish to pursue. Chances are you've already started this process when you were establishing your vision, but it is now time to go back and choose only those specific opportunities that you want your strategy to focus on. To do this, you'll need to understand the difference between market opportunities and product opportunities.

Your market opportunities will arise from the external part of your SWOT analysis. These are usually based on customer needs, industry trends, and opportunities to fill any gaps that may exist between what customers want and what they are currently getting. Product opportunities, on the other hand, are usually based on your own capabilities. These might reflect new technologies that you wish to pursue or any enhancements to existing products that you might want to make. That's not to say that product opportunities won't arise from customer needs, but opportunities that develop in this way will likely appear in the market column first.

When filtering your opportunities, I always recommend starting with the market opportunities and then moving to the product opportunities. This will help you to develop a more externally focused strategy than an internally focused one and also to use your inspiration rather than your motivation to help drive that strategy. It should be noted, however, that it is also perfectly acceptable to start with the product opportunities that you want to pursue and then match the market opportunities accordingly, although choosing in this order is likely to yield slightly different (and perhaps suboptimal) strategic results. I will talk about this more in Chapter 4.

You may also at this point be asking yourself: "Should developing my vision, goals, and objectives come before the SWOT analysis, or after it?" The reason I suggest doing the SWOT analysis first is because it enables you to explore all of your possible opportunities before deciding where you want to go. In this way, you are more likely to develop an inspired vision rather than a motivated one.

Once you have filtered the market and product opportunities with respect to your vision, goals, and objectives, you are ready to begin determining *how* you will actually go about pursuing those opportunities. But before jumping right into your strategies, you are going to want to learn as much as possible about the market and customers you intend to serve. We'll devote more time to obtaining this critical knowledge during the next step of our process.

IS THE PROCESS REALLY A CREATIVE ONE?

If all of this seems a bit formulaic, the reason is that in business it is not always easy to find your inspiration, particularly in the face of whatever internal factors may be motivating your strategic process. Therefore, the tools that I am presenting, and the order in which I am presenting them, are meant to help you find the inspiration that will help guide the rest of your strategic plan.

Keep in mind that strategy is not always something that you set out to accomplish. Inspiration (and motivation, for that matter) may present itself at any time, not just once a year because somebody asked you to put together a plan. Because of this, general managers or product managers or whoever is responsible for driving the results of a certain business, or part of a business, have to be thinking about strategy all the time. It is this dynamic nature of strategy that often throws the more traditional strategic planning process into disarray, but it can also lead to the development of highly inspired plans.

Some of the best strategies ever implemented were not developed in a boardroom and were not the result of a formal strategic planning process. They were simply inspired, written, and performed—just like some of the greatest songs you've ever heard. The best-laid plans sometimes aren't plans at all; they're inspired streams of reactions. And sometimes that yields incredible results.

The tools are meant to help spark your imagination, but they are not by any means required in a formal way if the situation doesn't warrant it. The important takeaway is the thought process, so that's what you should focus on as you enter the next step.

At this point, just try to answer the bigger question: "What is really driving my strategy, both internally and externally?" If you can answer that, believe it or not, you will have found your inspiration. You can always go back and fill in the blanks to validate your thought process, but never ignore your gut instinct. From this point forward, it will be your greatest guide.

If you choose to write out your inspiration formally, that is the metaphoric equivalent of writing the lyrics to your song. However, a song is but one musical form. Your inspiration can just as well be inside your head, and music alone can allow that inspiration to be expressed. Either way, you must now turn your focus toward writing that music.

But remember, your music will require artistry, and artistry requires passion, which you can usually find hidden among the unsolved needs of your target market. So before we begin writing our melodies, let's spend just a little bit more time exploring that world.

Finding Your Creativity

Ironically, for most creative ventures inspiration is not something that you actively need to find. Instead, it tends to seek you out. In business, however, we may need a little help opening the doors to the outside world in order to let in a little bit of that inspiration. With that in mind, here are some tips on how to find your creativity during this step:

- The tools in this chapter should be treated as guides rather than requirements. If you truly understand your company, your competitors, your customers, and your industry, you may already have a good sense for which opportunities will be most viable to pursue. Writing things down may help, but instinct has also guided many a great strategy. Don't be afraid to let it guide yours as well.

- If you are having trouble finding your inspiration, look no further than your customers. Visit them, observe them, and see what problems they're experiencing. You will be inspired to have a positive impact on their lives, and this, in turn, will inspire creative solutions to help you achieve that vision.

- Although the exercises in this chapter will certainly draw more heavily upon your Analysis and Recollection proficiencies, you must also utilize your Intuition and Artistry proficiencies if you hope to get any type of meaningful output from this step. Your creativity will be fueled by using some level of *all* of your proficiencies at every step of the process. If you limit these earlier steps to Analysis and Recollection only, you will block your view of what you can ultimately achieve, and stifle your creativity right along with it.

CHAPTER 4

GENRE

ANALYSIS	RECOLLECTION	INTUITION	ARTISTRY
Present	**Past**	**Future**	**Path**
Company/Capabilities	Influences	Vision	Strategy
Competitors	History	Goals	Story
Customers	Performance	Objectives	Resources
Industry	Experience	Target Market	Execution

◄──────── INPUTS ────────►◄──────── OUTPUTS ────────►

PREPARATION	PREPARATION	INSPIRATION	IDEATION
		GENRE	ARRANGEMENT
			ORCHESTRATION
			PRODUCTION
I	II	III	IV

What You Will Do

- Identify and understand your target market

It would be difficult to imagine a song being written without some level of consideration for its target audience. And the way a songwriter connects his or her songs with a target audience is by choosing to write within a certain genre. I will discuss the musical part of this process a bit later in this chapter, but before I do, let me briefly describe why this concept will also be so important for your strategic process.

Considering your future target market and the needs of that target market is often referred to as your *market strategy*. That encompasses the choice of which market you will pursue, how you ultimately will access that market, and how you will satisfy the needs of that market at a high level.

Market-focused companies will approach their strategic process by first looking at what their customers collectively need, then developing and marketing a solution that satisfies that need, and then managing all of their operations to provide that solution to the marketplace. On paper this sounds like exactly the right thing to do.

The problem is that market-focused companies may have a difficult time staying focused on the market as they continue to grow. When companies grow in terms of revenue, they also increase in size. With that comes a greater fiduciary responsibility to their employees and investors, along with more logistical challenges of trying to coordinate greater numbers of personnel. Although all of this certainly has its benefits, the downside is that companies may experience a natural shift in focus away from the market needs and onto their own needs. Over time their strategic priorities may inadvertently reverse themselves, whereby companies consider their own capabilities first, develop products that *they* believe customers will want, and then push those products onto the marketplace.

Few companies want to view themselves as putting their own needs above the needs of their customers, even though this in reality may be exactly the situation they are in. That's not to say that this isn't a valid approach to take. Companies that focus on being cost-leading commodity suppliers may be very content with considering their own capabilities first. So this approach is valid as long as it is intentional.

In the previous chapter, we used our vision, goals, and objectives to filter opportunities from the SWOT analysis and decide which of those opportunities we wanted to pursue. I chose to start with the market opportunities. But that is very much a choice, and the choice you make has everything to do with the strategic outcome you are trying to achieve.

If you wish to pursue an internally focused strategy, you will use your vision, goals, and objectives to filter the internal *product* opportunities you wish to pursue, without much consideration for what the market needs. You will then attempt to push that product into the market and establish a need for it. This approach could be appropriate if you wanted to achieve short-term financial results with little up-front investment or if you were trying to fully absorb the already invested costs of your manufacturing facilities or other internal resources.

If you wish to pursue an externally focused strategy, you will use your vision, goals, and objectives to filter the external *market* opportunities you want to pursue, without much concern for whether or not you are fully equipped to provide that solution. Taking this approach you are likely to invest larger sums of money to invent a new and innovative breakthrough solution that satisfies the market needs, secure in the hope that the market will eventually reward you for it. This is the type of strategy that is more likely to change the world.

If you wish to pursue a balanced strategy, you will filter a combination of both internal product opportunities and external market opportunities, paying close attention to balancing market needs with your company's internal capabilities. For most companies, this is the type of strategy that I recommend. If you plan to take this approach, I recommend, as discussed in Chapter 3, that you filter your market opportunities first and your product opportunities second. Doing so will ensure that you are giving strategic priority to the market needs without completely disregarding what your company is realistically capable of delivering.

The point of this chapter will be to provide further guidance on how to choose the market(s) you wish to pursue and also on how to get to know those markets a little bit better.

CHOOSING YOUR GENRE

The concept of genres is well known within the music world. In fact, with the advent of digital music, being able to categorize the vast amount of music that is now available to us has seemingly become something of a necessity. As of the writing of this book, the music research company

The Echo Nest was tracking 1,328 unique music genres (each of which can be sampled on the website EveryNoise.com).[1] But what purpose do all of these different genres really serve? Do they exist for the artists, for consumers, or for both?

Looking from the consumer side of the equation, genres can theoretically help listeners to more easily find and categorize their music. Back in the days of record stores, music was categorized by perhaps 20 to 30 different genres. This organization was helpful to an extent, but I can remember plenty of times that I was looking for a record in the wrong section because what I thought should be Rock was actually in the Heavy Metal section. So I may have thought the store didn't have the record I was looking for when in reality it was located under a different genre.

The same situation exists today in the world of digital music. Rarely will I search for music based on any of the 1,328 categories that I referenced earlier because, more than likely, my interpretation of at least some of those genres will be different than the interpretation of the artists (or companies) who categorized their music in the first place. The end result, just as with the record store, is that I might be looking in the wrong place for something that I really wanted to find. So as a tool for finding and cataloging music I think the genre system falls a bit short.

What I *do* use genres for is as a way to identify with the type of music that I enjoy. In this way the genre becomes more of a label or a brand that I proudly connect with. So I am a Jazz fan, a Ska fan, or a fan of Gothic Rock. And in this way I belong to my own private club of people who also have similar musical tastes and interests.

From an artist's point of view, I fear that many artists view genres as categories of musical *styles*. I, on the other hand, prefer to view genres as categories of musical *preferences*. That is an important difference and one that comes back to a concept we talked about earlier: the difference between focusing on your own products and focusing on your customers. Thinking that a genre reflects a musical style is the equivalent of thinking about the product first—that is, choosing a style and then finding someone who might like it. On the other hand, if you think of a genre as a customer preference, you are choosing to think about the market first—that is, thinking about what customers like first and then somehow connecting with that preference.

That's not to say that if I identify a segment that I want to appeal to that I can do so without having any capability in that area. Again it all comes down to balance. Look at what opportunities exist, and then balance that with your ability and willingness to provide whatever it is that the market wants.

For example, if I were a reggae artist, and I defined that as my style, I would be limiting my market opportunities to only those people who prefer the reggae genre. On the other hand, if I see that there is a growing market for reggae-pop crossover music, I can at least explore my ability (and willingness) to adopt a style that fits this preference and take advantage of a growing market opportunity.

Some artists might view this as selling out, and I am certainly not recommending that artists (or companies) always choose the most popular genre. What I do recommend, however, is that you try to view your product through the eyes of what customers want to buy rather than what you prefer to produce—that is, if you intend to make any money at it.

Most companies will say that they are customer focused, and I believe that is truly their desire. But, let's face it, right or wrong, there's a whole lot of "stuff" that just gets in the way of focusing on the outside world. What, with operations review meetings, quarterly investor calls, annual budgeting meetings, annual strategic planning meetings, and all of the legal and compliance issues, as well as Sarbanes-Oxley requirements, that's a lot of non-customer-focused things for companies to have to worry about. Also there are all of the issues that come up when you try to move tens of thousands of employees all in the same direction at the same time. I can't even seem to get 10 family members together for an extended holiday weekend without focusing nearly 100 percent of my time on trying to convince Grandma that I didn't mean what I said about her, keeping my parents from fighting with my brother, or preventing my cousin from leaving early because he can't deal with any of it any longer. That's just 10 people for three days, so try dealing with 10,000 people 365 days a year.

It is for this reason that company executives will rely on their product managers, marketing managers, and other business strategists to make sure that the customers are being looked after. And it is for this reason that you will want to put your customers front and center in your strategic plan. To do that, you'll need to know who they are.

MARKET SEGMENTATION

What exactly does it mean to "know your market"? We hear this phrase all the time, but how many times do we actually analyze what it's all about?

Knowing your market generally involves two main parts: (1) knowing *who your customers are*, and (2) understanding *what they care about*.

A market consists of a group of customers who want to transact business. Under this definition, practically the entire world population can be considered to be a market. That's a pretty broad target. So, in order to be able to manage things a bit more reasonably, companies will look to narrow down this focus by identifying only that portion of the population they wish to serve or who they believe can benefit from whatever it is that they are offering. These narrowed-down portions are commonly referred to as *segments*—market segments, to be exact. That's the easy part; I can literally break any given population into any number of different segments. The real question is, what criteria should I use to group them?

To answer this question we need to first understand that there will be several levels of groupings that have to occur. The first level will distinguish those people who *may* buy your product from those people who absolutely *will not* buy your product. An easy example of this is consumers of alcoholic beverages. In most countries, alcoholic beverages can only be consumed legally by people over 18 years of age; in some countries, that age is 21. Therefore, if you are a provider of alcoholic beverages, your first level of segmentation will occur by eliminating all people who cannot consume alcohol legally. We will consider what you are left with to be your Level 1 segment, as depicted by the triangle in Figure 4.1.

The next level of segmentation will determine what portion of the population a company actually *wants* to target or will physically have the *capability* to target. This is often a geographic segmentation, but there can be other factors as well. For example, perhaps our alcoholic beverage manufacturer will only want to target beer drinkers in the United States. In this case, this level of segmentation will have two criteria: one geographic and the other based on user behavior or preference. This allows companies to further narrow down their Level 1 segment into a Level 2 segment, as shown in Figure 4.2.

FIGURE 4.1

Level 1 Segmentation

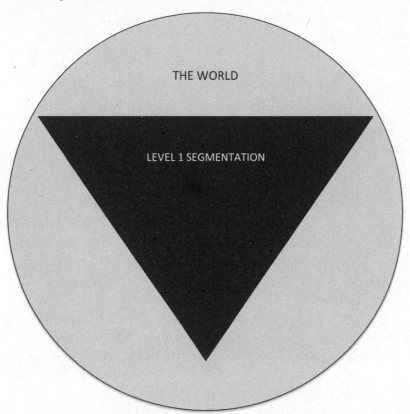

Now that we have a realistic picture of the world that we can actually supply our products to, we need to narrow our market down one more step to filter out those customers who we do not realistically believe we will be able to convert to our products. In this case, the segmentation is not necessarily based on locations or preferences but rather on pure numbers. Continuing with our example, if my company is a producer of beer, I know that there are hundreds, if not thousands, of other breweries that will all be fighting for the same target market. Furthermore, it is unlikely that my brewery will be able take over the entire market. So for this reason I'll need to narrow down the market one more step by estimating what percentage of the market my company will actually be

FIGURE 4.2

Level 2 Segmentation

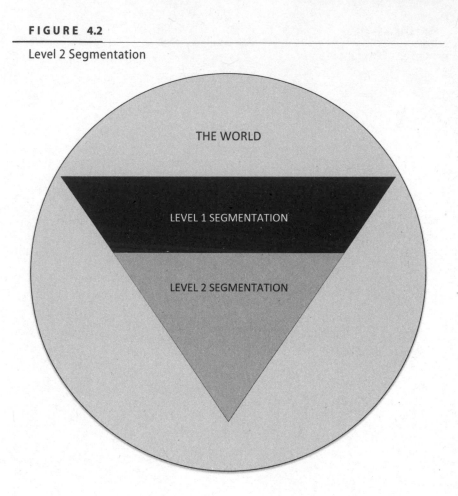

able to convert. This will become my Level 3 segment, as shown in Figure 4.3.

Now we have our base of potential customers, and now we can get down to the business of truly segmenting those customers based on how we believe they will ultimately buy our product.

These different segmentation levels are often referred to in marketing theory as TAM, SAM, and SOM, which can be simply defined as follows:

- **TAM** stands for *Total Available Market* or *Total Addressable Market.* This is the equivalent of my Level 1 segmentation and generally represents the part of the world that actually can or possibly will buy your product.

FIGURE 4.3

Level 3 Segmentation

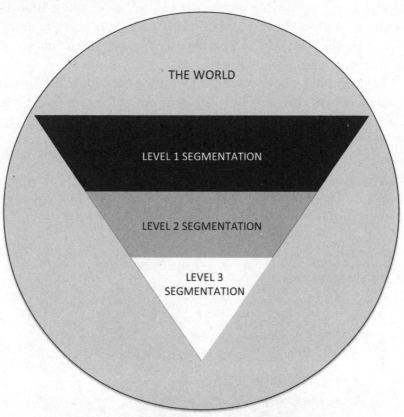

- **SAM** stands for *Serviceable Available Market* or *Serviceable Addressable Market*. This represents the part of the Total Available Market that a company can actually go after, based on capability, geography, and other factors. This is the equivalent of my Level 2 segmentation.
- **SOM** stands for *Serviceable Obtainable Market*, also sometimes referred to as *Attainable Market Share (AMS)*. This is the part of the Serviceable Available Market that you are actually expecting to capture and is the equivalent of my Level 3 segmentation. It should also represent your actual customer base.

Most of the time, you will see the TAM, SAM, and SOM discussion used in relation to forecasting. More specifically, this is a great way for businesses to financially predict how much revenue they can gain using what is called a *top-down forecasting* methodology—that is, starting with the universe and breaking it down bit by bit until you arrive at some reasonable prediction of the size of the market that you will actually be able to obtain. This puts an inordinate amount of focus on the numbers and perhaps not enough focus on *who* the customers in your target market really are.

In my model, I have dispensed with the mathematical formulas and the acronyms because what I really want to focus on is getting to know my Level 3 segment better. I want to know who they are; I want to know how and why they would want to buy my product; I want to know where they're hanging out. In essence, I want to take that Level 3 triangle and slice it up into more subsections, as shown in Figure 4.4. This will become my Level 4 segmentation, and this is how I will begin to truly understand my target customer base.

FIGURE 4.4

Level 4 Segmentation

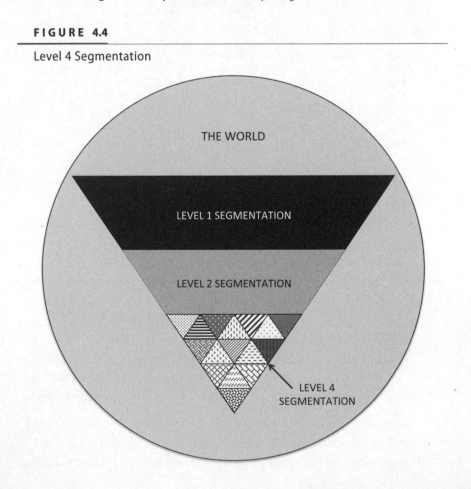

Before we talk about how exactly to group customers using this fourth segmentation level, I want to remind you that there are four levels for a reason; I do not want you to jump into this more traditional Level 4 segmentation exercise until you have first narrowed down your playing field using the first three levels. One of the reasons that I like to apply a top-down forecasting methodology to the subject of segmentation is because I might otherwise be tempted to segment the entire world based on their preferences, which of course could be a harrowing task. Companies are ambitious by nature, so it follows that they want to see the entire world as their collective oyster, accessing as many people in as many markets as they possibly can. Doing so, however, would be highly unrealistic, particularly without the right levels of resources, investment, or market presence. It is for this reason that I always encourage companies to first focus their target markets based on what is actually available to them and desirable to them. In this way, the final customer segmentation exercise will be much more palatable.

Note that all of this segmentation should be based on the market opportunities that you identified through your SWOT analysis and that you filtered using your vision, goals, and objectives. However, it is altogether possible as you begin to go through the actual segmentation exercise that you uncover additional market opportunities that you had not previously considered. In that case you should go back and update your SWOT analysis and your vision, goals, and objectives. Such is the strategic process. Each step builds from the last, and each step could well uncover additional information that will cause you to go back and start the process over again. Do not be afraid of this possibility, as this is all part of the iterative nature of strategic composition.

If you do end up reconsidering higher-level market opportunities (that is, opportunities that would otherwise have appeared in your higher segmentation levels), you should be aware that the higher up you target in this hierarchy, the more investment that will likely be required. For example, Level 1 opportunities will require the most investment because these are markets to which you do not currently have access. Level 2 opportunities will require the next highest investment, because you will have to work extra hard to convert more customers away from your competition. Level 3 opportunities—the level to which traditional customer segmentation is normally applied—will require the most reasonable amount of investment, because this is the level to which you currently have the most access.

Once you have finally determined what your target market will be, then you can move on to performing the Level 4 segmentation on that target market so that you can determine exactly where they are and what they care about.

Once you are at this level, there are literally hundreds of different criteria that you can use to group your target customers. These are the four most common:

- **Geographic.** Based on customer location
- **Demographic.** Based on objective characteristics, such as age, gender, ethnicity, economic status, and so on
- **Psychographic.** Based on subjective defining characteristics, such as lifestyle, personality, and interests
- **Behavioral.** Based on customer responses to given situations, such as how, when, or why a customer buys a product[2]

For business-to-business applications, there is a fifth methodology:

- **Vertical Market.** Based on a person or company's industry, profession, or trade

In general, geographic, demographic, and vertical market-based segments are all data driven, meaning that customers are grouped based on specific, factual, and undeniable data categories that are not subject to interpretation.

Psychographic and behavioral segments tend to be driven by emotion, meaning that customers are grouped based on how they act, feel, or respond to certain situations; therefore, emotional-based segments are all subject to interpretation, and interpretations are usually reached through a level of observation.

The common thread between all of these segmentation methods is that they are all based on common customer *needs*. As such, you should not segment customers based on any one characteristic just because it is convenient to do so. Instead, you should choose your segmentation models based only on those characteristics that represent a common need with respect to the product or service you will be providing to customers.

If you are developing a strategy for a preexisting product or service, you will probably have some existing, perhaps even presegmented, customer base to start with. Be careful not to assume that your current segments will remain valid for your future strategy, particularly if those segments have been defined on a corporate level. Each strategy will require its own unique segmentation model, no matter how inconvenient it might be to create. Chapter 2 examined the importance of observing your customers and understanding their problems. What you learn during that step may very well redefine any segment models that you or your company have already established. So you should remain open-minded on this account.

This relates back to our discussion on musical styles versus musical preferences. Predetermined, corporatewide customer segment models are equivalent to musical styles: they exist for the convenience of their creators. On the other hand, carefully chosen segments based on specific, strategic customer needs are the equivalent of musical genres: they exist based on the preferences of the customers. I encourage you, for the purposes of your strategic market segmentation, to always think in terms of genre.

In some cases, you will be developing a strategy for a product that has yet to be conceived. In those situations you will be starting with a target market and keenly observing the problems that they face. This market will likely be chosen based on balancing some core competency that you, as a company, already possess, and some target market that could likely benefit from that competency. As such, your Level 4 segmentation may be based on a combination of customer needs and how (and where) you choose to target those needs. Even so, you should wherever possible seek to define your segments in terms of how your customers will use your products rather than how you wish to provide them.

Sometimes, the subject of customer segmentation is reserved not for strategic planning but instead for strategic implementation (for example, for the purposes of developing marketing materials, creating promotional strategies, and writing customer-focused value propositions). While it is true that you will not have to dive too deeply into your segmentation models at this stage of the strategic process, it is absolutely imperative that you at least have a clear picture of which segments you will be targeting so that your strategy will be firmly aligned with the needs of your targeted market(s).

This will serve as a necessary guiding focus for your strategy, particularly as you enter into the next steps of the composition process.

With all of this in mind, now that you have a better idea of who the customers in your target market are, you need to spend some time getting to know them better.

UNDERSTANDING YOUR TARGET MARKET

One of the most difficult tasks you will face, especially in the later stages of executing your strategic plan, is learning how to speak to your target customers. By this I mean being able to speak their language and communicating with them in such a way that will allow them to relate more deeply to your company's products than to those of your competitors. Remember that we are all emotional beings. Ignoring that core part of the human psyche means that you will also be ignoring one of the main entry points into your customers' lives.

So if you know who your customers are, how can you now get them to trust you enough so that they'll want to make your product an integral part of their lives? The way to do that is to learn how to feel what they're feeling, which you can do using several now widely utilized techniques.

Many people in product management or marketing are familiar with the concept of using *customer personas* to assist in better understanding and relating to market segments. Personas attempt to capture the essence of customer segments by assigning a representative face, name, and personality to a typical customer within a particular segment so that you can get a better idea of how any of those customers might think, feel, and behave. In this way, companies will theoretically be better equipped to anticipate what a customer within that segment is likely to do under any given set of circumstances.

The use of personas was popularized by noted software developer Alan Cooper in his 1998 book *The Inmates Are Running the Asylum*. He promoted the use of personas to help software developers and product designers better relate to the typical personality and behavioral characteristics that a given product user might exhibit.[3] The practice has since been applied into many different business applications that might require a similar connection with a given type of customer or end-user. Prior to this application, advertising firms, marketers, and even playwrights had been utilizing comparable techniques for years, using common characteristics among large groups of people to embody singular character forms that could be used in any number of case studies, advertisements, or entertainment mediums.

Another approach that also seems to have arisen from the world of software development is to use what are commonly referred to as *user stories*. These are meant to be short descriptions or stories about how a customer uses certain products or features of a product. Like personas, user stories should in theory help companies relate to their end-user customers and the multitude of different product experiences that they are likely to have.

Both of these techniques are excellent tools for helping product developers relate to their customers in real terms. Perhaps to a lesser extent they also help marketers identify more completely with their market segments. However, in my experience, both of these techniques, in their current form, fall slightly short in helping product and business strategists truly understand their target markets. The reason is simple: the target for these exercises is a bit too narrow. In actually using and teaching those tools for many years, I feel that they sometimes force people too far into the individual user experience and too far away from the larger segment preferences. This might be useful for product development; however, for marketing and strategic applications, you generally need to think a bit bigger. Sure, it's nice to think about what Kathy in accounting would do in any given situation. But, in focusing so intently on Kathy, we might forget to think about how many Kathys there really are, and how significant that portion of the population is (or isn't) to our plan. So the exercise of getting to know your individual customer is a great one, as long as you remember to transpose that individual personality onto a much larger group.

What I propose, to expand upon the user story and persona concepts, is to create what I like to call a Team Card. Admittedly, I derived this name from my childhood hobby of collecting baseball cards. For some reason, I always cherished the team card. There was just something about being able to group all of these individual team members—each of whose cards I had collected and studied and come to know—and bring them together under one common umbrella. On the team card, I got the chance to see these players all grouped together; I had the opportunity to learn about what the team stood for and how the team performed together as a unit. And even though I knew that the team consisted of many different individuals, all with individual talents, skills, and personalities, there was something really captivating about seeing them all in one place at one time. I cherished the team card and the whole team concept in general. And, as it turns out, I'm not the only one.

Our desire to team up with people who have common goals, needs, and interests is about as natural to us as eating and breathing. It has been suggested that this core human desire dates back to an evolutionary need to surround ourselves with other people for the purpose of our own protection and survival.[4] It would naturally follow that this only works if the people we seek out have goals and interests that are in harmony with our own.

In a modern world, things aren't really that different. Not only do we naturally seek out "teams" that we can belong to on a regular basis, we also like to relate to one another in those same terms. Just as a fun little exercise, think of how many teams you currently belong to. Include in that list your company, your church, your community, your neighborhood, any sports teams or societies you belong to, your gym, your social media circles, any of the hundreds of websites that you currently have passwords to (don't get me started on that topic), as well as any of the probably dozens of sports teams, movies, bands, books, or clubs that you are a fan of. All of these affiliations link you to other people with the same common interests. The point is: we have a natural inclination to want to be grouped. When we do it in a negative way, we rightly call each other out on it. When we do it in a positive way, we give ourselves a logo and boast about our commonalities. It is this latter group that I want to expand upon.

The Team Card exercise allows us to quickly and easily group our customers in a positive way, by focusing on what makes them similar, giving them a collective identity, and bringing out a few fun facts that will help guide our strategic process. The reason I want you to think in terms of a card is because I do not want you to write an essay for each group. Instead, you should provide only as much information as would fit on the back of a Team Card.

The Team Card exercise forces us to automatically think in terms of a larger group while still focusing in on the individual characteristics that bind that group together. With that said, here's what I like to include on my Team Card, which is visually represented in Figure 4.5.

FIGURE 4.5

Team Card Template

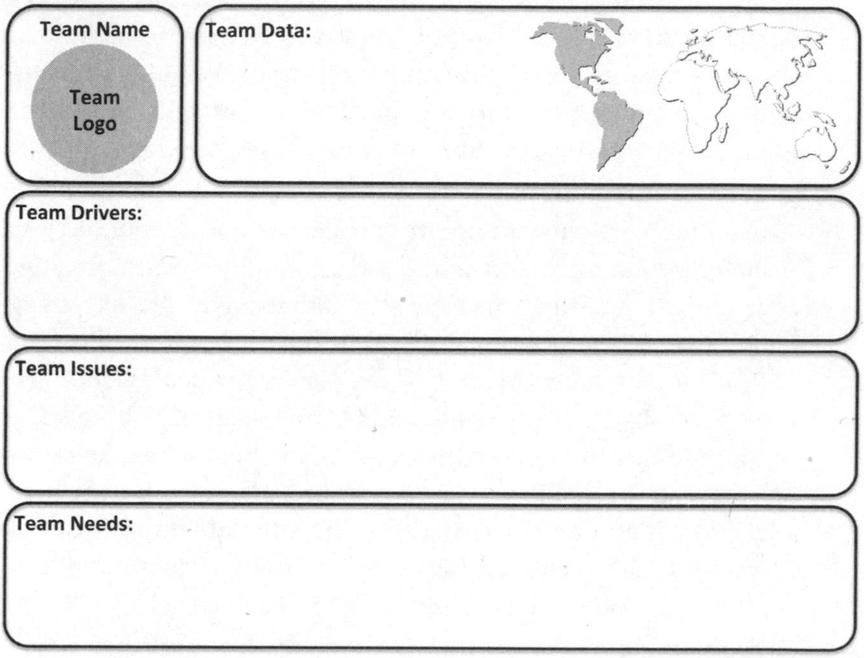

- **Team Name and Logo.** Nothing brings together a group of people like a symbol! It can be nothing more than a small picture or icon that is instantly relatable to the defining characteristics of your team. Creating the team logo gives you the opportunity to represent as many common customer characteristics, needs, and interests as you can in a quick sketch. In some ways, your logo will be the visual version of the segment's persona. You should also choose a segment name that can be easily associated with the most important characteristics you are attributing. As an example, the consulting firm Deloitte LLP has published several comprehensive reports on the U.S. healthcare market, one of which contains a detailed view of six distinct consumer segments. With segment titles such as Sick & Savvy, Casual & Cautious, Online & Onboard, and Content & Compliant, these are excellent examples of names that get right to the heart of what each segment stands for in just one short phrase.[5]

- **Team Data.** This is where you will capture any of the data-driven segmentation criteria that we discussed earlier, which includes geographic data, demographic data, and vertical market information. Do not feel that you have to include *all* of this data, as you should only indicate the range of information that is common to this particular segment, and only if that information is relevant to your strategic vision.

- **Team Drivers.** In this section you should indicate the things that this particular segment cares most about. These could include such factors as school, work, family, wealth, prestige, or any other feelings or aspirations that might drive this segment to take action. In short, find out: *What does this team stand for, and what do team members care deeply about?* For business-to-business applications, this section will speak to company cultures, how they represent themselves, how they behave, and what is most important to them. For business-to-consumer applications, this section will relate more closely to some of the psychographic or behavioral segmentation criteria that we discussed earlier.

- **Team Issues.** This section is the place to indicate the typical challenges or pain points this team has to deal with on a day-to-day basis. Items such as financial issues, health issues, problems at work, or any other everyday frustration can be considered here, but only inasmuch as they relate to the product opportunities that you are considering. This is an important point because this list can become quite broad if you do not keep it focused on the subject at hand. For example, using the previous healthcare example, if I am analyzing any one of those segments, I will want to restrict my observations to the issues that this team has around healthcare and, perhaps even more specifically, the particular healthcare-related product opportunities that I am considering.

- **Team Needs.** This is perhaps the most difficult section to complete, because you might be inclined to *solve* the problems that you identified in the previous section. We are not quite ready for that, however. Somewhere in between problems and solutions are needs. To best illustrate this, I will refer to Harvard Business School professor Theodore Levitt, who is often quoted as having said, "People don't want to buy a quarter-inch drill, they want a quarter-inch hole." In fact, in his book *The Marketing Imagination*, Levitt himself attributes this observation to a gentleman named Leo McGinneva.[6] Whatever the origin, the saying has been quoted, in some form or another, literally hundreds of times, to help put a rather simple but often overlooked concept into context: the drill is a possible means to an end, but the core need is for the hole. Before you can solve any customer problems through your strategy, you first have to understand what customers truly need.

Using this famous drill analogy as an example, the corresponding Team Card categories might look like this:

Team. Residential Cabinet Installers

Team Drivers. They care about providing the highest-quality workmanship, protecting their own reputations, and providing the safest and longest-lasting installations possible for their clients in order to get referrals and repeat business. Doing so allows them to support their families, grow their businesses, and increase their personal wealth.

Team Issues. Cabinets and furniture must be secured to any number of different building materials from metal studs, to brick, to concrete blocks, to drywall, to wood. Oftentimes, the material is unknown or a hole cannot be safely drilled, leading to last-minute design changes or potentially unsafe installations. Also, pipes are often drilled into by mistake, causing additional damage, repairs, and frustration on the part of the end customers.

Team Needs. To provide a clean, fast, and accurate hole in almost any building material and without damaging any nearby pipes or other structures. The hole must ultimately allow for cabinets and furniture to be attached to walls safely, securely, and reliably.

In this case we can see that the needs directly arose from the issues but did not yet translate into solutions. The issues will give the reason for the needs, which is a critical piece of information to have. But the solutions are yet to be developed and in fact will be addressed through your strategies. In this way, the Team Cards will provide the perfect bridge to the strategies that will be developed in the next step of our process.

We also see that the need, in this case, is much more compre-hensive than just having a hole. By walking through this exercise, we discover that what this segment really needs is a hole that can be created without damaging any surrounding structures and that will allow cabinets and furniture to be safely secured to walls. So the need is not the quarter-inch drill *or* the quarter-inch hole. It is actually to secure furniture to a wall! This opens the strategist up to a whole new array of strategic possibilities that might not have been uncovered if we simply stopped at the hole, let alone the drill.

Keep in mind that as in the example just mentioned, the Team Card exercise should be applied to a fairly specific scenario lest it become too broad of an exercise to meaningfully connect to your strategy. Therefore, you should perform the Team Card exercise within the context of a product opportunity that you are considering, and directed at the specific set of market segments that are most likely to benefit from that opportunity. You may well uncover additional opportunities as a result of this exercise, but you still need to provide yourself with some contextual boundaries to start with so that the exercise will be more manageable. It is also not necessary for you to consider every single market segment that could ever use your product or service. This is why it is useful to perform the Team Card exercise only with respect to your Level 4 segments, because it will allow you to focus your strategy more effec-tively on solving the problems of just those markets that you intend to serve. Your solution may eventually find success in other, perhaps unintended, markets as well, but you can then go back and refocus on the specific needs of those customers when and if your strategy calls for it.

Before you embark on this exercise, I give you one caution: keep it simple! Over the years, I have seen persona and user-story exercises taken to new heights of complexity, only a portion of which actually added any real value to the outcome. Complexity might help to employ more people, but it generally doesn't help companies to make more money. The Team Card exercise is meant to be *simple*. So I encourage you to keep it that way. Have fun with it, and don't make more of it than it's meant to be, which is just a quick and easy way to learn how to speak your customers' language. And, in so doing, you will be able to reach them in ways that your competitors can't.

REALIGNING OPPORTUNITIES

Now that you better understand your target market, you will need to realign your identified product and market opportunities. Before doing this, it is worth discussing the difference between an opportunity and a solution. Using the drill example, one of the product opportunities that you identified during your SWOT analysis may have been to develop a brand new way to create a hole. Another may have been to enhance your existing drill. These are not full solutions. Rather, they are broader categories of how you might solve a problem through product development or enhancement. In this way, the opportunities you choose will help to guide your strategic solutions rather than define exactly what those solutions will be.

Because your opportunities will serve in this critical capacity, it is important that you go back and realign them with respect to what you have learned through your market exercises. This will ensure that your vision, goals, and objectives are aligned as well, and that your collective inspiration and genre are firmly established before you proceed with developing your strategies. After working through your segmentation, you may, for example, find that your objectives cannot be fully met by pursuing the market opportunities that you had originally chosen, in which case you'll need to revisit these opportunities altogether. Or perhaps your chosen market opportunities can only be met by pursuing product opportunities that you hadn't originally conceived of or that you had previously rejected because you didn't feel that they were aligned with your vision. Again, these will need to be realigned so that you have an updated picture of both the market and product opportunities you want to pursue.

It is entirely possible that new market insights gained through this step will cause you to go back and redefine your vision, goals, and objectives altogether. This is perfectly acceptable as well, and in fact even encouraged, since you will not have had as much information then as you do at this point in your process. As you learn more, and as conditions evolve, your plan will need to evolve as well. This will happen now and at every step that follows.

You may be questioning why, then, I didn't ask you to perform a deep dive on the market prior to performing your SWOT analysis. This is somewhat a matter of preference, but I have found it to be more effective to use the SWOT analysis as a brainstorming tool and then use the outputs of that tool to help guide further exploration of the market. Doing this in reverse can result in studying market segments that are too broadly defined or that are not necessarily aligned with your overall vision.

Coming out of this stage, you should have a clear vision, clear goals, clear objectives, a clear view of the market opportunities you want to pursue, and a firm understanding of the product opportunities that will be required to support those market opportunities. In short, you now have all of your "whats" aligned. It is now time to glue them all together and begin working on the "hows."

The foundation of your song is now in your head. It's time to begin writing your melodies.

Finding Your Creativity

Artists must fully consider their landscape, environment, capabilities, and customer needs before they can begin designing their structural masterpieces. But they will still be stretching their creative muscles even through these seemingly less inventive preliminary steps. Here are some tips on how you can do the same:

- Remember to tap into your Intuition proficiency to consider not only how your customers feel and behave presently, but also how you anticipate they might feel and behave in the future—particularly in response to whatever you have planned for them. Creativity in this step will come from predicting future reactions based on what you observe in the present and what you know from the past.

- As you move closer toward ideation, you will be drawing more upon your Artistry proficiency. Remember that true artistry is not just about having passion; it's also about being able to express that passion in a way that inspires other people to care. And you can only do that if you know who they are, what they feel, and what they ultimately need. Your strategy is your artwork. If you want people to care about it, you must first show that you care about them.

- Although a book typically moves from chapter to chapter, your creative mind does not have to follow that same convention. In practice, you will likely be roaming freely among all three of the steps we have covered so far (preparation, inspiration, genre). This is absolutely encouraged both now and as you move through the rest of the creative process.

- Remember to have fun! There are times that I have intentionally avoided choosing a right and a wrong way to go about doing things. I can tell you what practices, in my experience, have yielded the most successful results, but I will stop short of definitively saying that you should or should not take a certain approach. Doing so would go against the very grain of the creative process I am hoping to instill. So feel free to experiment with your own methodologies as you explore the tools and frameworks I have provided. Who knows, maybe you'll help me write the next edition of this book!

CHAPTER 5

IDEATION

ANALYSIS	RECOLLECTION	INTUITION	ARTISTRY
Present	**Past**	**Future**	**Path**
Company/Capabilities	Influences	Vision	Strategy
Competitors	History	Goals	Story
Customers	Performance	Objectives	Resources
Industry	Experience	Target Market	Execution

◄──────── INPUTS ────────►◄──────── OUTPUTS ────────►

PREPARATION	PREPARATION	INSPIRATION	IDEATION
		GENRE	ARRANGEMENT
			ORCHESTRATION
			PRODUCTION
I	II	III	IV

What You Will Do

- Compose your strategies
- Develop your Go-to-Market Plan

Once I begin writing a song, things just start to flow naturally. To the untrained eye, it may appear as though somebody has just turned on a faucet and the ideas have just started to pour out, seemingly from out of nowhere. However, upon closer inspection, one begins to see that these ideas are actually based solidly in the preparation, inspiration, and genre steps that we've been working on up to this point. So the creative output isn't some form of magic; it's actually quite prescribed. You just have to allow all of these elements to work together and fuel them with enough passion to drive creative results.

If I were to draw my own 2 × 2 matrix to somehow capture how to do this, my dimensions would be knowledge and passion, with ideas resulting at the intersection between the two. I have a database of knowledge in my head to draw from, and I have a passion that is inspiring this knowledge to come together in a way that has never been expressed before. That's how I write songs, and that's how I compose strategies.

Figure 5.1 illustrates this matrix in relation to writing music.

FIGURE 5.1

The Melody Matrix

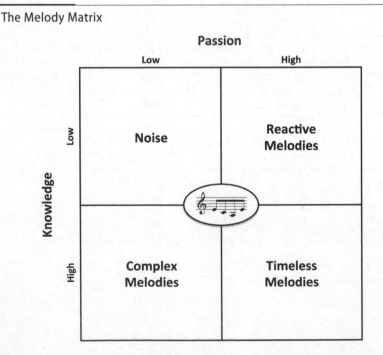

Using music as our guide, a composer's knowledge will allow melodies to be crafted that will draw upon tried-and-true musical theories and concepts, as well as the most current needs of the audiences that those melodies will ultimately serve. On the other axis, passion will allow a composer's raw feelings and emotions to be expressed, without regard for how the resulting melodies will connect musically with an audience. Intersecting these contributions will result in the following:

- **Timeless melodies.** Intersecting high passion and high knowledge results in classic melodies that will always be remembered, replayed, and referred to time and time again.
- **Complex melodies.** Intersecting low passion and high knowledge results in overly complicated melodies that may have little feeling and, therefore, no real melodic "hook."
- **Reactive melodies.** Intersecting high passion and low knowledge results in melodies that are born out of raw emotion but may have little musical substance.
- **Noise.** Intersecting low passion and low knowledge will result in nothing more than background noise.

This is just a theory, of course, based more on observation and experience than on science. But if we apply this same matrix to the concept of developing strategic plans, it's difficult to ignore the parallels.

Timeless strategies are based on a strong base of foundational knowledge; they are driven by people with strong passion and an inspired vision of who they want to be and how they want to get there. Complex strategies tend to be highly engineered, but they may lack the passion that will be required to drive any real change. Reactive strategies are fueled by a high sense of urgency, but they may not be based in enough facts or data to be completely effective. And strategies that are based on little knowledge and little passion will be nothing more than background noise.

As with all things, there may be a place for all of these types of strategies, but the strategies that I want you to compose are the timeless ones. To do that, you'll need to intersect the knowledge that you've built (through the preparation step) and the passion that you've found (through the inspiration and genre steps). Both elements are there; you just need to find a way to bring them together and express them. This is where your true Artistry lives, and this is the proficiency that you will be drawing upon more heavily from this point forward.

To help you do this, I am going to introduce you to one more strategic theory that typically helps me to formulate strategies from all of the foundational information that I have collected up to this point. It is based on a model put forward, once again, by Kenichi Ohmae in *The Mind of the Strategist*. Here, Ohmae introduces us to his 3Cs model or, as he refers to it, "The Strategic Triangle." In this model, Ohmae suggests that effective business strategies must focus on the 3Cs: Customers, Competition, and Corporation.[1] Even before I was aware of Ohmae's model, I have always considered, quite consciously, each of these three elements in almost every strategy that I have ever developed. However, my way of looking at these dimensions is just a bit different than his and, because of that, I want to introduce you to my derivative of this model here.

In my view, every business strategy should be able to answer three basic questions:

- How will we add value for our customers?
- How will we add value for our company?
- How will we face our competition?

To answer these questions, I like to think in terms of three strategic perspectives as follows:

- The Customer Perspective
- The Company Perspective
- The Competitor Perspective

My theory here is that it will not be enough to simply ask our three questions; instead, these questions must be asked from the point of view of the three different subjects of each:

- As a customer: "What value will I receive?"
- As a company: "How will we benefit?"
- As a competitor: "What effect might this have on me?"

In addition to these three perspectives, I tend to view every business strategy as having both a market dimension and a product dimension; that is, I am selling some product or service to some base

FIGURE 5.2

Strategic Perspectives

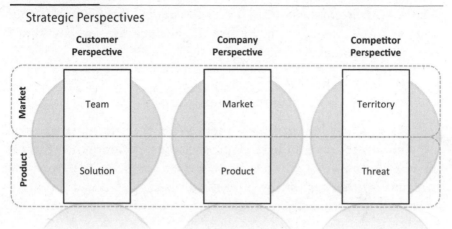

of customers. Following the strategic perspectives concept, I need to view both of these dimensions through the same three customer, company, and competitor viewpoints. Therefore, what my company views as its market and product, our customers will view as their team and solution, and our competitors will view as their territory and threat. This is illustrated in Figure 5.2.

In summary, there are two dimensions to consider (market and product), as viewed through three strategic perspectives (customer, company, and competitor). From these five basic elements, all of your strategic ideas will evolve.

STRATEGIC MELODIES

Somewhere between what you want to achieve and the specific actions you will take to achieve it is a summary description of *how* you intend to go about doing this, stated in just a few concise statements. These statements serve as a way to do the following:

- Provide high-level direction as to how you will achieve your vision, goals, and objectives.
- Describe what your overall future plan is all about.
- Categorize your actions.

Oftentimes, these statements take the form of a bullet-point list, with each point being referred to as a *strategic initiative* or *strategy*.

However, in the spirit of the creative approach I am taking, I am calling these *strategic melodies*. These will capture the essence of your plan, at the intersection of the five dimensions that we envisioned through our strategic perspectives:

- Product / Market
- Customer / Company / Competitor

As you may have guessed, there is no exact formula that will tell you how to write these strategic melodies, no more than there is an exact formula that you can use to write a song. So the best way to explain how this part of the process works is to step you through a hypothetical example using all the tools we have at our disposal so far.

Situation

Let's say that I am a product manager for a company that makes luggage. My company has an existing line of laptop bags sold into broad consumer markets, and we are looking to grow this part of our business. We have already completed our analysis on customers, competitors, industry, and internal capabilities, and, based on this information, we have established the following vision, goals, objectives, and market situation:

Vision

We want to be the customer's first choice for high-quality, fashionable, and innovative luggage and travel solutions that can accommodate portable laptop computers.

Goals

- Grow our market share of laptop bags in North America.
- Offset declining profitability in the broad consumer segment.
- Identify sustainable growth opportunities for specific focused markets.

Objectives

- Increase overall North American market share of laptop bags from 20 percent to 35 percent in three years.
- Increase overall profitability of our laptop bags from 35 percent gross margin to 40 percent gross margin in three years.
- Increase market share of business users in North America from 5 percent to 20 percent in three years.

Market Situation

Through our analysis, we have found that business users comprise a target market with unmet needs and sustainable growth opportunities. These users want a product that is easier to carry, puts less stress on their backs and shoulders when they travel, and has a professional look and feel that they can feel proud to wear and use. This analysis caused us to clarify a specific objective around this targeted market segment, being that this is also a segment that we are currently serving with our broader consumer brand.

Through this exercise, and drawing upon some of the strategic theory and influences that we have been exposed to, we believe that we want to solve the market problem with a new, differentiated laptop bag that will focus on this specific market. The question is, how will we go about doing this?

Let's start with our *customer perspective*. This is the lens through which the market and product opportunities from our SWOT analysis will be focused, as shown in Figure 5.3.

What we see is a market-focused differentiation strategy beginning to develop through this perspective.

Next, let's focus through our *company perspective*. This is the lens through which the strengths and weaknesses from our SWOT analysis will be focused, as shown in Figure 5.4.

FIGURE 5.3

Customer Perspective

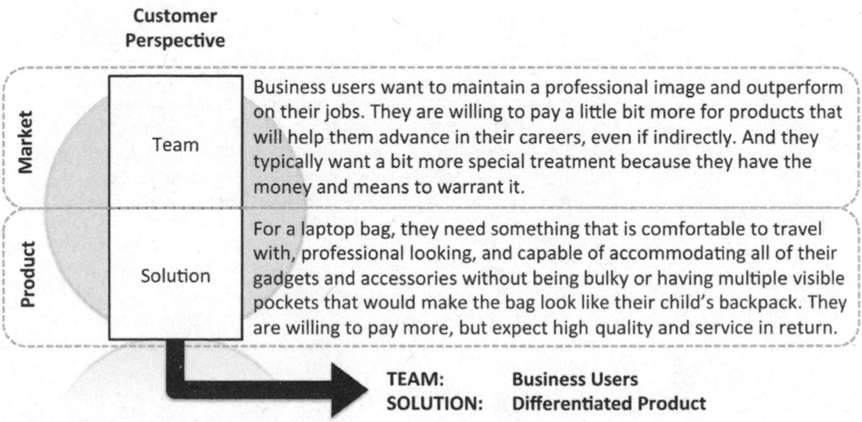

Market	Team	Business users want to maintain a professional image and outperform on their jobs. They are willing to pay a little bit more for products that will help them advance in their careers, even if indirectly. And they typically want a bit more special treatment because they have the money and means to warrant it.
Product	Solution	For a laptop bag, they need something that is comfortable to travel with, professional looking, and capable of accommodating all of their gadgets and accessories without being bulky or having multiple visible pockets that would make the bag look like their child's backpack. They are willing to pay more, but expect high quality and service in return.

TEAM: Business Users
SOLUTION: Differentiated Product

FIGURE 5.4

Company Perspective

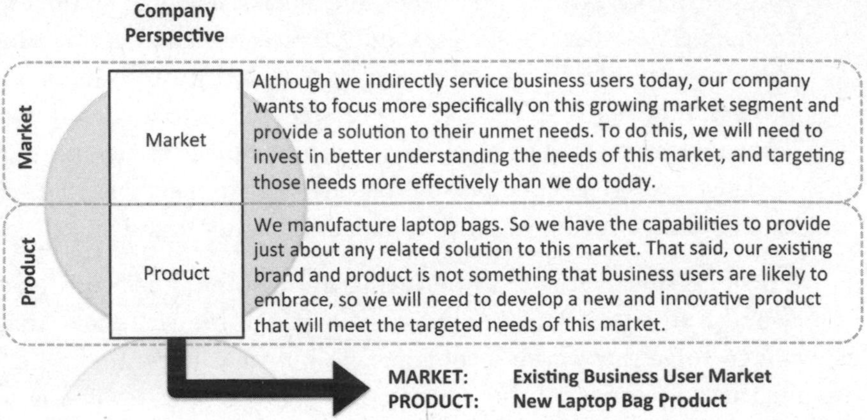

**Company
Perspective**

	Market	Although we indirectly service business users today, our company wants to focus more specifically on this growing market segment and provide a solution to their unmet needs. To do this, we will need to invest in better understanding the needs of this market, and targeting those needs more effectively than we do today.
Market		
Product	Product	We manufacture laptop bags. So we have the capabilities to provide just about any related solution to this market. That said, our existing brand and product is not something that business users are likely to embrace, so we will need to develop a new and innovative product that will meet the targeted needs of this market.

MARKET: **Existing Business User Market**
PRODUCT: **New Laptop Bag Product**

What we see is a product development strategy of providing a new product into an existing market beginning to develop through this perspective.

Finally, we'll focus on our competitor perspective. This is the lens through which the threats from our SWOT analysis will be focused, as shown in Figure 5.5.

We now see a strategy developing based on facing competitors directly and redefining the products that the business user market has become accustomed to.

FIGURE 5.5

Competitor Perspective

**Competitor
Perspective**

	Territory	Competitors view the business user market as an important source of high-margin revenue. They have invested heavily to establish their positions in this market, and are not likely to give up this "territory" easily. They also have the advantage of having an established infrastructure that intimately knows the needs of this market.
Market		
Product	Threat	Competitors currently supply high-quality products that business users want and need. If someone else entered this arena with a superior product, competitors would not lower their prices because their brand images would suffer. So they would likely try to discredit the new brand and design a competing product, which could take some time.

TERRITORY: **Competitive Business User Market**
THREAT: **Superior New Products/Brands**

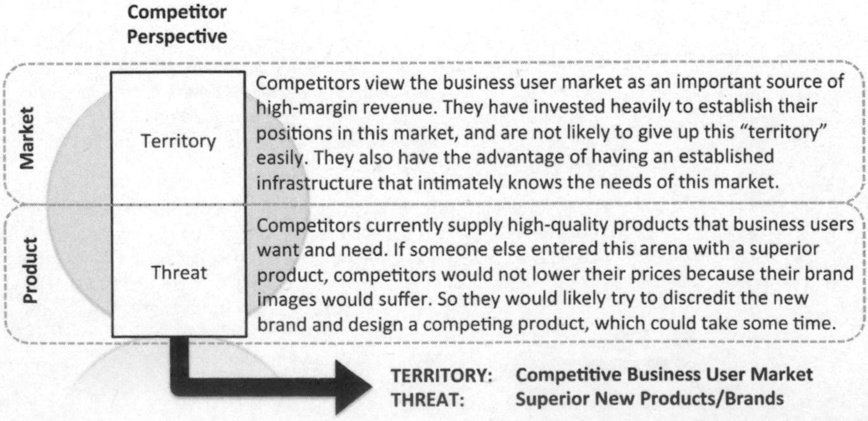

I have drawn upon the already-established strategic frameworks that I presented in Chapter 2 to help define the strategies that were being viewed through each of these lenses. More specifically, I used Michael Porter's generic strategies model to help define my customer perspective, I used Igor Ansoff's product-market growth matrix to help me categorize my company perspective, and I used Kenichi Ohmae's strategic advantage model to help capture what I want to do from a competitive perspective. Just as in music, we can take established and proven theories and combine them in new and creative ways that will yield unique results.

Of course, the examples I have presented are simply overviews of what each of these perspectives might look like. In practice, you can be as detailed as you want, considering all of the many different options that could exist when viewing your situation through each of these lenses. You might also find it helpful to state each perspective in first-person narrative form, taking on the persona of each as you do. This will further enhance the exercise and help you to truly get into the mindset of your customers, competitors, and even your own company.

Visualizing our product and market through these perspectives, our strategic melodies begin to flow, providing a framework for our entire strategy as follows:

- Provide a differentiated laptop bag focused on the specific needs of high-end business users, with constantly evolving features that will be difficult for competitors to react to.
- Promote a premium brand targeted toward high-end business users that leaves a permanent impression on customers that competitors can't discredit.
- Continue to look for specific problems of the business user target market and solve those problems in ways that nobody has thought of before.
- Consistently focus on quality, style, and simplicity over cost.

That's it. Four simple bullet points arising from our baseline analysis, our SWOT analysis, our vision, goals, and objectives, a firm understanding of our chosen target market, and a healthy processing of all of those inputs: balancing Analysis, Recollection, Intuition, and Artistry to arrive at the melodies that will serve as the foundation for our entire strategic song. You can use the strategic perspectives model if it helps you, or you can simply balance your knowledge of the past and present to help you anticipate what the future should look like. However you go about it, your strategic melodies should be broad, overarching statements that provide sufficient direction to guide every action that could possibly be carried out, but without specifically stating what each of those actions need to be.

Note that there is not a direct correlation between the strategic perspectives and your strategic melodies. In other words, I did not develop a strategic statement specifically for each strategic perspective. That is by design. The strategic perspectives are provided as a way for you to process information. The outputs will be completely dependent on what you learn and what you feel as you process this information.

Because there is no exact formula to follow in this situation, you might be asking yourself how many strategic melodies you should have. There is no definitive answer to this question, but here's a bit of overall guidance for you to follow:

1. Your strategic melodies should clarify your target market and your product solution.
2. Your strategic melodies should be able to answer, either directly or indirectly, the following three questions:
   - What will we do for our customers?
   - What will we do for our company?
   - How will we face our competition?
3. Your strategic melodies should be both simple and memorable.
4. Your customers should be able to sing your strategic melodies back to you without ever having been told what those melodies officially are.

In many of my workshops, I ask people to tell me what they think Apple's strategy is, and inevitably some variation of the following three points are presented:

- **Innovation.** Develop breakthrough, high-end, high-margin, beautifully designed products.
- **Simplicity.** Sell products that are simple for anyone to choose and simple for anyone to use.
- **Lifestyle.** Focus on providing a complete infrastructure that ties customers directly to Apple.

I honestly don't know what Apple's official internal strategy is, although it has certainly been surmised many times. And the reason, I believe, that so many people seem to be so comfortable doing so is because Apple consistently demonstrates some form of this strategy through its actions, if not through its words. As consumers, we understand how Apple will serve its customers, how it intends to compete, and how the company will benefit. We know the markets it wants to pursue, as well as the types of products it wants to provide. And perhaps most important, nearly anyone can recite Apple's strategy without ever truly knowing what it officially is or was.

Perhaps more widely publicized is the strategy of Southwest Airlines. The main elements of this strategy (as it stood in 2003) were published in the excellent textbook *Crafting and Executing Strategy: The Quest for Competitive Advantage*, by Arthur A. Thompson Jr., A. J. Strickland III, and John E. Gamble. In fact, this reference only served to confirm and expand upon what I, as a customer of Southwest Airlines, had already deduced the company's strategy to be:

- Gradually expand into new markets
- Focus on direct, point-to-point flights
- Provide friendly, casual, low-price service
- Economize on costs wherever possible[2]

Even in my interpreted version, this is a clear example of how (1) the product and market are both clearly defined, (2) each of the three strategic perspective questions is answered, and, (3) the points are simple, memorable, and capable of being sung by nearly any customer of the company. As with most successful companies, this strategy continues to evolve and, as it does, customers should be able to detect any new melodies and sing right along with them.

Try this with other prominent companies that you do business with and you'll likely be able to deconstruct their strategies as well. Some of the strategies will be successful; others will not. You should be able to deconstruct that aspect as well.

As you begin to develop your own strategic melodies, you should keep this important point in mind: your melodies need to be catchy—so catchy, in fact, that people can't stop singing them. This includes your company, your customers, and even your competitors. Avoid writing complex melodies that are too heavily weighted toward your own knowledge, and avoid writing overreactive, knee-jerk melodies that are too heavily weighted toward any specific passion. You should infuse high levels of both of these elements, but make sure they are kept in balance. Doing so will lead to the timeless strategic melodies that will ultimately inspire action, growth, and long-term results.

If you are still having trouble developing your strategies, I offer you a simple summary formula that I often use to tie all three strategic perspectives together:

- Your *customers* need something.
- Your *competitors* are supplying something.
- Your *company* should fill the gap between them.

In that gap, if you search hard enough, you'll find unmet, sometimes even unknown, customer needs. And in that gap is where you'll also find your strategic melodies.

STRATEGY VERSUS TACTICS

At about this point people usually ask me whether or not their strategies are too tactical. Here's my general response: "I think that business people spend far too much time trying to answer this question."

Somewhere along the way, the idea of being tactical seems to have taken on a negative connotation in the business world. This makes little sense to me because taking action should be a good thing! But because of this misplaced notion that being tactical is somehow undesirable, I find that strategists spend a disproportionate amount of energy worrying about whether or not their strategies are too tactical. I reiterate: tactics are good. You shouldn't be afraid of being action oriented.

Where the negative implication most likely comes from isn't from having tactics but rather from *not* having a strategy. Without a strategy, your tactics appear random and unexplained. The same effect will also happen if you have a strategy but don't communicate it effectively. Simply put, if nobody understands your strategy, then your actions will seem out of place. And then you will likely be accused of being too tactical. Your strategy should provide the context for your actions. Then your actions will be embraced in a positive way. It's as simple as that.

Although it will not be necessary for you, as the strategic composer, to lay out every action that could possibly result from your strategies, you might find that you need to go just one level deeper to guide how your strategies will ultimately be implemented. To do this, it may be helpful to develop a high-level plan—one level below your strategic melodies—that can be used to guide the more detailed actions that will ultimately be developed and carried out by your implementation team. This will help outline at a high level how you will translate your strategies into marketplace behaviors.

GO-TO-MARKET PLAN

Most students of business have, at one time or another, heard of the 4 Ps of marketing: product, price, promotion, and place. They can be loosely defined as follows:

- **Product.** This is what you are selling to the market and can be tangible (such as a manufactured good), intangible (such as a service), or a combination of both.
- **Price.** This is how much a customer will pay for your product (monetary or otherwise).
- **Promotion.** This is how you will let customers know that your product exists and also convince them that they should buy it.
- **Place.** This is where you will make your product available to your customers.

Often referred to as the "marketing mix," the 4 Ps date back to the 1960s and can be attributed to marketing professor and author E. Jerome McCarthy.[3] When McCarthy outlined the 4 Ps, the idea of a marketing mix was already in existence, that phrase being coined by marketing and advertising professor Neil H. Borden after drawing inspiration from a research bulletin written by another business professor, James Culliton. In this 1948 bulletin, Culliton describes a business executive as a "'decider,' an 'artist'—a 'mixer of ingredients,' who sometimes follows a recipe prepared by others, sometimes prepares his own recipe as he goes along, sometimes adapts a recipe to the ingredients immediately available, and sometimes experiments with or invents ingredients no one else has tried."[4]

Not surprisingly, the 4 P model has been built upon further and modified many times since its introduction. Over the years, some thought leaders have added additional Ps, including packaging, positioning, people, and process. Other derivative models have suggested replacing the 4 Ps with more customer-centric terms. Whatever mnemonic you choose, the concept of having a marketing mix is consistently applied among all of these frameworks—that is, each element is like a lever that can be pushed or pulled, and each lever will almost certainly affect the others. In this way, it is Culliton's original inspirational picture of an artist who mixes ingredients that continues to resonate with me.

A good example is the Apple iPad. When the iPad was first introduced, it was certainly a breakthrough product, and it was priced accordingly between US$499 and US$829.[5] Considering that some laptop computers were already in the sub-$500 price range, introducing what, at the time, could easily have been perceived as a large smartphone priced anywhere from one to two times the price of a fully functioning computer was a pretty bold move. That said, what would have happened if Apple would have introduced the iPad at a price of $99? More than likely, people would have seen it as more of a toy than as a tool. Similarly, if the product was designed as a lower-end product made of cheap plastic and featuring a nonresponsive interface, the price would have had to be adjusted to reflect this reality and to match what consumers would ultimately expect from such a device. So price and product were at least to some degree interdependent.

At that time, the iPad was only available at Apple online and retail stores and through "select Apple Authorized Resellers."[6] This essentially translated into a limited placement strategy, which also certainly added to the cachet of the iPad being a high-end exclusive product. If the iPad had been more widely distributed, it might have been seen as less of a breakthrough product and more of a commodity product, which may also have had some impact on its price. Add promotion into the mix, and you have a perfect recipe for managing a product's performance (and perception) in the marketplace.

All of this makes the marketing mix a very effective vehicle to help guide the ultimate actions that will be used to carry out your strategy. Using the marketing mix in this forward-looking way will result in what is sometimes referred to as a *Go-to-Market Plan*.

The Go-to-Market Plan will generally provide high-level guidance for each of the four marketing mix elements. Because these are still guiding statements, they are generally considered to be a part of the overall strategy, which is why I like to consider them at this stage of our process.

For further direction on how you can create your Go-to-Market Plan, let's explore each of these marketing mix areas in a bit more depth.

Product

Your product is whatever you are making available to your customers. It can be a tangible product like a television, an intangible product like a bank account, or an all-encompassing environment like a theme park. The important thing to know about your product is that it is never any one thing. Instead, it is whatever overall experience your customer has in relation to your company.

Let's consider a mobile phone. If I am a manufacturer of mobile phones, I cannot specify my strategy with respect to just the physical product, because that will make up only one very small part of a customer's overall experience. Customers will purchase the mobile phone at a wireless carrier's store, where they will wait a certain amount of time, be treated a certain way, and receive a certain amount of support to get them started. That becomes part of the experience. Then they will open the product box, examine the included accessories, and glance through the instruction manual. And that becomes part of the experience. Then they will turn the phone on, activate it, transfer their contacts and pictures, and begin using the included software on the phone. That also becomes part of the experience. Then they will begin interfacing with the phone, making calls, observing how well people can hear them, observing how well they can hear others, and thoroughly testing all of the various features, functions, and controls that the phone has to offer. That too becomes part of the experience. They'll find out how easy the phone is to use, feel how light or heavy it is, and think about how awkward or convenient it is to put in their pockets, jackets, or purses. That becomes part of the experience as well. Then they'll drop the phone (accidentally, we hope) and see how well it holds up. And if it didn't hold up, they'll get the phone serviced and see how convenient the repair process is. That also becomes part of the experience. In using the phone, calls will drop, important calls will be missed, and, if they're really lucky, the phone may mysteriously dial someone on its own. And that becomes part of the experience. When they need technical support on any or all of those things, that will become part of the experience as well.

Sometimes marketers refer to three levels of a product, which can be summarized as:

- **The core product.** This is the primary benefit that a customer receives from a product.
- **The actual product.** This is the tangible product that a customer buys, including the design, brand, packaging, and quality.
- **The augmented product.** These are the intangible added benefits that a customer receives such as service, support, warranty, and so on.[7]

In our mobile phone example there are actually many other factors to consider, particularly in today's high-tech world, where many products interact to provide a collective, often inseparable experience for customers. As I write this paragraph, my computer is running word processing software, which is automatically backing up to a cloud storage service over my high-speed Internet connection. When something isn't working as expected, I have no idea which of these products is the culprit. And I don't really care. Because of that, I'm likely to blame the wrong one and switch to another product as a result. So every company in that chain has to pay close attention to my entire collective experience and, in the ideal case, work together (whether directly or not) to ensure that I receive the best experience possible.

While the three-level approach may be helpful to some, I tend to view products in terms of a more singular experience, with each touchpoint connecting to other interconnected "dots" in that total experience chain. And although each of these individual dots (such as packaging design, user interface, warranty, service, and support) are important to specify, I tend to view those more as specific actions than as strategies. At this stage, what I like to focus on is the overall user experience. In fact, I go as far as to say that my customers' experience *is* my product and that the tangible thing they hold in their hands is only a means to that end. It follows, then, that my strategy will need to provide guidance on what that experience should be for my product—from beginning to end—as well as what that experience needs to be for any other product with which my product will also interface. This is an important consideration in today's modular, high-tech world, and one that I have captured visually with the honeycomb diagram depicted in Figure 5.6.

FIGURE 5.6

The Overall Product Experience

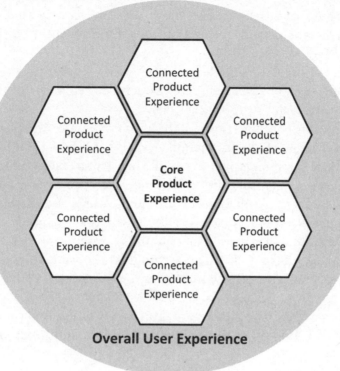

Overall User Experience

Another aspect of your product involves the timing of any revisions, upgrades, improvements, or enhancements you intend to make. It is common to release several versions of a product or to slowly release different styles or variations of your product over a set time schedule. This could serve to control your manufacturing supply, spread out your demand, or increase your share by slowly converting (or reconverting) more and more of the market with incremental improvements over time. A classic example of this could be seen throughout the 1990s with new families of faster computer processors being released for the consumer market every year (and sometimes multiple times within any given year). Each upgrade brought with it more power, faster speeds, and better performance, which eventually created a need for consumers to upgrade their home computers on every third or fourth release. The trend in hard-drive storage followed closely, as did software programs, most of which were updated annually at a minimum. Today, this trend of rapid product updating can be seen with smartphones and other high-tech devices. All of these are examples of carefully planned product upgrades with the purpose of attracting new customers and reattracting existing customers who want to take advantage of the latest that technology has to offer.

These preplanned releases are usually captured on what is referred to as a *product road map*, which is often a part of the ever-evolving strategic Go-to-Market Plan.

One last consideration for the product part of the plan has to do with the cost of the product or service that is being provided. You might have a strategic melody (as in our laptop bag example) that requires you to consider user experience over cost. In this case, your Go-to-Market Plan will focus on product features and enhancements that align with this strategic intent. On the other hand, if you were implementing a strategy of economizing wherever possible, your Go-to-Market Plan might include things like consolidating products; reducing labor and material costs; and eliminating other frills that might not be important to your target market. These cost-saving measures would all become an integral part of the product you intend to offer and, as such, would be incorporated, at some level, into your Go-to-Market Plan.

Price

Pricing is an inexact science, which generally makes it a form of art. As such, there are volumes that I can write (and that many others have already written) on this topic alone. But to try to frame this up in a simple way, let's take a quick look at this idea of customer value, as explored through the concept of the customer value proposition.

Although its origins are not completely clear, the term *value proposition* most likely arose from the idea of a "unique selling proposition," the definition of which was solidified by author and advertising guru Rosser Reeves in his 1961 book *Reality in Advertising*. Reeves's definition was centered around three main points:

1. It must point to a specific benefit.
2. It must be unique (something that competitors do not offer).
3. It must be meaningful to large numbers of people.[8]

Thus the idea of promoting products in terms of some unique and specific customer benefit was born—or at least popularized.

One of the challenges with the unique selling proposition concept is that it generally approaches this idea from the standpoint of selling rather than buying. As such, the tendency might be to put the company's interests above those of its customers. The implication is that if a company can show that its product does something that uniquely benefits customers, then those customers will want to buy it. A subtle yet meaningful evolution of this concept can be seen in the idea of a value proposition, which simply takes this *selling* proposition principle and turns it into a *buying* proposition.

Following this line of thinking, a value proposition is typically stated not only in terms of a benefit that a customer will receive, but also in terms of the quantifiable value a customer might ultimately derive from that benefit. This can be stated in terms of financial gain, time or labor savings, or even an emotional status or feeling. Once you understand the value of your product, you can use that value to help determine your price.

In the absence of a strong value proposition, you may be tempted to price your products based solely on costs and desired profit margins. Doing so would likely result in either pricing your products higher than customers are willing to pay or leaving margin dollars on the table because your products were not priced as high as you could have demanded. Pricing to customer value provides a better alternative that will result in maximizing your prices with respect to the ultimate value your products deliver.

When attempting to set a price based on value, you will quickly find that a 1:1 relationship does not exist between these two factors. For example, if your product will save a customer $1 million over his or her lifetime, it is very unlikely that he or she will be willing, or even able, to pay $1 million for that product up front. The reason is that the $1 million benefit does not come without some level of sacrifice—in this case, waiting a lifetime to receive it. So the customer will not be willing to pay anywhere near that price.

When determining overall price, you generally need to subtract whatever sacrifice a customer must make from whatever benefit they will receive. So:

$$\text{Benefit} - \text{Sacrifice} = \text{Overall Value}$$

Most discussions around value proposition focus only on assigning a value to the benefits. However, I contend that you must also assign a value to the sacrifice, and then use the difference between these to help set your price. You will still be pricing your product with respect to the benefit a customer receives, but you will now be offsetting any sacrifices to arrive at higher or lower relative values and, accordingly, higher or lower relative prices. This can be visualized as shown in Figure 5.7.

The purpose of this chart is simply to help you think in terms of a product's relative value rather than just the value of its benefits. Products with high relative value will have prices that more closely match the value of its benefits, while products with low relative value will have prices that are adjusted quite a bit lower than the value that their benefits will bring. Every product comes with some level of sacrifice. Even going to a store to buy something or waiting several days to receive something in the mail represents a sacrifice of time or emotion on the part of the customer. The idea is to determine the value of this sacrifice and then use that value to help adjust your pricing accordingly. Of course, doing so will be much more a matter of

FIGURE 5.7

Relative Value Graph

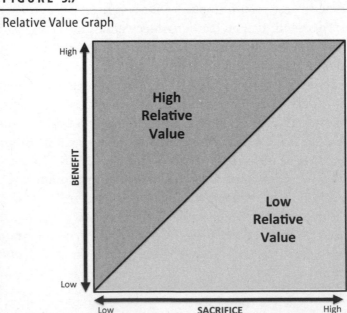

feeling than of math, and so you must, once again, draw upon your instinct and intuition to help guide you through this exercise.

When I purchased my home, there was a constantly running list in my head of all the benefits that I would receive: location, school district, commute, safety, convenience, status, resale, layout, square footage, amenities, and so on. Each benefit equated to a value, and all of that added up to a price that I was willing to pay. If any of those items were missing, I took that off the benefit list and adjusted my price accordingly. Sometimes the items were available, but I had to do a little extra work or spend a little extra money or time to get them. In that case, I had to subtract the value of those sacrifices, which then caused me to revalue the entire purchase. A different buyer may have placed a different value on those things and might therefore have been willing to pay a different price. And therein lies the conundrum for companies: every customer will have a slightly different value proposition. So it is up to sellers to (1) fully understand the benefits and sacrifices that will impact the majority of their customers, and (2) place an overall value on those benefits and sacrifices in order to establish a price that most people will be willing to pay.

Once you have determined the price of your product based on its overall customer value, there is another factor that you'll need to take into consideration: the basic laws of supply and demand. High value will only translate into premium pricing if there are not too many other products available that can provide the exact same value proposition. In this case, it is important to consider the *entire* value proposition and not just one part of it. This includes any value that will be derived from the features, function, brand, or any other emotional connections that a product may have to its customers. This is also where a direct connection to promotion will exist, because you can only differentiate the value of your product if you let people know what that unique value is. The more different your product is, the more rare it will be, and the higher price it will generally be able to demand, assuming the original customer value was there to begin with.

There are other aspects of how you will execute your pricing that will be determined during the implementation stages of your strategy. These will include your pricing logistics (how you will actually go about attaining your pricing through bundling, discounting, or promotion), as well as your price timing (how you will vary or alter your pricing over time to achieve your desired price position). These details will become a part of your implementation plan, since, in most cases, these actions must be dynamically carried out in response to changing market conditions and reactions. At this point, you just want to provide some high-level guidance on how you intend to price your product with respect to its overall value so that all of these eventual actions can be guided by some overarching pricing strategy.

Promotion

With product and price fully considered, we now want to think about how we will promote our product. The good news is that each subsequent element becomes more clearly focused as we move through the mix. Knowing what we now know about our product and price makes it much easier to think about how we will strategically promote our product in order to support these other two marketing mix elements.

At this stage of the game, we want to consider our overall message more than the specific promotional activities in which we will participate. As with the other mix elements, there will be time to talk about these details when we begin preparing our action plans. For now, we just want to provide some high-level guidance regarding how we intend to get our message to our target market and what in general we would like for that message to say. To do this we will need to consider how our product will be positioned.

Positioning is a concept that was popularized by Al Ries and Jack Trout in their book *Positioning: The Battle for Your Mind*.[9] The idea behind positioning is that companies can influence the unique space that their product occupies in a customer's mind. That is accomplished by developing strategies that will speak not only to the value that a product brings but also to ways in which that value compares to competing products or solutions. What makes positioning interesting is that it can be applied to any number of entities, from products to brands to processes to companies to countries and even to people. The idea is to establish a position that makes your offering stand out from the crowd.

In relation to messaging, I like to think about positioning my products in terms of four main parameters:

- Direct competitors
- Indirect competitors

- Customer needs
- Customer preferences

Any one of these forms of positioning can be combined with the others, or they can be addressed independently of one another. In this way, products can be mapped to these positioning relationships, as shown in Figure 5.8.

Using the model in Figure 5.8, a product can be positioned with respect to any (or all) of these four parameters, which can be described as follows:

- **Positioning with respect to customer needs.** In this form of positioning, you are carving out a specific customer need and identifying your product as the unique solution for that need. A classic example of this type of positioning can be seen with over-the-counter pain medicines, where there are solutions aimed at different symptoms and different types of pain (for example, backache, headache, muscle ache). If you position here more effectively than anyone else, your competitive position will be ensured as well.

FIGURE 5.8

Strategic Positioning Relationships

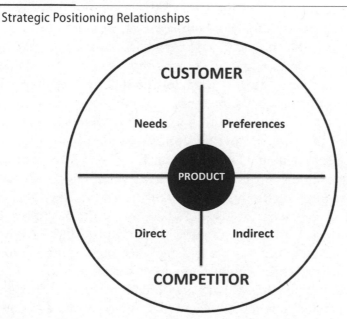

- **Positioning with respect to customer preferences.** This type of positioning attempts to associate your product with the trends, styles, and socially embraced norms of your target market. This endeavor might involve adopting a given demographic's cultural or social styles in your logos, packaging, or advertising. Restaurants are well known for taking this approach based on whatever region or demographic they are attempting to target. Again, if you accomplish this more effectively than anyone else, your competitive position will be ensured as a result.

- **Positioning with respect to direct competition.** This type of positioning involves establishing exactly how you want your customers to view your product with respect to a competitor that provides a substantially similar product or service to your own. You can choose to position yourself similarly (for example, Avis vs. Hertz) or somewhat differently from your competitor (for example, Pepsi vs. Coke), and you can also choose to apply your position broadly (for example, "We have the best burgers in town!") or directly against another competitor's product (for example, "Don't settle for those pan-fried burgers!").

- **Positioning with respect to indirect competition.** In this form of positioning, you compare your product not to other similar products but to other similar *solutions*. An example of this might be a manufacturer of household irons positioning its products against wrinkle-free shirts rather than other brands of irons. This form of positioning might also involve comparing certain aspects of your overall product experience with other noncompeting companies that also offer that same experiential aspect. Author Tom Connellan outlines a great example of this in his book *Inside the Magic Kingdom: Seven Keys to Disney's Success*. His very first "key" observes that Disney does not just strive to provide the best customer experience in the theme park industry. Instead, it strives to provide the best customer experience out of any company that its customers might compare it with.[10] Anyone who has visited one of the Walt Disney theme parks can clearly see this general rule in action, and it is a great example of how to position yourself with respect to your indirect competition.

There is literally an endless array of positioning arguments that you can take, but I find that most of them fall into some combination of these four categories. As Figure 5.8 shows, it is not necessary for you to position yourself in any *one* of these categories exclusively. If you choose to position with respect to a customer need, you should also explore how that overlaps with their preferences, and then refine your message accordingly. You should then check to see if other direct or indirect competitors are already taking that same approach and again revise your plan accordingly.

You may also choose to position your product against other products within your own portfolio. Returning to the pain reliever example, a company might have one product targeted to relieve cold symptoms, another targeted to relieve sinus symptoms, and still another targeted to relieve allergy symptoms. Although these products may all have overlapping ingredients, they can each be positioned differently with respect to different customer needs. You might also choose to competitively position your own products against one another using a "good, better, best" approach or even by marketing the same product under two different brands.

It shouldn't be difficult to see why positioning will form a key part of a company's promotional strategy, because the only way you can actually position yourself is by reaching out to your customers and letting them know where you stand. And just as with product and price, what I am attempting to do by introducing this concept is to provide you with a bit more "meat" in the promotional part of your strategy, so you don't just say something like, "We will advertise our product through print ads, brochures, and word of mouth." Yes, believe it or not, this is what most promotional "strategies" that I see look like. But again this tells you nothing about how you intend to win whatever war you may be fighting. By incorporating how you intend to position yourself into your promotional strategy, you will be giving some much-needed direction regarding what your promotions will actually say. It is the *message* that we are concerned with here, and your positioning can help get you there.

Place

On the surface, *product placement* might be defined as "how a company makes its product available to the marketplace." Although this statement is technically correct, I prefer to state this in terms of the customer's perspective. So product placement becomes "anywhere a customer can get our product." This may seem like a subtle difference, but it is important because, when considering where your product will be made available, you will also need to consider whether or not your prospective customers will actually go there to get it.

Have you ever taken a long trip? Most likely you have. And when you took that trip, especially if there was some discomfort involved (which there almost always is), you did so only because there was some compelling reason for you to be wherever it is that you were going. Sometimes people travel for business. Although not many people love this part of their jobs, they do it because it's part of what needs to be done in order to make a living. So taking these long business trips becomes a necessary means to a financial end. Other times people travel for pleasure. In these cases they take the same long and arduous journeys because there is some pleasurable experience waiting for them on the other side. When people travel for pleasure, they are doing so because there is no other way for them to obtain whatever unique experience they are seeking at that time.

If neither of these conditions existed—that is, if people could make a living or they could get a uniquely pleasurable vacation experience without having to travel—then they would not likely make those trips. Likewise, if these same conditions could be accessed in a more convenient way (for example, if either of these end results were closer to home), then people would likely choose that option instead.

What I'm setting up is a relationship between fulfilling a given need or desire and doing so as conveniently as possible. The more we need or want something, the more trouble we are willing to go through to get it. That seems pretty obvious, but now let's apply it to our placement strategy.

If you have a product or service that people absolutely need—that is, they feel they can't live without it and they can't get it from anywhere else—then they will be willing to withstand fairly high levels of inconvenience to get whatever it is that you have. In these (often rare) cases, you can be very selective about where you offer your product or service, because people will travel relatively great distances or go through relatively high levels of inconvenience to get it. On the other end of the spectrum, if you have a product or service that people consider to be somewhat commonplace—that is, it satisfies a need or want that can be fulfilled by many other different products or solutions—then you will practically have to deliver it to their doorsteps in order for them to buy it from you. More realistically stated, in these cases you will have to make sure your product is ever-present wherever your target market normally hangs out.

It is hoped that, based on the work you did in Chapter 3, you already know where people in your target market are and where they like to go. Now all you have to do is overlay that information on top of how uniquely your product fulfills a given customer need.

Even given this analysis, you might be inclined to believe that the more places you can sell your product, the more sales you will ultimately get. This may be true in some cases, but this approach also comes with sacrifices—namely, the more places you sell your product, the more your prices are likely to suffer because each of those places, or channels, will be competing for the same customers. In addition, making your product too ever-present could take away any of the cachet that you might have otherwise created had you decided to make that product just a little bit less attainable. This ties back to the supply-and-demand discussion we had in relation to pricing.

So far, we have examined where geographically you want to sell your product (based on where your target market is) and how present you want your product to be within that geography (based on how much inconvenience people will be willing to go through to get that product). Let's call these factors "geography" (where) and "convenience" (ease). The next thing we need to consider is the type of experience you want your customers to have, which will clearly be affected by your choice of channels. If, for example, I am selling very high-end appliances, I am not likely to choose a lower-end retail chain as my main channel partner because the experience will be in direct contrast to that which I want to associate with my high-end products. Instead, I might choose to sell through a channel that will better support a buying experience of luxury goods. As a consideration for our placement strategy, let's call this the "experience" factor.

Another key part of product placement has to do with availability. The objective of this concept is to determine how long customers are willing to wait between the time they buy your product and the time they receive it. In the days when physical storefronts were the norm, product availability was limited to whether or not a store had a given product in stock. Consumers generally expected that certain types of products would be readily available, whereas other products, such as large, unique, or custom-manufactured goods (for example, furniture and automobiles), would require some wait time.

In today's world, customer expectations of product availability have shifted. This change is fueled, in many ways, by the convenience factor of being able to shop for and receive virtually any product in the world without ever having to leave the comfort of one's own living room. In this way, the concept of having a product in stock has been replaced in many cases with the concept of getting that product delivered to a customer's doorstep faster than anyone else. Still, this factor of availability, although it has evolved, is a key consideration when choosing how your product will be dispatched to the world.

When an overall placement strategy is determined, these four factors of geography, convenience, experience, and availability are the main elements for which I like to provide guidance. They are summarized in Figure 5.9.

Although I have referenced more traditional tangible goods to help illustrate each of these placement factors, their definitions may take on slightly different meanings for intangible goods. For example, for downloadable music content, the definition of *geography* will translate into the type of currency that is accepted or the different languages that the website features; *convenience* becomes how intuitive the interface is and how easy the website is to navigate; *experience* might include the performance or speed of the download; and *availability* might reflect how many different songs or artists are featured on the website at any given time.

FIGURE 5.9

Placement Considerations

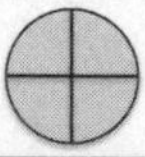 ⊕	**Geography**: In which regions will your channels be located?
 ⚙	**Convenience**: How easily can your customers access your channels?
 ☺	**Experience**: What kind of environment will your channels provide for your customers?
 ?	**Availability**: How long are your customers willing to wait for their products?

As with the other marketing mix elements, there are many other factors that can be considered. I have found, however, that developing a high-level plan around the aforementioned four main placement factors will help to provide the right level of strategic guidance for almost all of the placement actions that will ultimately be initiated in support of your strategy. Saying "we want to make our product available through our existing channels" does not a strategy make. Your implementation team will need to know *why* those channels are important and *how* those channels will help you achieve your overall strategic objectives. Considering the four placement factors will help you to communicate why and how more effectively.

SUMMARIZING YOUR STRATEGY

Let's review where we are in our process and think about how we got here so far:

1. We started with a strategic motivation and a baseline analysis of our customers, competitors, company, and industry.
2. We ran that baseline through a SWOT analysis, which we used to help us anticipate what market and product opportunities might exist that could satisfy our strategic motivation.
3. We then turned our strategic motivation into a set of vision, goals, and objectives that could be used to inspire, rather than simply motivate, our strategy.
4. We used our vision, goals, and objectives to filter the opportunities from our SWOT analysis and focus in on the market and product opportunities we wanted to pursue.
5. Based on our chosen opportunities, we took time to really understand the target market for those opportunities and to validate our vision, goals, objectives, and opportunities with respect to the needs of that target market.
6. Next we created our strategic melodies, intersecting our knowledge and our passion to come up with simple high-level strategic statements that provide guidance on *how* we want to go about pursuing our chosen opportunities.
7. Finally, we completed our strategy by developing a Go-to-Market Plan that provides strategic guidance on how we will ultimately implement actions around each element of our marketing mix.

This process is captured in the strategy workflow diagram shown in Figure 5.10.

At this point, it's a good idea to go back and review your strategic melodies to ensure they are in line with your vision, goals, objectives, and target market and that they are written at the right level (that is, not too high and not too low). There's a vocal technique called *melisma* that is commonly used in today's popular music. This is when one syllable is sung between several successive notes. When applied sparingly, this technique can produce a truly beautiful effect. If melisma is overapplied to a melody, however, it can become downright distracting; causing, in extreme cases, the melody to be hidden, confused, or altogether lost in all those additional transitional notes.

To be more direct, you should make sure that your strategic melodies do not have too much melisma. That means ensuring that your melodies remain true to their original intent and that they do not contain any unnecessary words or details that will only serve to distract people from your core message. Keep your strategic messages short, simple, and easy to digest, but still include the right level of detail to both hold people's interest and deliver whatever message you are trying to convey.

FIGURE 5.10

Strategy Workflow

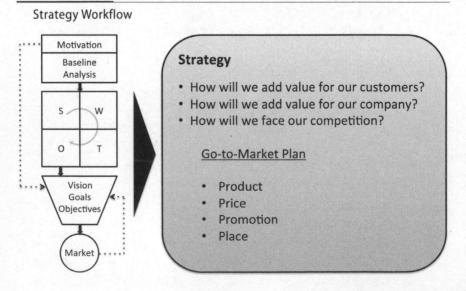

Remember that your strategic melodies should encompass some elements of past, present, and future. It's not enough to base your strategy on what happened yesterday or even what's happening right now. Good strategy will always consider everything that we know at any given time and use that information to try to anticipate what will happen next. And *great* strategy not only anticipates what will happen next but also considers any number of outcomes that might occur as a result. If your strategy is too broad, it will lack context, and you will lose your ability to predict. If your strategy is too detailed, it will be overly restrictive, and you will lose your ability to react. So, to coin a phrase, your strategy has to be "just right."

To ensure that your Go-to-Market Plan follows a similar model, you should provide a high-level summary for each of your marketing mix elements to accompany your strategic melodies. Doing so will make the Go-to-Market Plan easier to communicate, implement, and dynamically adjust as needed. To create an effective summary, you should break your plan down to only the most salient points by answering the following key questions:

- **Product.** What is the core product you are selling, and what overall customer experience do you want to convey?
- **Price.** What overall value will customers receive, and what price do you expect to demand?
- **Promotion.** What is the main message you are trying to convey, and how will you position your product against customer needs and preferences, direct or indirect competitive solutions, and your own product portfolio?
- **Place.** What are your main expectations around geography, convenience, experience, and product availability through your selected channels?

You've made it this far, which means that you've composed the heart of your strategy! But the process is far from over. Your strategy is meaningless until it is implemented, and it can never be implemented until people understand what it's all about. At this point, your strategies are just melodies inside your head. Now it's time to organize those melodies into a song that you can share with the world. Our next step, then, will be to create our strategic arrangement.

Finding Your Creativity

Where exactly do ideas come from? Certainly not out of thin air. In fact, most ideas arise out of some combination of what you've been exposed to, what inspires you, and what you're trying to accomplish. If that sounds familiar, it's because these are exactly the steps we covered throughout the first three stages of our process. When it comes to the fourth step of idea formulation, your creativity will emerge through your ability to put those things together in a way that hasn't been done before. Here, then, are some tips to help you find that creativity during ideation:

- When I am writing a new song and ideas begin to flow, I am always conscious of not repeating a melody or chord structure that I have written in the past, or that perhaps someone else had written before me. This is where creativity lives in the songwriting process, because you are always checking and balancing your melodic ideas to ensure that they are truly original. In business, however, I am constantly amazed at how many strategists seek to copy exactly what others have done rather than building upon that knowledge and creating something truly original from it. The message is this: be inspired by what others have done, but don't copy it.

- As with the previous steps, I have presented tools in this chapter to help you formulate your thoughts and ideas more easily. However, as is also the case with the other steps, try not to get too caught up in the process. Business strategy is all about understanding what your customers want, what your company wants, and what your competitors will likely do in response. If you can give customers something they need but that they aren't currently getting, you will have found your creativity. Ensure this aligns with your capabilities and goals, anticipate how competitors will react, and then you will have found your strategy.

- The marketing mix is meant to be a bridge between your strategic and your tactical plans. It will serve as a way to group your tactics to ensure that they align with one another and with your overall strategy as well. But tactics are not devoid of creativity—far from it. Truly original product features, pricing actions, promotional plans, and placement options are all opportunities to explore creative approaches and differentiate your plan even if your higher-level strategies overlap something that has been done before.

CHAPTER 6

ARRANGEMENT

ANALYSIS	RECOLLECTION	INTUITION	ARTISTRY
Present	**Past**	**Future**	**Path**
Company/Capabilities	Influences	Vision	Strategy
Competitors	History	Goals	Story
Customers	Performance	Objectives	Resources
Industry	Experience	Target Market	Execution

← ——— INPUTS ——— →←——— OUTPUTS ——— →

PREPARATION	PREPARATION	INSPIRATION	IDEATION
		GENRE	ARRANGEMENT
			ORCHESTRATION
			PRODUCTION
I	II	III	IV

What You Will Do

- Develop your strategic story

At this point in our songwriting analogy, we have a collection of really strong inspired melodies, and we have some connective tissue (in the form of our Go-to-Market Plan) to help hold those melodies together. We certainly have the makings of a great song. But that song has no structure. And at this point neither does our strategy.

You may have heard the phrase "structure follows strategy." This is based on a thesis presented by business history professor Alfred D. Chandler Jr. in his 1962 book *Strategy and Structure*. The original observation was that companies develop the structure of their businesses based on the strategy that they are trying to pursue.[1] This observation soon became a sage piece of advice to which many companies still subscribe. It follows that we need to write our strategies first and then apply a type of structure to those strategies to enable their implementation. To do this, we first arrange our strategic melodies so they can be more easily communicated; then we orchestrate our collective strategy so that it can be more effectively carried out.

There are generally three distinct steps that all lend themselves to any musical composition process: composing, arranging, and orchestrating. Because these terms are so closely related, the definitions of these three functions vary somewhat, depending on the style of music to which they are being applied. In most cases, these functions can be broken down as follows:

- **Composing.** The act of writing melodies, chord structures, and song structures
- **Arranging.** The act of organizing (or reorganizing) song structures and instrumentation to achieve a particular sound
- **Orchestrating.** The act of assigning and writing different instrument parts for a given musical composition

There is a hierarchy to these definitions, because the art of composing can also include arranging and orchestrating, whereas the art of arranging can also be inclusive of orchestrating. In this way, the definitions can be visually depicted as shown in Figure 6.1.

This hierarchy fits perfectly within our framework because the strategic process will include formulating ideas (melodies), arranging a story, and orchestrating parts to enable performance. Each is accomplished in three distinct steps, and each step contributes to the greater overall compositional process.

FIGURE 6.1

Composing Hierarchy

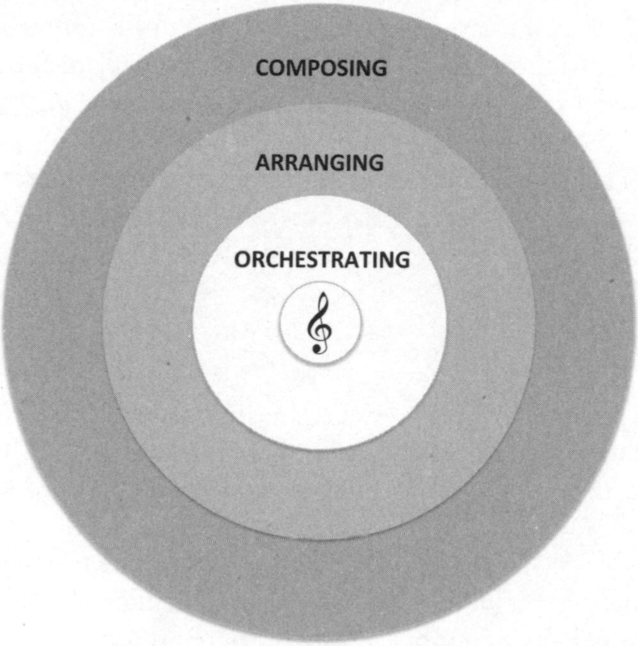

We have our strategic melodies. Now we want to arrange them into a song that can be orchestrated and performed. To fully appreciate this analogy, let's dive a bit deeper into how typical songs are structured, or, using my definition, how they are arranged.

The backbone of most songs consists of melodies, with each of those melodies having elements of both pitch and rhythm. When I arrange melodies into songs, there are three basic things that I do:

1. I complete the song by filling in the gaps between my melodies (adding verses, bridges, and any other connections) to create a cohesive composition.

2. I then assemble the parts into a logical order or pattern that will ultimately allow me to tell my story or convey whatever message I am trying to get across.

3. Finally, I enhance my song by adding harmonies, voices, additional rhythms, instrumentation, and other tonal elements that will allow the overall message to be conveyed in the most emotionally effective way.

This last step is the one most commonly associated with musical arrangement, although all three steps absolutely apply within the context of my definition. These are the same three steps that you will apply to your strategic melodies. Structure follows strategy. Arrangement follows ideation. And all of this will result in strategic songs that your organization can perform to achieve your vision, goals, and objectives.

Capturing these three steps to arranging and translating them into terms that we can apply to our strategic melodies, we have:

1. Complete
2. Assemble
3. Enhance

Figure 6.2 provides a visual outline of each of these steps. As you can see in the illustration, these three steps will ultimately allow you to arrange your strategic ideas in the form of a strategic story that can be communicated easily and effectively.

When we hear a song that we really love, it usually contains a combination of sounds that we find pleasing in some way. No different than any of our other senses, there are sounds we hear that feel good to our ears, and there are other sounds that simply do not. Of course this experience can be very subjective and is extremely hard to put into words, but for now it's enough to say that certain songs will probably sound good to a large majority of people and others probably won't.

When you find a song that sounds good, you tend to play it over and over. And with all of those repeat performances, your mind is making associations between what you are hearing and what you are feeling during those moments. In the simplest of terms, that song is becoming a soundtrack for whatever is happening in your life. Think of your memory as a sponge that is soaking up any number of inputs from any number of your senses at any given time. When those inputs become interlocked and associated, they are burned into your memory in such a way that is often difficult to separate back into its respective parts.

Stories serve the same purpose. When we hear a story, we are instantly making an association with an emotion that we've felt or an experience that we've had. We relate to it, and so it becomes an instant part of our psyche. Once the story is "burned in," we remember it and

FIGURE 6.2

Strategic Arrangement

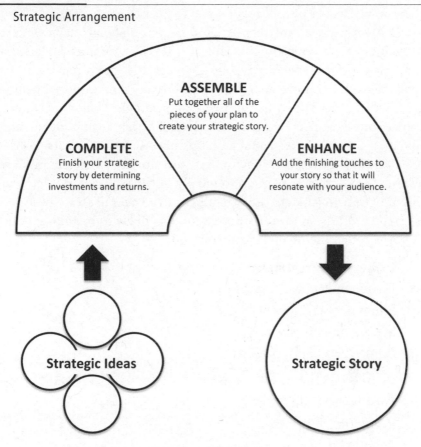

draw upon it over and over again. This allows the overall intent, or message, of that story to be both remembered and acted upon—both of which will be critical to effectively implementing your strategic plan.

So now let's take these three steps, explore each one a bit further, and see how they can all come together to create your strategic arrangement.

COMPLETING YOUR STRATEGIC STORY

As Greek philosopher Aristotle observed, every story has a beginning, a middle, and an ending.[2] Following the process up to this point, you've written your beginning and middle, but you still have to write your ending. In terms of your strategy, this will include any resources and investments that may be required to implement your plan, as well as the overall results you expect to get in return.

Note that a strategic plan is different than a business case. A business case typically consists of a detailed financial plan that is developed for a specific product or business idea when an actual investment decision needs to be made. Usually one or more business cases will be developed in support of a strategic plan as it is being implemented. A strategic plan, on the other hand, provides overall guidance as to how a product or business will achieve its desired goals and objectives. In this context, the financial investments and returns for a strategic plan are typically outlined at a very high level and only to help validate the feasibility of the overall strategy.

Toward this end, your strategic plan is likely to include some or all of the following financial information:

Projected Investments

Development investments

Equipment investments

System investments

Infrastructure investments

Projected Ongoing Expenses

Personnel expenditures

Promotional expenses

Support and/or service costs

Revenue and Profitability Projections

Annual revenue projections

Annual growth rates

Annual margin projections

Projected future market share

Investments and costs should be presented with respect to both magnitude (how much each will cost) and time (when they are expected to be incurred). It will also be important to ensure that the impact of any investments or expenses has been considered in your future profitability projections.

Once you have outlined, at a high level, how much your company will need to spend, you should be fully equipped to reveal what the expected result will be. This is your opportunity to prove the viability of your strategy by showing that your vision, goals, and objectives will be met.

Most strategic plans are designed to look three to five years—or longer—into the future. Because of this, the accuracy of your projections is, unfortunately, not likely to be very high. To ensure that your story is credible, you need to support your projections with whatever key assumptions you used in their development. The more fact-based your assumptions are, the more believable your plan will be and the more accurate your projections are likely to be as well.

Since this will be such a critical part of your story, let's explore some of the key assumptions that can be outlined around the three most important projections you will make: revenue assumptions, margin assumptions, and market share assumptions.

Revenue Assumptions

When companies grow above expectations, they almost always celebrate their successes. When they fail to meet expectations, they usually blame the market! Both reactions may be right, or both may be wrong. To find out which is which, you might need a little more information.

When providing a revenue growth forecast, I always break the growth into three main areas:

1. **Price.** This includes any increase (or decrease) in prices that have been applied to the existing customer base. Companies usually have clear records to show what pricing changes have been initiated in this way.

2. **Market.** This is the growth (or shrinking) of the overall market, meaning that existing customers are buying more (or less) volume of your product overall. Companies usually have records on this based on customer volumes or through industry sources that publish information on overall market trends.

3. **Share.** This is reflected in the growth of business with new customers or the loss of existing customers to competitors. Companies may have information on this, or it may also be deduced if you know your price and market trends (since share would make up the remainder).

TABLE 6.1

Revenue Assumptions Example

	Forecast	Actual
Price	5%	5%
Market	0%	15%
Share	5%	−5%
TOTAL:	**10%**	**15%**

Growth will always occur among a combination of these three categories. Breaking down your projected revenue growth in this way will allow you to outline how you intend to achieve your forecast. It will also enable you to track your performance against that forecast and take the proper corrective actions in the specific areas where action may be required.

For example, let's say that I forecasted my business to grow 10 percent from year 1 to year 2. If my business actually grew 15 percent in that time period, I might be likely to celebrate. However, a closer look at my forecast might reveal a breakdown, as shown in Table 6.1.

Looking at the breakdown in Table 6.1, I see that I met my pricing objective but the market grew significantly more than I anticipated. This means that 15 percent of my growth happened as a result of existing customers buying more product, while at the same time my business shrank by 5 percent as a result of at least a portion of those customers moving to my competitors. Looking at it this way, not only should I not be celebrating, I should be actively trying to understand why I lost share and trying to figure out how I can recover that share in the future.

Putting revenue assumptions like this on the table will not only help build credibility for your plan but will also help guide you and your strategic team as your plan is being implemented and its results are being measured.

Margin Assumptions

Your margin assumptions will come from three main places:

- Price
- Costs
- Investments

Nothing will have a quicker impact on your margin than your price. It is important, then, that you state your pricing assumptions up front. These may include how you intend to vary your price over time, what value your products will bring to customers, what competitors' reactions are likely to be, what discounts, rebates, and promotions are anticipated, and any other pricing impacts that you may or may not have built into your plan.

Costing assumptions will revolve around the cost to produce your product. These will typically include assumptions about material costs, labor costs, or any additional factory expenses that may be required to carry out your strategy.

Major investments or capital expenditures will typically affect your margins in the form of depreciation, particularly if those investments are for equipment that is required to manufacture or service your product. These should be stated and calculated for any investments that you are presenting as part of your strategy.

These three items will likely make up the majority of your margin assumptions. If you are building your plan for an overall business rather than for a specific product line, however, you will likely be measuring the overall profitability of your business as well as the margins of your product. In this case, you will also want to clearly outline the impact of any additional ongoing system, infrastructure, or personnel expenses that may be required to implement your plan and that would typically be reflected outside of your product margins.

Market Share Assumptions

Market share is simply your product sales stated as a percentage of an overall market size. That seems simple enough to calculate, but there are some complexities that go along with it. First of all, you must determine if you want to measure your sales numbers in terms of dollar revenues or unit volumes. If you choose to measure share in terms of revenue, then you will need to take any anticipated price increases or decreases into consideration as well (both for your product and for the overall market). This measurement may be preferred by some organizations, but it does add a level of complexity when you are attempting to project your share into future years. Choosing to measure share based on volume will give a more accurate picture of your true unit share or gain, but it may not reflect how well you are actually translating those unit sales into real dollars that your company can use. Whichever methodology you choose, you must state both your sales and market numbers in similar terms, and you must indicate any related assumptions accordingly.

Once you have determined which type of share you will be measuring, you will then be tasked with obtaining overall market numbers. This is often difficult to do because competitors rarely share their sales or volume numbers with the public down to a product level. So at best you will need to make some high-level assumptions about your competitors' performance based on market feedback, win-loss analysis, and any other industry sources that you might be able to find.

Next you have to determine what your definition of the market is. For example, if I am selling USB outlets that can replace standard electrical outlets, I can either state my share in terms of only other competitors' USB outlet device sales or I can state my share in terms of *all* electrical outlet device sales. The choice would largely depend on the type of strategy I am trying to implement. If I were trying to grow my business by taking share from other USB outlet competitors, then I might use this to define my market. On the other hand, if my strategy was to convert all electrical outlet users over to USB outlets, then I might want to measure my share against a market that is inclusive of both. All of these assumptions must be clearly stated so that your market share numbers can be accurately interpreted.

One last consideration for market share is to be sure that you tie your market assumptions to your revenue assumptions as well as to your share assumptions. For example, if you state that your market is growing from $1 billion to $2 billion in five years, and you also state that you are growing your share from 25 percent to 30 percent over that same time period, your resulting revenue projection will be $600 million, as shown in Table 6.2.

TABLE 6.2

Market Share Assumptions, Example 1

	Market	**Share**	**Revenue**
Year 1	$1.0B	25%	$250M
Year 6	$2.0B	30%	**$600M**

TABLE 6.3

Market Share Assumptions, Example 2

	Market	Share	Revenue
Year 1	$1.0B	25%	$250M
Year 6	$2.0B	**20%**	$400M

If you had actually projected a more conservative revenue growth of, say, approximately 10 percent per year (from $250 million to $400 million), without tying this back to the projected market growth, you would inadvertently be implying that you are actually *losing* 5 points of share, as shown in Table 6.3.

More than likely, this isn't your plan. But if you aren't careful and you forget to reconcile your market, market share, and revenue numbers, you can lose credibility quickly in front of a sharp audience. Of course, I wouldn't mention this if I hadn't witnessed this scenario play out many times, so don't say I didn't warn you!

Now that your parts are complete and your assumptions are all laid out in front of you, it's time to begin assembling all of these different pieces and bringing together your strategic story.

ASSEMBLING ALL OF YOUR STORY ELEMENTS

No matter what source you read, most will agree that there are five main elements that make up a story. Although the origin of this particular theory is a bit unclear, five traditional elements are most commonly cited:

1. Theme
2. Setting
3. Character(s)
4. Plot
5. Conflict

More than likely, these elements were derived, in some shape, form, or fashion, from Aristotle's *Poetics*, which dates back to approximately 335 BC and is one of the earliest accounts of dramatic theory and structure. In it Aristotle notes six parts that make up a dramatic tragedy. These are (depending on the translation) plot, character, diction, thought, spectacle, and song.[3]

Clearly there is a strong correlation between Aristotle's observations and the five elements that are commonly mentioned nowadays. And so it is, as with any of these analyses, that the five story elements have been debated, reduced, added to, and redefined in just about every way imaginable over the years. But arguing the basic theory would be missing the point. Whatever you choose to call them, these five basic elements, in some form or another, are present in just about every story that has ever been told. More important, if these five elements are not present, then you probably won't be telling a story; instead, you'll be giving a narrative that is unlikely to connect with your audience.

To ensure that we can align our stories properly around these elements, let's explore each one in more depth.

Theme

Every story should have some reason for existing. Most people would agree that the best stories, at their core, show you something that you didn't know, feel, or think about before. The theme, then, is that reason for a story's existence. Sometimes, we refer to this as the moral of the story. It can be a lesson. But it can also be a feeling that you're left with, like what remains with you for days after an amazing movie that took you on a very emotional journey. In short, all of this makes up your theme. It's what you want your story to be about, the emotion you want to evoke, and the impression or message you want to leave people with when it's all said and done.

Setting

Your story has to take place somewhere and at some point (or points) in time. This is your setting, and it goes hand in hand with your theme. Where and when your story takes place will be an integral part of setting the mood for your story. For example, if I am writing a love story, I can place my characters in a romantic, dimly lit room with strawberries, champagne, and candlelight, or I can put them in a dirty cave full of insects, bats, and mud. I can tell the exact same story, but by setting that story in a romantic room, I'll be telling the story of love, passion, and desire. By setting that story in a cave, I may still be telling the same love story but now it will be in the face of hardship, discomfort, and challenges that must be overcome. And that will add a completely different element that will evoke a completely different emotional response. The same can be said about time. A story told in medieval times will set a different mood than one set in the year 2112. In fact, we've all experienced stories that have been handed down generation after generation in which similar characters go through similar situations with similar messages. By changing the setting, the story takes on a completely different feel.

Character(s)

We have a theme and we have a setting; now we have to add somebody or something that will ultimately interact with or within this environment. That will be our character. The setting is just a static backdrop, but characters will allow our story to come to life. The trick is, a character doesn't have to be a person or even a living being. A character is anything that you give action to. You can tell an entire story in which the main character is a rock. But if the rock doesn't experience anything, then it will just be part of the setting. The minute that rock experiences action, it becomes a character. That doesn't necessarily mean the rock will be an *interesting* character; but it will be a character nevertheless. The key to creating effective characters is to give them a purpose for being. To do that you need to make your audience care about them. We've all heard critics talk about mediocre movies in which the characters were never fully developed. What this generally means is that the author didn't reveal enough aspects about that character to make the audience care about what happens to him or her. So a character experiences some sort of action, but a good character, as part of a good story, experiences action that we care about.

Plot

The plot is the action that your characters experience. Many people mistakenly confuse the plot with the story itself because, admittedly, the plot is one of the most important of these five elements. When we think about a plot, we usually think about whatever the characters go through. It is their journey, so to speak. But just as there are some characters that are more interesting than others, depending on how effectively you can connect your audience's emotions to them, so there are some plots that are more interesting than others, depending on how well you develop the action throughout your story. The way this is typically done is by creating some level of our next element: conflict.

Conflict

Conflict is what makes a plot interesting. When you think of conflict, you are likely to picture a type of battle. In the context of a story, that is certainly one form of conflict, but it is by no means the only one. A conflict is actually any level of discord or disparity that needs to be resolved. So a battle is certainly the easiest form of conflict to understand. There are two sides, with each one seeing something differently than the other. So you establish why they see things the way they do, you establish that there is some level of discord between these two viewpoints, and then you have your conflict that needs to be resolved. Simple. But what about conflict of a less obvious sort? Let's say we have two characters who are in love. They're not in a battle at all (at least not until after they've been married for a few years!). So can you have a viable story if both characters see things the same way? Yes and no. They certainly don't have to be at odds with each other, but they have to be experiencing some sort of disequilibrium in order for any kind of action to take place. For example, perhaps they want to be together all the time but they can't. That sets up a conflict—not between the two characters, but between the characters and their ability to get what they want. Or perhaps they have parents who won't allow them to see each other. This also creates a tension that needs to be resolved. If all you had were two characters who felt exactly the same way about each other and experienced exactly the same things at exactly the same times, your story wouldn't move. To really bring this point home, think about what you learned in your high school physics class. In order for something to move, you need to have some form of potential energy that exists. A rock sitting on the ground has no potential energy between it and the ground, and so it has nowhere to go. But hold that rock above the surface, and now there is potential energy, in the form of gravity, between it and the ground. If you drop the rock, you will be able to turn that energy into movement. Conflict is just like potential energy. Without it, there can be no movement, and without movement, there can be no story.

Those are the elements of a story, and, on the surface, they appear to be fairly complete. Upon closer inspection, however, you may notice that these five elements are not all created equally. Our first three elements—theme, setting, and character—are all static. In short, they are our storytelling nouns (people, places, and things). The last two elements—plot and conflict—are both in motion. So they are our storytelling verbs (figuratively, not literally). This is an important distinction, because for our verbs we need to describe not only their existence but also their motion. And to do that, we will need to introduce yet another storytelling concept: the concept of a dramatic arc.

THE STRATEGIC ARC

Having all five of our elements absolutely gives us a story, but it doesn't necessarily give us a *good* story. To create a good story, we need to make people care about what's happening to our elements. And to make people care, we need to take them on an emotional journey. That's where the dramatic arc comes in.

In 1863, a German novelist and playwright, Gustav Freytag, wrote a book entitled *Die Technik des Dramas*, translated as *The Technique of the Drama*. In this book Freytag provided a critical analysis of the well-known five-act narrative structure used by many playwrights, including William Shakespeare. In one particularly compelling section of Freytag's book, he lays out what has come to be known as Freytag's pyramid, whereby he gives both names and motion to each of these five-act dramatic story parts.[4] This is sometimes referred to as the *dramatic arc*, a version of which is shown in Figure 6.3.

FIGURE 6.3

The Dramatic Arc

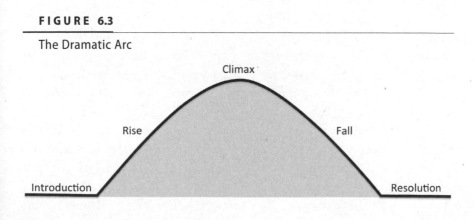

Although there have been many different interpretations of this general idea over the years, the basic principles remain thoroughly unchanged. The five events of the dramatic arc can be summarized as follows:

1. **Introduction.** Sometimes referred to as *exposition*, this is the stage in which the main story elements such as characters, setting, and any applicable back stories are introduced.
2. **Rise.** During this stage the main story elements interact with one another, building tension through conflict as they go, and working toward a peak point of interest. This is the stage of complication, or, in simpler terms, the building up of something that will eventually need to be resolved.
3. **Climax.** The climax is often referred to as the *turning point*. It is the point in the story where the tension comes to a peak and a change occurs that will allow the conflict to work toward being resolved.
4. **Fall.** After the climax, the conflict begins to reverse itself, working toward a final outcome. In some cases, the final outcome is left unknown until the very end of the story.
5. **Resolution.** In this final stage the conflict is finally resolved. This is sometimes referred to as *dénouement* (the final outcome), *revelation* (when the unknown becomes known), or *catastrophe* (where the main character meets with some tragic ending).

This is storytelling in a classical sense. You need to have a theme, a setting, characters, a plot, and some type of conflict, and the action of the story needs to follow some sort of dramatic arc.

But before we get too technical about all of this, just as with strategic theory, I contend that these theoretical approaches will only get you part of the way there. The real trick is to learn to tap into your creative center and develop your story intuitively, not because it follows a framework, but because you truly care about it. If you care, so will your audience. And that's how great storytelling is really done.

I absolutely believe that a great story has to contain all of the elements that were mentioned previously. But I prefer that you use these tools as more of a checklist to validate that you have a great story rather than attempting to build your story as a result of them. This is a critical distinction because, by following the theory alone, you run a greater risk of overthinking your task and, in so doing, potentially missing the point of what it is that you're really trying to accomplish. This is similar to writing your melodies based purely on knowledge and without any passion.

In my experience, a story does two things really well, both in relation to your audience:

1. It connects to them.
2. It entertains them.

I remember a particularly moving scene in Disney Pixar's animated movie *Up*. Anyone who has seen that movie will immediately know the scene that I'm referring to, but if you haven't seen it, you may want to skip over this next paragraph for fear of a spoiler alert!

In a matter of only a few minutes (just over four to be exact), we are told the story of two characters, Carl and Ellie, as they take their life's journey from marriage into their golden years. This is a story within a story and, as such, all of the five elements are prominently featured, and the dramatic arc is brilliantly on display—right down to the final tragic ending where Ellie passes away, leaving her husband alone in his retirement years, after never quite achieving what they both had set out to achieve. The end of this short story, as it turns out, sets up the arc for the main story that the movie ultimately goes on to tell, but this brief montage is so effective that it could easily stand alone as its own movie as well.[5]

When I first saw this scene in theaters, I doubt if there was a dry eye in the house. Still, to this day, it is the only scene in just about any movie that makes me cry out loud. The reason, yes, is partly due to the use of the classic storytelling techniques that I spoke about previously. But almost all movies use those same techniques, and almost none have had such a profound effect on me. What makes this particular scene so incredibly effective is the fact that the story elements connect so deeply with things that I myself feel—namely, my undying love for my wife, as well as the sense that I will likely never be able to accomplish everything that I want to. These are feelings that many of us have, and many of us have them so deeply that, when they are put into motion in front of our very eyes, it's hard not to imagine ourselves in the shoes of the characters going through these same emotions. We connect, and, in so doing, we understand—and we remember.

The second thing that makes this scene so effective is the speed with which the writers take us through the dramatic arc. Not that faster is always better, but if you can use the arc to expose your characters, take them through a conflict, bring that conflict to a climax, resolve the conflict, and reveal a tragic ending all in a time span that allows you to never lose grip of your audience's attention, you will undoubtedly keep them that much more entertained. And in so doing, your message will land that much more powerfully.

The reason I like this particular example is because the storytelling techniques used in books and movies are usually too lengthy to translate into a business setting, where people's attention spans are infamously short. For a strategic story, you not only have to connect and entertain but also do so practically at the speed of light! That means that brevity will have to be another defining characteristic when you translate these techniques over to your strategic presentation.

Conveniently enough, the strategic process that I've been taking you through follows the dramatic arc to a tee. So, as far as the action of your story, it is already laid out for you, as shown in Figure 6.4. From this point forward, I will refer to this as the *strategic arc*.

Note how the dramatic arc in Figure 6.4 aligns perfectly with the story elements of the Creative Strategy Generation framework shown above it. To provide a bit more detail on how to make a story

FIGURE 6.4

The Strategic Arc

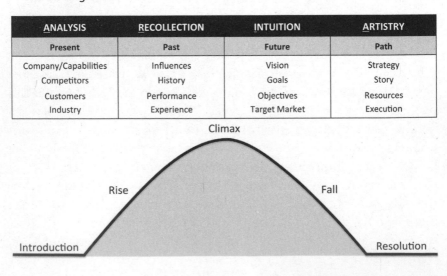

ANALYSIS	RECOLLECTION	INTUITION	ARTISTRY
Present	Past	Future	Path
Company/Capabilities	Influences	Vision	Strategy
Competitors	History	Goals	Story
Customers	Performance	Objectives	Resources
Industry	Experience	Target Market	Execution

Climax

Rise   Fall

Introduction   Resolution

out of all this, what follows is a brief outline that you can use to directly model the action of your strategic story (with the symbols in parentheses indicating the position that each element occupies on the strategic arc.):

Introduction (__)

- State the performance of your product or business today.
- Introduce the customer, competitor, and industry factors.

Rise (/)

- State the problem that you are trying to solve.
- Tell us about any history, references, or experiences that you plan to draw from.
- Build to your vision, goals, and objectives.

Climax (*)

- Tell us what your customers need.
- Tell us what you intend to do. Make it impactful!

Fall (\)

- Present the details of your strategy and how you intend to implement it.
- Outline the investments and resources you'll need.
- Anticipate how your competitors and customers will react.

Resolution (__)

- Reveal the financial impact that your strategy will have after it has been successfully implemented.
- Tell us how both the company and customers' problems were solved.

At this point you have the framework for your story. But you may not have the framework for a *good* story, because you still need to both connect to and entertain your audience in order to fully engage them. What follows then, are some tips on how to do this, building off of the same concepts we have examined so far:

- **Connect with your audience.** To truly connect with your audience you need to know something about them and to focus your story on characters and situational elements that they can relate to. For example, if your product is a robot used on an assembly line for automobile parts, you might start your story by asking, "Did you ever wonder how the car you drove to work today was actually built?" Immediately, you will have connected your audience to your product by making it relatable to something that they personally experience every day. You can use this same technique when introducing customers into your story. Try using the techniques that we talked about in Chapter 4 by giving personalities to your customer segments that your audience can relate to. Then, when you take these characters through the strategic arc, your audience will be traveling right along with them.

- **Keep your audience entertained.** Telling your story in an entertaining way will involve ensuring that all parts of your strategic arc connect fluidly together and in a way that excites your audience. If you go through your strategic arc in bullet-point form, you will never hold your audience's interest. Instead, you need to provide the right amount of connective tissue between all of your main points and tie them all together around a common point of interest. Otherwise, your story may still be there, but your audience will never hear it. It is also important to tell your story with both excitement and passion. If you don't care about your strategy, your audience won't care either. Similarly, if you *tell* your story as if you don't care about it, the end result will be the same.

- **Keep it succinct, and repeat where necessary.** Here, I'll take a page out of our songwriting book. Most popular songs are between three and five minutes long. They stir your emotions, make their point, make it again, and then conclude. Your strategic story should follow similar suit. As a strategist, you might be tempted to let your audience in on your every thought, particularly if that audience consists of your bosses and company executives. You might feel that you have to show your audience that you know, in fine detail, what you're talking about and that you've done all of your homework. Believe me, they'll know—but not by you presenting mounds of boring data and backstories that nobody can digest. Instead, your deep knowledge of any topic can most effectively be demonstrated through your ability to break down that knowledge in a way that everyone can easily understand and absorb.

- **Be brutally honest where required.** Oftentimes, company leaders approach the strategic process with preconceived notions. Consequently you may be inclined to present a strategy that you think your bosses would want to pursue but that really doesn't support the baseline information that you've gathered. Or, perhaps more commonly, you'll present a result that doesn't match your story but that *does* match the result your executives have asked you to produce. This is dangerous thinking in terms of strategic planning. If your company has absolute targets that must be met, then by all means you should put a strategy in place to meet them. But be sure to outline the true resources and investments that will be required to implement that strategy. Or be sure to show the true result that will be achieved without them. In short, make sure that the ending matches the story and that the entire thing is believable from beginning to end.

- **End with the ending.** When putting together your strategic story, never put your anticipated financial results at the beginning of your story. Follow the strategic arc: start with where you are today, set up the problem, reveal your solution, tell people how much it will cost, and then end with how much they'll get in return. If you lead with the results—or, worse, the costs—your audience will be much more likely to start asking you for details that will inevitably be covered later in your story. You'll then be forced to share information out of order and without the impact that your story is designed to give. Leave the idea of an executive summary for your term paper. Your strategic presentation needs to tell a story, and telling that story in the right order will be critical to its success.

Now that you've put all of your strategic elements together in a way that can be easily communicated, understood, and remembered, there is still one more element that can be added to help bring your story to life in a way that nobody will ever forget: the oft-referenced sixth story element of *style*.

ENHANCING YOUR STRATEGIC STORY

Style is the way in which a story is told. This includes the tone that is used, the rhythm, the grammar, the sentence structure, the point of view, and any other number of elusive elements that help to drive a story in support of its plot. In terms of our strategic story, the style will serve to enhance the impact of your story—both when you go to present your strategy and when you go to implement it. So let's take a little time to find out what some of these stylistic elements might consist of.

First, on the musical side—just to set the stage. The style of a song will be dictated by the way it is executed. If, for example, you take a song and apply different instruments, rhythms, or harmonies to it, you'll get a completely different emotional effect. Many examples of this can be found in the remix versions of popular songs where slow, heartfelt ballads have been turned into driving, energetic dance songs just by altering the rhythm and adding some selective electronic instrumentation.

Your strategic story will be affected by similar stylistic elements or enhancements that can also serve to alter the entire feel of, and ensuing response to, your strategic plan. Because your style can include any number of subtleties, let's just focus on the three that will likely have the greatest effect. They are tone, energy, and harmony.

Tone

In a literal sense, tone refers to the quality of a sound, which in and of itself is nearly impossible to define. So we do so by relating it to something that we *can* define—more specifically, how a certain tone makes us feel. A sweet tone makes us feel happy, a soothing tone makes us feel calm, a harsh tone makes us feel uncomfortable, and an angry tone makes us feel mad. In music, the type of instrumentation that you use will have a direct effect on the tonal qualities of a song and consequently on the feelings that it imparts to its listeners.

Music most likely takes its cues from human speech patterns. A sweet musical tone is thought to sound that way to our ears because when a human being is feeling happy the tonal qualities in his or her voice take on similar characteristics to that which we consider to be pleasant sounding. These qualities are then mimicked in music, and we relate to them accordingly. Other emotional sounds likely follow similar connections to human speech.[6] Whatever the relationship to music, one thing is clear: how we feel about something will have a direct effect on the tone of our voice, and the tone of our voice will in turn have a direct effect on how we make other people feel.

Because of this correlation between expression and impact, the term *tone* has been expanded to other applications. For example, I am writing this paragraph using a certain tone. If I change the phrasing and punctuation of my sentences, that will have a direct effect on the tone that you interpret:

- How do you feel?
- How are you feeling?
- How do you feel now?!
- Are you feeling OK?

All of these sentences are asking the exact same question. However, each one is written using a different tone. By changing the phrasing, punctuation, and sentence structure, I go from an inquisitive tone, to a concerned tone, to an angry tone, to a casual tone. You are only able to interpret this because my written word is a representation of my spoken word. So, you are "speaking" my words in your head as you read the sentences and, depending on how I write each phrase, you translate my written words into tonal speech qualities that each make you feel differently about the question I am asking you.

So tone begins with sound, which originates from speech, which can be represented in words.

But there is another form of tone that cannot be ignored: your body language. Like the tonal qualities of your voice, the expressions you make with your physical body will be a direct reflection of how you feel and how you are likely to make others feel as a result. When we are angry, our faces become stiff and intimidating, our bodies stand upright in a show of strength, and our muscles become tense so that we can best defend ourselves against a possible counterattack. Similarly, if we are happy, our bodies are loose, relaxed, and approachable, evoking a demeanor that others will immediately be drawn to. And if we are excited we become aggressively nonthreatening, remaining flexible and vulnerable yet still ready to spring into action should the chance immediately present itself.

Albert Mehrabian, a professor emeritus at UCLA, published two separate studies in 1967 that have since come to form the

"7-38-55 rule." This says that one person's interpretation of another person's feelings is essentially determined by the following:

- 7 percent words
- 38 percent tone of voice
- 55 percent body language[7]

Translating this to our discussion, how we receive another person's verbal message would theoretically be 93 percent determined by a combination of both their audio tone and their visual tone. Whether or not such exact percentages can be so broadly applied, the key point here is that the way in which we interpret a message will be dictated by the way we *feel* about that message. And the way we feel about a message will be dictated by the way the *communicator* of that message feels, which ultimately will be reflected in both his audio and visual tone.

So what, then, is the secret to adjusting your tone? Simply put, your tone cannot be faked, and it cannot be hidden, neither in music nor in strategy. How you feel will be reflected in your story. There is absolutely nothing you can do about that. What you *can* do, however, is make sure that *you* feel the same way about your strategy that you want others to feel about it. And you can do that by reviewing the section in Chapter 1 on Artistry. Make sure that you have found your passion in your strategy; if you haven't, then keep working on your strategy until you do.

Whatever you feel, your audience will feel as well. And when members of the audience say that you're passionate about your product or business, you'll know that you're setting the right tone.

Energy

If tone is your instrumentation, than energy is your rhythm. The same melody played at two different tempos or underscored by two different drumbeats will have completely different emotional impacts, just as in the remix example mentioned earlier. In the case of your strategy, the rhythm of your story will be set by your energy level.

You may be thinking that I'm going to tell you to always maintain a high energy level. Not true. It *is* true that your energy level will be infectious, and if your high energy is a high *positive* energy, then this is certainly the ideal situation. But I have seen plenty of examples of negative high energy as well. Such energy can manifest itself in the form of panic, anxiety, overt aggression, or even being overly comedic in a situation in which that behavior might not be appropriate.

Every strategy will call for a different approach and a different energy level. It will be up to you to find the right balance for your particular situation. Although high positive energy is usually preferable, there may be situations that call for lower energy levels. Such might be the case if you are presenting in a more formal or an appropriately somber setting, or if you want to convey a feeling of calm, controlled professionalism.

The best advice I can give you is to make sure you are passionate about your strategy, know what rhythm you want to set, and then be constantly aware of how your energy is affecting that rhythm. If any of those things are out of alignment, your audience will pick up on it, and the effectiveness of your strategic story might be put in jeopardy.

Harmony

In music, harmony is another stylistic element that will help define a song's arrangement and, consequently, how that song will sound and feel. Strictly defined, harmony is any combination of musical notes played simultaneously, usually in conjunction with the melodies of a song. The result is almost always a richer and more powerful sound and therefore a richer and more powerful song. But that doesn't always have to be the case.

Without getting too deep into music theory, musical notes are nothing more than sound waves traveling at certain frequencies that are within the range of our normal hearing. Waves traveling at different frequencies will be heard as different pitches. The closer together the frequencies are, the harder our ears will have to work in order to discern them. So there are ideal spacings between frequencies that are more comfortable to our ears than others when two or more different notes are played together. Each unique spacing between frequencies will induce a different musical sound, which will evoke a different emotional response. So the key to writing harmony is to choose a combination of simultaneously played notes with spacings that work together to produce whatever sound or emotion you are trying to achieve.

Few hit songs have been successfully produced with one single voice and absolutely no other instruments at all. Instead most songs feature different instruments and different voices all collaborating together in harmony to produce an overall sound that helps bring the song to life.

For your strategy this concept will manifest itself in the form of all the other team members with whom you will collaborate to implement your plan. In the next chapter, we'll talk about how you will assign specific roles and parts to each of these players in order to drive them all toward a common end result. At this point, you need to know what kind of accompaniment you'll need and what types of different "instruments" you believe will be required to achieve the overall sound and feel of your strategic song.

As with all of our other story elements, these three styles of tone, energy, and harmony are inseparable in their mission. All will collectively help to convey your message, and all will affect the impact that your story will ultimately have when it is communicated.

THE STORY THAT NEVER ENDS

Writing a book is difficult because you have only one chance to tell your story. Once that story is committed to print, it may be years before you can update or evolve it based on whatever feedback you might receive. The nice thing about your strategic story is that you will always have a chance to dynamically evolve it—that is, as long as you allow it.

Whenever I enter into a strategic consultancy, I give the same disclaimer. I tell my clients that they will love me in the beginning of the process, hate me in the middle, and love me again at the end. The hate part usually comes right around the time I'm offering feedback on a strategic story that a client feels is complete but that I, as the audience member, feel needs more work. This is exacerbated by the fact that the story usually evolved the way it did because of advice that I gave!

The reason this happens is because, just as with a song, you never know how a story is going to feel until you hear it. Every story has a flow and a dynamic and an impact; all of which will be heavily influenced by the elements we examined throughout this chapter. All of the pieces may even come together a little bit differently every time you tell your story, and this may continue to happen until you have told it enough times to truly get it right. In short, you need to allow yourself the flexibility to let your story continue to evolve. I like to say that the process is emotionally iterative, and it really is true. There are times you will absolutely hate the process of massaging your story. But when you hit the mark and everything flows together in just the right way and your story has just the impact that you intended, there is no better feeling in the world. (That, by the way, is when the client loves me again!)

Once that happens and you have a song that's ready to be performed, it's time to begin rallying the troops around the parts that each of them will play to collectively help bring your song to life. In short, it's time to orchestrate your strategy.

Finding Your Creativity

You may think that creativity only applies to coming up with inventive, new ideas. But there is a big difference between great melodies and great songs. So here are some tips to help you find your creativity when you are putting all of your strategic ideas together:

- A piece of art may be unique, but it will only be considered to be creative if someone appreciates that uniqueness. To achieve this, the artist must find a way to connect to what other people are feeling. Your strategic story is no different. Pull yourself away from the details and think about the overall purpose of your strategy and what you are ultimately trying to achieve. Then think about how you can make other people understand that importance by connecting it to something that they feel strongly about as well. Creativity lives in the connection between unique and impactful; you won't find it in just one of those alone.

- There are many creative ways to tell stories—some of which may not yet have been conceived. Don't be afraid to deviate from the standard slide presentation that has become the norm for most businesses. The use of video, music, props, or other interactive forms of media may not be common, but their use can help draw your audiences in to your message and leave them with an impression that they won't soon forget.

- Your strategy not only has to connect to others, it has to connect to you as well. Don't try to put your story together based solely on templates or a formula. These can be used as a guide, but, ultimately, every strategy must have its own unique story. Put your story together in a way that feels right to you, even if that doesn't follow the exact order that I have suggested here. If your story doesn't flow well for you, it isn't likely to flow well for anyone else either.

CHAPTER 7

ORCHESTRATION

ANALYSIS	RECOLLECTION	INTUITION	ARTISTRY
Present	**Past**	**Future**	**Path**
Company/Capabilities	Influences	Vision	Strategy
Competitors	History	Goals	Story
Customers	Performance	Objectives	Resources
Industry	Experience	Target Market	Execution

←———— INPUTS ————→←———— OUTPUTS ————→

PREPARATION	PREPARATION	INSPIRATION	IDEATION
		GENRE	ARRANGEMENT
			ORCHESTRATION
			PRODUCTION
I	II	III	IV

What You Will Do

- Assign and guide your resources

If arranging is the art of knowing what you want a piece of music to sound like, then orchestration is the art of providing directions to all of the different instrumentalists so that your desired sound can be achieved. For our strategic process, the person who develops the strategy will more than likely be the same person who orchestrates that strategy. However, the fact that, in music, orchestration is often a completely different role certainly speaks to the complexity of the task at hand.

Technically speaking, orchestration is defined as the practice of writing music for an orchestra, which itself has a fairly strict definition with regard to the number and types of instruments that it will contain. However, the practice of orchestration is not limited to this exact configuration of instruments. In fact, the term has come to be applied to the practice of writing for whatever instruments the music calls for, from large ensembles to small rock bands. More precisely than that, orchestration has come to be known (as discussed in the previous chapter) as the assigning and writing of musical parts, even if some of those parts are not played by a human being. A case in point is the practice of computer orchestration where musical parts are assigned, written, and then fed into a computer program that translates those parts into electronic sounds. This, in fact, is the technique that I use for much of the music that I compose, since I do not have ready access to the New York Philharmonic! So orchestration is really about these things:

1. Knowing what the composer's vision is
2. Choosing what resources will be needed to carry out that vision, and assigning roles accordingly
3. Understanding the capabilities and limitations of those resources
4. Providing clear directions and guidance so that those resources can all work together to achieve the composer's vision

I hope it is clear as to why this analogy applies so perfectly to our strategic composition process.

With this backdrop, let's step through each of these four basic steps so that we can better understand this critical concept of bringing together an "orchestra" to help carry out your strategic plan.

KNOWING THE VISION

Although music composing, arranging, and orchestrating are three separate tasks, they are not always three separate roles. In practice, it is perhaps more typical to have a composer/arranger who works with a separate orchestrator or a composer who works with a separate arranger/orchestrator. In either case, because two separate people will usually be carrying out these three different activities, the meetings that take place between them will be critical to creating an overall musical composition and performance that is in line with the composer's original vision.

Perhaps one of the most common of these relationships can be found between composers and orchestrators in the world of musical theater. Musicals tend to be composed and at least partially arranged by one individual and then orchestrated by another. This allows the composer to focus on the high demands of writing what is the equivalent of a modern-day opera, carefully integrating music and action to tell an entertaining story to the audience. This process generally requires a lot of upfront research, intense collaboration, and multiple rewrites as the story is slowly tested, rehearsed, and modified for the limitations of what ultimately will be a relatively confined space. With all of this activity, musical theater composers, more often than not, will require the help of someone who can then take their music and bring it to life through an orchestra or ensemble of some shape and size. Many times, at least part of the arranging (as we've defined it) has already been completed, or at the very least contemplated, by the composer. The structure of the songs has been determined, the feel and emotion of the songs has been set, and the overall sound of the music has more than likely been envisioned. This allows the orchestrator to focus on bringing the three stylistic elements of tone, energy, and harmony to life through instrumentation, rhythm, and collaboration.

When working in this way, it is critical that the orchestrator thoroughly understands all of these intricacies that are in the composer's mind. This is usually accomplished through a series of meetings and working sessions wherein these individuals will closely collaborate to ensure that the original intent of the music is translated into the sounds that audiences will ultimately hear. Because you will serve in both of these roles for your strategic process, it may be helpful for you to think about how you as a composer/arranger might prepare for such a meeting if someone else was orchestrating your strategy.

The first step is just to take mental note of the things you determined in your arrangement:

- What do you want your strategy to achieve?
- What is the overall theme of your strategic story?
- How do you want your strategy to come across?
- Whom do you think you'll need help from?

Make sure the answers to these questions are clear in your mind, because these are the things you will need to know when choosing the resources that will help make all of this come to life.

CHOOSING RESOURCES

The number-one key contributing success factor for your strategy will be the people who will help you implement it. I've learned some difficult lessons throughout my career about trying to do too many things on my own and, believe me, every single time that I have collaborated with others, the result was better than when I tried to do it all by myself.

Collaboration isn't always easy, but it is almost always more rewarding than doing something by yourself—as long as you seek to truly understand the people you're collaborating with. One of the reasons that people may find it difficult to collaborate has to do with the fact that it takes time, effort, and emotional fortitude, especially in the early stages. The time is in finding the right people to collaborate with; the effort is in working with those people to share your vision and to gain a common understanding of how you can best collaborate together; the emotional fortitude is in the fact that you have to accept some level of disagreement and pushback that you wouldn't have otherwise had to deal with. Given all of this, sometimes you may feel that it's just easier to avoid collaborating altogether.

But that would be a bad choice, for several reasons:

- Collaboration introduces skills and capabilities that you may not possess.
- Collaboration leads to ideas and perspectives that you might not otherwise have been aware of.

- Collaboration simply gives you more human resources to work with. This translates into more time and energy that can collectively be dedicated to achieving your objectives.
- Finally, collaboration can be a lot of fun, providing education, camaraderie, and another person or persons with whom to celebrate your successes.

Viewed through this lens, there are many more reasons to collaborate than not. However, those reasons will quickly diminish if you choose the wrong people to collaborate with or if you misjudge the contributions that each of those people should make.

In a musical environment, every instrument—and every player, for that matter—will bring a certain sound to the finished piece. It is the orchestrator's job to know which sound is associated with each instrument and to also know how to combine all of these different sounds to achieve the desired overall musical effect. This will involve having not only a deep understanding of what each instrument brings to the party but also an intimate understanding of the overall objectives that you are trying to achieve so that the right instruments can be brought into the mix at any given time. In terms of your strategy, this translates into fully understanding what each collaborative function does and what each will contribute to achieving the overall objectives of your plan.

Fortunately, companies, like orchestras, are all organized in similar ways: there are some fairly standardized functions within each organization, and for the most part what those functions *do* is also fairly consistent from company to company. Although this is by no means an exhaustive list, I will attempt to outline the most common of these functions, along with what they will more than likely contribute to your overall strategic plan.

Product Management

The product management team, if one exists in your company, will more than likely be responsible for running the business of your products. As such, this team is usually responsible for product strategy, with a product manager acting as the owner of that strategy. Product Management usually exists in bigger, more complex organizations that have large numbers of products or product portfolios. The goal of the product management team is to help companies maintain a sharp focus on individual products and portfolios within what is usually a larger matrixed organization. To do this, product managers are typically tasked with running their product as if it were its own mini-business: utilizing shared resources from other departments to act as their product business staff. Note that not all companies have a separate product management team. Sometimes the marketing team maintains ownership of product strategies. Other times, particularly in small to midsized companies, the product business is led directly by the general manager or by a similar business unit leader. Whatever the structure, when I refer to the product management team, I am referring to whichever team owns the product strategy.

Marketing

Marketing generally has two components: an inbound portion and an outbound portion. Inbound marketing involves gathering information on what is happening in the marketplace, including customer, competitor, and industry insights. If it exists as a separate function, the inbound marketing team will serve as a critical resource to the strategic composer throughout the preparation phase. Outbound marketing most often involves the promotion portion of the marketing mix. Many marketing teams, however, have some level of responsibility for price and place as well (if product is handled by a separate team, as noted earlier). As such, outbound marketing teams play key roles in helping determine and implement many of the specific actions that will support the Go-to-Market Plan.

Sales

The sales team is primarily responsible for convincing someone to buy your products or to utilize your company's services. If it is Marketing's job to broadly let prospective customers know a product exists, it is the job of Sales to follow up with these prospects (often called "leads") on an individual basis and turn them into paying customers. From the standpoint of the strategic process, the sales team will usually represent a company's front line. As such, members of this team will typically provide critical inputs throughout the strategic process as to which actions can feasibly be taken to achieve a desired strategic result, based on their vast experience of what may or may not have worked in the past.

> NOTE: The traditional model of Sales and Marketing is changing. The model that many of us are familiar with is that the marketing team is responsible for mass-messaging to large numbers of people, mostly through some form of advertising or promotion, and the sales team is responsible for one-on-one follow-up and interaction with customers who are attracted to those promotions. Today, people are communicating differently. With the advent of social media and the Internet, the line between mass messaging and personal interaction is becoming blurrier by the day. That's not to say that both functions aren't still required, but it does mean that, in some instances, Sales and Marketing are more and more becoming less and less two separate entities.

Operations

Traditionally, the operations team is responsible for manufacturing your product. But this team can take many forms, depending on what type of product or service you are trying to bring to market. If it is a manufactured product, this team will consist of your manufacturing plants, as well as your supply chain and logistical functions. If your product is a service, your operations team will consist of the people who are actually responsible for providing whatever service you are offering. In addition to the obvious implementation aspects of this function, your operations team can also provide key inputs to your strategy regarding any additional investments that may be required to support existing capabilities or resources. One of the most important considerations when working with Operations is to ensure that the functional goals and objectives of this team are firmly aligned with your strategic goals and objectives. Oftentimes, operations teams will be concerned with supplying a product or service at the lowest possible cost. The key word here is *possible*, implying that there is a limit to how low that cost should actually be. For example, will the cost be limited only by the technical specifications of a product, or are there other considerations, such as service, support, delivery, quality, customization, or breadth of portfolio that will need to be strategically maintained? These are some of the alignment issues that typically have to be sorted out between the strategy owner and the operations team.

Engineering

Engineering can have many facets. I have seen this term applied to research, development, technical support, field engineering, applications engineering, industrial engineering, and any number of other technical disciplines. Many of these roles may even fall into one of the other functional categories that I am presenting in this section. From the standpoint of our strategic process, my definition of *Engineering* is the team that takes a product idea and turns it into something that can be sold to a customer. As such, this team will have a lot to say about what can and cannot be feasibly developed, as well as how much money will be required to produce and maintain your product. Engineering will also be instrumental in carrying out your product action plan, in that the product management team will define the big picture of what you want to achieve (turning their product roadmaps into product requirements), while the engineering team will define the specific technical specifications for a product that will meet those requirements.

Service

Service involves any function that provides support for a product after it has been made available to customers. This can include Customer Service, Field Service, Technical Support, or even any number of contracted repair centers or other service providers. Service teams will usually be involved in the implementation of your strategy, and because of that they must be perfectly aligned with whatever message you want the marketplace to receive about your product. Service teams will also be able to contribute valuable information about any service-related investments that may be needed to support your plan.

Support (Internal)

No strategic plan will be successful without drawing upon the expertise of internal support functions. The main purpose of internal support teams, from the standpoint of our strategic process, will be to provide key expertise that the strategy owner might not otherwise possess. In this way, these functions will act as consultants for your plan but will also be instrumental in implementing your plan from the standpoint of both supporting whatever unexpected situations might arise, as well as helping you track the success of your plan. These are the most common internal support functions that you will draw upon:

- **Finance.** Provides guidance on your company's overall fiduciary responsibilities and objectives, as well as key information on how all of the financial aspects of your plan (revenue, costs, expenses, investments) will come together to achieve your objectives
- **Human Resources (HR).** Provides guidance related to the human skills and capabilities that exist in your company and what, if any, additional skills, training, or personnel might be required to implement your plan
- **Legal.** Provides guidance on compliance issues, patent issues, and any other legal implications that could affect your plan, as well as ongoing support for any unexpected legal issues that might arise throughout your implementation stage

Information Technology

The information technology (IT) team primarily manages the technology that is used to run a company's business. Traditionally, this function has focused on the systems that served as part of a company's internal technology infrastructure. With the explosion of technology that has occurred in recent years, however, this infrastructure has expanded into all of the systems, devices, and software that drive every employee's job function, as well as many of the systems, programs, or apps that are used by a company's external customers. All of these are considered products—some internal, and some external. Therefore, it is not uncommon for people in IT departments to serve in one (or more) of the following four roles:

- **Internal Product Management.** If they are developing a strategy for a technology used by internal employees
- **Engineering.** If they are developing a product that will be used by external customers
- **Service.** If they are providing support for a technology used by external customers
- **Support.** If they are providing support for a technology used by internal employees

Because of these complexities, it is not uncommon for IT departments to be both very large and also to be split by, at the very least, an internal and an external component in order to perform any or all of the above roles.

Remember, every musical composition needs to have a certain sound. The composer has a vision of what this sound needs to be based on the overall feeling that the song needs to convey—which itself is based on the inspiration, the genre, the idea, and the arrangement for that song. The orchestrator's job, then, is to choose the right mix of instruments to achieve that sound.

Now that we know what each instrument in our strategic orchestra does, we need to know how to balance those instruments in order to achieve the sound we're looking for. To do this, we need to consider not only which functions to draw from but also how to position those functions with respect to one another.

Assigning Roles

When choosing the parts that my strategic orchestra will play, I like to assign each team to one of the following four roles (listed in order of strategic influence):

- **Leaders.** These are the people who will help to lead and oversee the strategy.
- **Drivers.** These are the people who will mainly be responsible for implementing the strategy in the marketplace.
- **Supporters.** These are the people who will provide critical deliverables to the strategy.
- **Accentuators.** These are the people who will enhance the effectiveness of the strategic implementation.

These four roles—which make up my LADS model (**L**eaders, **A**ccentuators, **D**rivers, **S**upporters)—may also be accompanied by a singular owner role that will be occupied by the person who owns the strategy from beginning to end. This strategy owner might be a product manager, a general manager, or even a CEO, but this role will always be held by an individual rather than a team or function. The owner is the person who is ultimately responsible for both developing and carrying out the strategy, so, in most cases, it is probably going to be you!

The role that each team or function will perform should be aligned with the overall intent of the strategy. Going back to our strategic melodies, if, for example, you are pursuing a market-focused strategy with new products in new markets, the role assignments might look like this:

- **Leaders.** Product Management
- **Drivers.** Sales, Marketing
- **Supporters.** Operations, Engineering
- **Accentuators.** Service, Support

A strategy based on maintaining a cost leadership position with existing products in existing markets, on the other hand, might look something like this:

- **Leaders.** Product Management
- **Drivers.** Operations, Engineering
- **Supporters.** Sales, Marketing
- **Accentuators.** Service, Support

This is really just a type of responsibility assignment matrix, not unlike the commonly used RACI analysis (Responsible, Accountable, Consulted, Informed), or the expanded RASCI (which adds *Support*) or CAIRO (which adds *Omitted*) models.[1] The LADS model that I am proposing is more applicable to teams, and so it is a very effective way to guide how each function will contribute to the overall implementation of your strategy.

The only reason for assigning roles in this way is so you can have a clear idea of what you, as the strategy owner, will need from each team as you work toward your production phase. This will also help define how you should interact with each one (and how they should interact with each other) as the strategic implementation unfolds. In my experience, this is a critical step in ensuring that each team works together harmoniously toward a common end goal.

Once you have determined what instruments your orchestra will consist of and what roles each will play, it's helpful to draw a quick map so that everyone will always remain aligned as the strategy is being implemented. To do this, I like to think again in terms of a standard orchestra layout, where usually the conductor is front and center, the high strings (the drivers of the melody) are to the left, the low strings (the supporters of the melody) are to the right, and the woodwinds, brass, and percussion (the accentuators of the melody) are down the middle. This layout varies slightly from orchestra to orchestra, but usually the idea is to have melody to the left, backbone to the right, and highlights down the middle.

Without being overly literal, I like to use this same basic guide to lay out the map of my strategic team, adding the role of leaders directly in front of, and as a virtual extension of, the conductor or owner. To do this, I follow the template shown in Figure 7.1.

It may seem odd to lay out your strategic team in the form of an orchestra, but let me give you one truly compelling reason to consider this approach. The reason that an orchestra is laid out in a semicircle is so that all of the players can see one another while still remaining focused on the overall vision and direction that is being communicated by the conductor. So each section has its own role, but each role must also rely on all of the other roles, as well as the conductor, in order to come together to create music. If you have ever heard an orchestra (or any other musical group) that is out of alignment, you'll recall that it is an absolute catastrophe to listen to. In rock music, there is perhaps no greater compliment than to say that a band sounds "tight." Roughly translated, you're saying that the band is completely

FIGURE 7.1

Strategic Orchestra Map

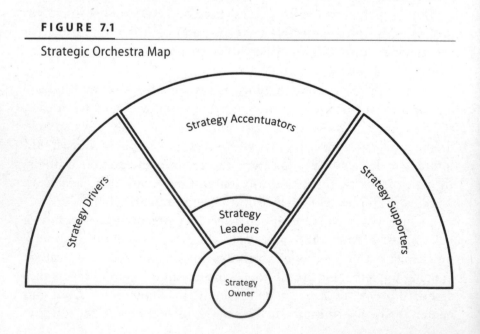

aligned, all working together toward a common goal. And even if that goal is not your particular cup of tea, you'll still acknowledge that they sound great together.

If you work for a large company, you've probably heard of (or experienced) *organizational silos*—usually within a negative context. This is when individual functions become more concerned with serving their own goals and objectives over those of the company as a whole. In reality, if a company tried to operate without any silos at all, it may lack form, structure, or functional purpose. But if organizational silos become too strong, they can prevent internal departments from all working together toward a common overall vision. Laying out your strategic implementation team in the shape of an orchestra, if only symbolically, may be the first step toward striking just the right balance between these two extremes.

Taking this one step further, once you've assigned your strategic roles, you can begin to draw your map by filling in the team names and physically arranging them with respect to the other teams with whom they will most closely need to work. Applying the roles that we might establish for a differentiated new product strategy, we can arrange our map as shown in Figure 7.2.

This is just one of many possible configurations. It will be your job as the strategic orchestrator to choose your orchestra,

FIGURE 7.2

Strategic Orchestra Map Example

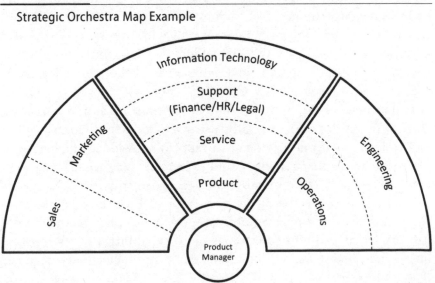

assign their roles, and lay them out according to the needs of your particular strategic plan. Doing so will help clear the path for a cohesive strategic implementation team that has only one thing in mind: working together to achieve the vision, goals, and objectives of your strategic plan.

UNDERSTANDING YOUR RESOURCES

Now that you've chosen your resources and laid them out according to your strategy, it is important that you take some time to fully understand the true capabilities of those resources before you go about the task of orchestrating your plan.

When writing for an orchestra, the orchestrator must deeply understand the range of each instrument that he or she is writing for. Every instrument has a certain range of notes that it can play, which may also vary somewhat based on the level of skill that each individual player has. This means that all of the instruments must work together to produce the full range of notes and sounds that will be required by any given piece of music. Knowing how and when to combine these different parts will be one of the keys to an orchestrator's success.

In addition to note range, the orchestrator must also be keenly aware of how each instrument is capable of being played. For example, a player's hands can only move so swiftly from one note to another on any given instrument, and each instrument has different capabilities in this regard. This has to do not only with the agility with which a player can manipulate the instrument but also with the physical spacing of notes on some instruments versus others. So all of these elements must be carefully considered.

I remember my first attempt at writing for a string quartet. I wrote the entire piece digitally, using the *sounds* of violins, cellos, and violas but without having any practical knowledge of whether or not these actual instruments could ever really play what I was writing. Later, when I asked members of a real string quartet if they could realistically perform the piece, they informed me, as nicely as they could, that it would be absolutely impossible to play! It wasn't until I dutifully learned all of the ranges and capabilities for the instruments for which I was writing that I could produce a piece of music that could actually be played.

The point is that you absolutely have to understand the ranges of the teams that you are leading through the strategic process if you want to have any chance of orchestrating a plan that can be effectively implemented. The best way to do that is to talk to them, meet with them, communicate with them, and bring them in on your plan. For very large teams, this can be done through the team leaders. For smaller teams, you may be able to manage this knowledge transfer yourself. Whatever the case, this is a critical step that absolutely cannot be overlooked, because if you give directions to a team that they either can't follow or can't perform, they won't always come back to correct you. More often than not, they just won't do whatever it is that you're asking them to do.

So what happens if your plan requires capabilities that your team simply doesn't possess? This is when you have to invest.

Unfortunately I have seen many strategic plans that simply don't consider whether or not a company possesses the capabilities needed to execute it. Companies have great ideas and high aspirations, but they don't always want to admit when they aren't capable of doing something.

I remember working with a company that was deep into the implementation stage of a strategy to provide electronic devices for a specific industrial application. This company sold mechanical components in this particular market; in fact, it was one of the share leaders in this space. Being intimately familiar with this market, they rightly identified a need for electronic devices that would be used in conjunction with some of their mechanical products. As it turned out, other electronic device manufacturers had all but ignored this market, leaving an open opportunity for somebody else to provide a solution to a very real market problem. All the stars were aligned, so this company forged ahead with its strategic plan.

On paper everything looked perfect. The company had planned to outsource much of the development and manufacturing of the product, keeping ongoing fixed costs low. The market share projections were fabulous, the margins looked very attractive, and the expected return on investment was nearly double what the company was getting from any of its other investments. And none of this was smoke and mirrors. This company had done its homework and really had a good plan on its hands. Throughout the process, strategic planners and implementers did everything right. They had a great story, had assembled all the right people, and they were able to rally their teams collectively around their common strategic goal. The product was developed on time, released to the marketplace, and outpaced all projections in a very short period of time.

But, unfortunately, they weren't able to brag about all of this success. The reason is that, several years into the implementation, something had gone terribly wrong. A quality problem with the supplier had, almost overnight, caused mass quantities of these electronic devices to fail. The problem with the product itself was bad enough, but this issue was also starting to affect the leading share position the company had with its mechanical products.

In the end, it was decided to kill the electronic device product and shut the line down. But that's not the part of the story I'm trying to tell. The important part of this particular story had to do with the root cause of the problem. Way back in the strategic planning process, through all of the celebration of this hidden gem of an opportunity that they had found, people missed something. They failed to consider their own capabilities. They knew that they could neither develop nor manufacture electronic devices without a lot of investment. So they rightly decided to outsource these capabilities. This, as it turns out, was a good decision and helped to keep upfront investment costs low. What wasn't such a good decision, however, was the failure to recognize the need for a sustainable infrastructure to support and service the product after it was released. Had they factored this into their strategy, the additional ongoing expenses would likely have resulted in an unprofitable plan or at best a longer payback period than they were willing to accept. They knew the market, they understood the need, but they failed to understand their own capabilities. Therefore, the strategy failed as well.

This particular story helps to outline a critical point. Yes, sometimes companies actively mislead themselves about the true investment that will be required to fully implement a plan with an otherwise attractive return. But many times companies just overlook their own weaknesses. It's difficult for any of us to admit that we might not be able to accomplish something with the capabilities that we currently possess, particularly when we're excited about the end goal. And, believe me, I'm the first person to say that *anything* is possible. But you'll never hear me say that anything is possible for *free*. That just wouldn't be realistic.

Now is the time for you, as the strategic composer and orchestrator, to take a good, hard look at your own internal resources—be they people, systems, knowledge, or infrastructure—and compare your capabilities to whatever will truly be required to meet your strategic objectives. If there is a gap, you can take one of two directions: you can account for the investment or you can change your strategy. That's it. But now is the time to make that choice.

When everything lines up and the strategy still makes sense, now you're ready to start providing direction to the orchestra.

PROVIDING DIRECTION

Returning to the music analogy, once all of the instruments have been chosen and the capabilities are well understood, the final step in the orchestration process will be to provide directions for each of the instruments in the form of a notated musical score. This score will typically include a written part or parts for each instrument type, with every musical direction meticulously notated, from notes to rhythms, to volume changes, and sometimes right down to the expression with which each note should be played. In this way, the score takes a composer's structured song and ensures that just about any group of instrumentalists can put that song into action exactly as the orchestrator intended. This level of detail is typical for classical music, musical theater, or any style of music that is intended to be played the same way by multiple different instrumentalists at multiple different times.

Other styles of music, on the other hand, tend to be much more dynamic. Orchestrations for jazz or rock music, for example, may be less specific than for other genres, and in some cases may not even be written out at all. These musical performances rely much more heavily on the individual skills of each musician, as well as the dynamic interplay between them. So orchestration in these situations often happens in real time as the performance evolves. Sometimes the entire compositional process is a collective one, with more than one performer developing not only the orchestrations but also the melodies and songs themselves. In these cases, the formal notation of each and every orchestration may be unnecessary because the same resources will be composing, arranging, and orchestrating all at the same time.

In business I find that the majority of situations will call for an approach that is somewhere in the middle of these two extremes. What this means is that as you begin to turn your strategies into actions, it will be up to the teams who are helping to implement the plan to also help design the specific actions that will ultimately drive that plan. Not only is this evolution encouraged, it is required. In most large organizations, once the strategy goes into the implementation stage, strategy owners simply cannot manage every aspect of continuously adjusting and readjusting every single action by themselves. If they try, they will almost certainly sacrifice the company's ability to act and react quickly in the marketplace.

One of the mistakes that I often see strategists make is that they feel they need to single-handedly develop not only their high-level strategies but also the more granular tactics that go along with those strategies. The whole point of developing the Go-to-Market Plan is to provide high-level strategic direction for each of the marketing mix elements. Doing so will allow you to provide crisp and well-communicated guidance for almost any action that will be taken while still allowing your action plans to evolve over time as market and competitive conditions change. Remember, you have to think like a chess player. Every single move is not going to be strictly mapped out. Instead, your strategy should allow for any number of different moves to be chosen as situations present themselves. The faster you can adapt, the more effective your overall strategy will be. Calling upon your team to help dynamically develop your tactics will allow for this level of strategic agility.

Following this model will provide you with these key benefits:

- You will gain access to ground-level skills and expertise that you yourself may not possess.
- Your team will buy in on your strategy because they will feel like they have some part in creating it.
- The company decision makers and stakeholders will have more confidence in your strategy once they see that your team also supports it.
- The entire team will feel they have collective ownership of the strategy, which also means they will take accountability for making sure the strategic results are achieved.

Against this backdrop, your role in the orchestration process will be to both understand and *enable* resources by providing whatever high-level direction they may need in order to help carry out your strategy. To do this, your role must begin to shift from orchestrator to orchestra conductor as your strategy moves into the implementation stage.

Bringing our analogy full circle, let's explore what some of these strategic orchestrations, or actions, might look like in relation to the high-level guidance that was provided in your Go-to-Market Plan:

- **Product actions.** Specific features, function, aesthetics, packaging, manuals, service, support, versions, releases, and so on, including the timing and availability of each
- **Pricing actions.** Specific pricing, timing, variations, competitive positions, bundling, discounts, rebates, pricing promotions, and so on
- **Promotion actions.** Specific messages, campaigns, mediums (radio, television, billboard, print ads, social media, viral videos), branding, and so on
- **Place actions.** Specific geographies, partners, methodologies (online, telephone, physical distribution, retail), exclusivity, programs, and so on

There are many more actions that could be conceived, but these categories should provide some idea as to the types of actions that your orchestra will help you not only carry out but also create. And this will be made possible by the context provided in your strategic melodies and Go-to-Market Plan, supported by the guidance you will continue to provide as you conduct the orchestra throughout the implementation phase.

Depending on the type of strategy you are putting together, you may or may not decide to put these actions to paper. Again, this decision will be based on how much flexibility you want to give your team, which will likely be based on factors such as how big that team is, how dynamic your strategy needs to be, and how quickly your team needs to be able to move. As mentioned earlier, you can choose to notate every action up front, as in classical music, or you can allow team members to dynamically develop their own actions around the framework of a higher-level plan, as in jazz music. My personal preference is to work somewhere in between these two extremes.

To capture this I like to produce what I call a *strategic score*. This is a high-level summary of each action (orchestration) as it relates to each Go-to-Market Plan element, the time frame (tempo) for completing each element, and the functions (instruments) that will ultimately be responsible for performing each action. For an example of what this strategic score might look like, see Figure 7.3.

Keep in mind that this particular tool is meant only to provide the key actions that will be required by your strategy. This allows

FIGURE 7.3

The Strategic Score

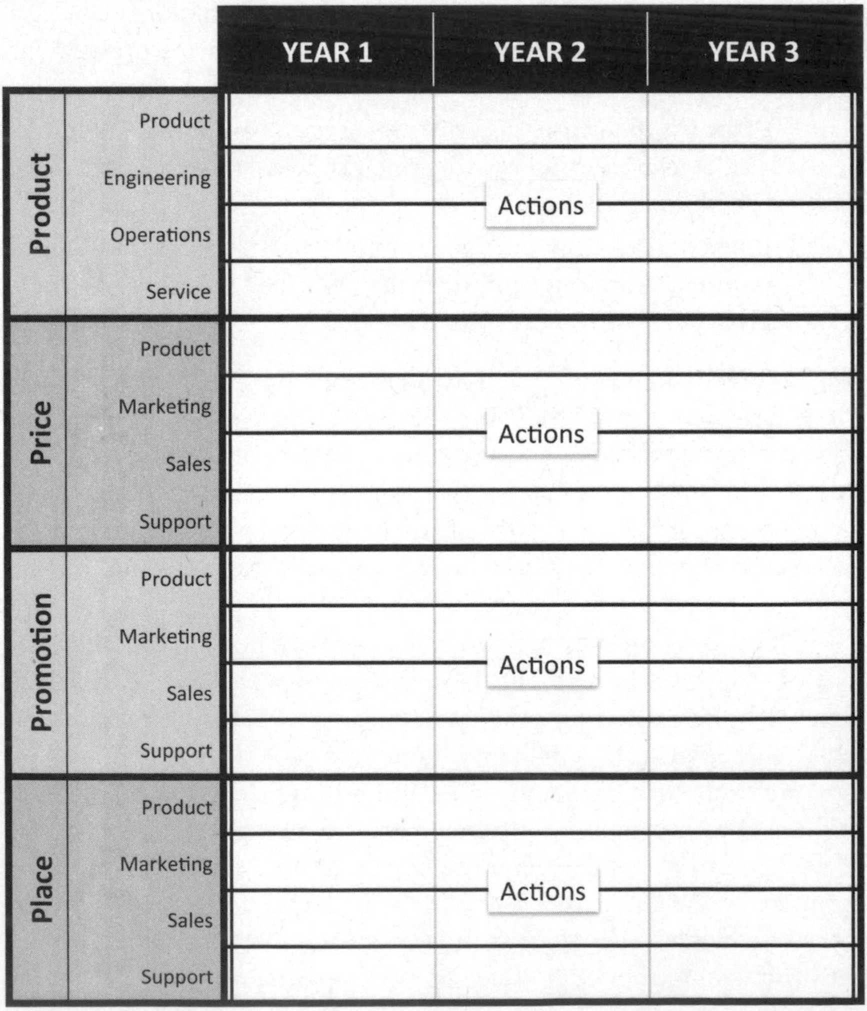

			YEAR 1	YEAR 2	YEAR 3
Product		Product			
		Engineering		Actions	
		Operations			
		Service			
Price		Product			
		Marketing		Actions	
		Sales			
		Support			
Promotion		Product			
		Marketing		Actions	
		Sales			
		Support			
Place		Product			
		Marketing		Actions	
		Sales			
		Support			

team members to also develop their own actions along the way, as long as those actions are in line with the strategic intent of your plan. In music, this is referred to as *improvisation*, or the act of creating music spontaneously, while still working within a given set of boundaries. This technique often results in some of the most unique, inventive, and successful music ever performed, and it is highly recommended for at least some portion of your strategic composition as well.

In the end, it will be up to you, as the strategic orchestrator, to communicate your score to the teams. And if everything goes as planned, it will be up to you, as the strategy owner, to conduct your orchestra through the final phase of your strategic process as well. Your strategy will be nothing more than a dream until you turn it into a performance. It's time, now, to put your strategy into full production.

Finding Your Creativity

Orchestrating the same piece of music in different ways will produce very different results. The same can be said of your strategic orchestrations. Here, then, are some tips to help you find your creativity as you prepare to orchestrate your strategy:

- When orchestrating a piece of music, a good orchestrator will only utilize those instruments that will add value to the overall sound, style, and message that he or she is trying to communicate. Why, then, should it be any different for corporate strategies? Don't feel as though every function in your company needs to be involved in the execution of every strategy you compose. Doing so may lead to overlapping team members all competing for the same parts. Creative strategic orchestration can be most effectively achieved by streamlining your ensemble to fit the purpose of your plan.

- The typical departmental roles that I've described in this chapter may be the de facto standard for most organizations, but they aren't the only options that exist. Stringed instruments that are plucked instead of strummed or bowed take on a more percussive quality, thereby changing their traditional roles. Similarly, when keyboards were invented that could effectively mimic other instruments by way of digital sampling, entirely new creative possibilities were opened up to composers and orchestrators alike. Challenging the traditional roles of standard company functions might just have a similar effect.

- Always see the orchestration of your strategy as part of the creative process. It's not enough to have ideas; you'll also need to execute those ideas in a meaningful and impactful way. Toward that end, the more you choose to collaborate with the targeted teams and functions that can help you achieve your vision, goals, and objectives, the better chance you'll have of being able to implement your strategy in an exciting new way. Draw upon those teams as you orchestrate your strategy, and they will help you forge your creative path.

CHAPTER 8

PRODUCTION

ANALYSIS	RECOLLECTION	INTUITION	ARTISTRY
Present	**Past**	**Future**	**Path**
Company/Capabilities	Influences	Vision	Strategy
Competitors	History	Goals	Story
Customers	Performance	Objectives	Resources
Industry	Experience	Target Market	Execution

←———— **INPUTS** ————→←———— **OUTPUTS** ————→

PREPARATION	PREPARATION	INSPIRATION	IDEATION
		GENRE	ARRANGEMENT
			ORCHESTRATION
			PRODUCTION
I	II	III	IV

What You Will Do

- Implement your strategy
- Measure the results

A producer is perhaps one of the most misunderstood roles in the entertainment industry, which is interesting because this is the only industry I know of that actually uses this term. I think the confusion stems from the tendency to associate a producer with "someone who produces something." In fact, that's not exactly how the term, as we know it today, is usually applied. What a producer actually does is to ensure that a production takes place. In very broad terms, the person in that role is responsible for taking an idea for a production, ensuring that financing is available, lining up resources, managing schedules and budgets, overseeing all aspects of the actual production, and having the final say when creative decisions have to be made along the way. If you believe that, as the owner of your strategy, you will have similar responsibilities when your plan goes into production, then you are definitely in the right frame of mind!

Different industries within the entertainment business each have slightly different definitions of what a producer does, ranging from having mostly financial and business responsibilities to overseeing more of the creative decisions. There are also different levels of producers that might focus on slightly different aspects of a given production. An executive producer, for example, might deal with more of the business-related issues, whereas other types of producers (associate producers, supervising producers, line producers, co-producers, and so on) might handle other, perhaps more creative parts of the production.

All of these producer roles, in one way or another, are considered to be general managers over one or more aspects of a production. In this way, the role of a producer will encompass some level of leadership, business, and creative/visionary responsibilities.

It should come as no surprise that the implementation of your strategy will be the equivalent of your strategic production—that is, you will be taking a creative vision and turning it into a reality. It should also come as no surprise that your role at this point in the process will be much like that of a producer. As such, you will be overseeing all aspects of your strategic production, ensuring that all of the different implementation pieces come together in line with your original vision.

As the process shifts from orchestration to production, there are three main steps that you will have to take in order to bring your idea to life:

1. You need to convince investors and stakeholders that your strategic plan is worth pursuing. For this, you'll need to know who those stakeholders are, and you'll need to persuade them to commit their hard-earned time, money, and resources to your plan.

2. You need to perform. To do this, just like the conductor of an orchestra, you will need to take the stage, inspire your team, and passionately lead the implementation of your strategy.

3. You need to track and measure the results and make adjustments as necessary. This will require a firm understanding of your overall objectives, a keen eye on the performance of your plan, and acceptance of a level of accountability that reaches beyond any official position that you may have within your company.

With this agreed, let's explore each of these three areas more closely as we work toward bringing our strategic composition to life. In summary, they are:

1. Convincing investors
2. Performing
3. Measuring results

CONVINCING INVESTORS

If you've made it this far in the process, you should have a strategy that both you and your future implementation teams truly believe in. Your challenge now will be to convince your strategic stakeholders to believe in it too.

You may be in a position to finance your strategy yourself. But more often than not, the ability to implement your plan will be contingent upon your company or some outside investors supporting and financing your plan. This could come in the form of a one-time investment, such as a bank loan or an *angel investor* or, as in the case of larger companies, in the form of a general commitment of both money and resources over a long period of time. In this latter (and more common) case, getting buy-in on your strategic plan does not mean that every subsequent business case related to your plan will automatically be accepted. There is a much higher probability,

however, that these future business cases will be funded if they are
tied back to a fully supported strategy.

In Chapter 6 we examined how to put together your strategic
story, which culminates in how much the plan will cost and what
will come as a result. Your investors will likely think of this in terms
of what is commonly called a *return on investment*, or *ROI*. There
are several different ways to analyze what kind of return any given
investment will yield. The official calculation looks at how much
money you make as a percentage of how much you invest. But this
is not the only way in which returns can be analyzed. For example,
you can look at how long the investment will take to pay itself back,
how much money a company will net out of the investment over
any given period of time, or how a given investment compares to
other investments that could otherwise have been made with the
same amount of cash. Although it is unlikely that your investors will
be thinking in these detailed terms at this stage of the game, they are
definitely going to be interested in how much they have to give versus
how much they will ultimately get. And this is the stage where you'll
need to translate your strategic story into an actual strategic presentation to help bring it all together for them.

In Part 3 of this book, I provide a compilation of tools that will
help you master the strategic process that I've outlined. Among those
tools is a guideline for your strategic presentation that will allow your
story to be told effectively, succinctly, and with the impact required
to persuade investors to believe in your plan. As you are presenting
this story to your potential investors, I urge you to keep the following key points in mind, based on some of the most common mis-
steps that I have witnessed during this stage. Most of these tips apply
to people working in large, publicly traded companies, although the
lessons can be applied to smaller companies and private investment
arrangements as well:

1. Remember that the financial resources you seek do not always
   belong to the decision makers. Your executives are there to
   represent the interests of the true owners of the company:
   its shareholders. As such, your executives do not have an
   obligation to provide you with funding. Instead, their obligation is to ensure that the shareholders' money is wisely spent.
   If your strategy does not get executive support, it is up to

you to understand the reason and then work to identify a strategy that is more in line with shareholder interests, as represented by your executives. Remember, your shareholders' money isn't owed to you; it is up to you to earn the right to invest it, and it is up to your executives to retain the right to decide who does. Even if you are a small business manager applying for a loan, that money does not belong to the loan officer. That person is a representative, and it is incumbent upon you to fully understand whatever interests they are representing.

2. Once you have been given the authority to invest your shareholders' money, you need to act as if it is personally yours. The reason your executives act as if they own the company's money is because they have been entrusted with taking personal accountability for how that money is handled, and if they fail in that task, they will not be entrusted with it again. You need to adopt the same line of thinking for your strategy. If you were running a small business (as I currently am), every financial decision you make could put your company out of business. If you spend your money unwisely, you will not be able to pay your employees. That's a fact. There is no bailout plan. The only bailout is to create a better strategy. No matter the size of your company, taking that same level of accountability and ownership over whatever money is entrusted to you will be critical to the success of your strategy.

3. Perhaps most important, your company is investing in both your strategy and *you*—and usually in fairly equal parts. Your executives or investors want to know that *you* believe in your idea before they will ever think of taking a chance on it. To measure this, they will be analyzing your level of personal accountability, observing your passion, and gauging whether or not you've done all of your homework and truly understand your customers, competitors, and company. Then they will be judging your ability to personally lead your strategy, keep the implementation team motivated, drive through any barriers, and remain truly accountable for achieving the results. The shareholders have entrusted their money to the executives, and now the executives are entrusting that

money to you. If you don't show your investors that you're unconditionally ready to take on that challenge, their money will never change hands, mostly because they don't believe that the customers' money will change hands in return.

What all of this equates to is one pure and simple rule: you need to lead your strategy. You are the general; if you are truly willing to take on that role and all of the responsibilities and accountabilities that go along with it, then your strategy will be green-lighted. Only then will you be ready to perform.

PERFORMING

Chances are, you as the strategy owner will also be the one leading the strategic implementation team. More than likely, most of that team will not work directly for you. Such is the dilemma of anyone who owns a strategic plan. This includes business managers, general managers, and even CEOs.

There is a common misconception that just because a person sits at the top of an organization, she or he will have no trouble getting things done. This couldn't be farther from the truth. In fact, it might arguably be *more* difficult to prompt people into action from that position because employees may automatically assume they are being *told* what to do, which is in fact exactly the opposite of what people generally want. And it is exactly the opposite of what organizational leaders should want to do.

Telling employees what to do rarely results in anything positive. Think about your own experiences in this regard. Have you ever been directed to do something that you didn't fully understand or embrace? Chances are, you did it reluctantly and only to the absolute bare-minimum requirement, or you found a way not to do it at all. Neither of these reactions will help a company grow. Instead, a true leader needs to *inspire* people into action, and this can be done regardless of structural hierarchies. The idea is to have people work not for a person, but for a shared vision. This is the type of environment that great leaders will strive to create.

Your strategic team will want this same type of inspiration from you. In addition to being inspired, they'll also want to know what role they play in the bigger picture, they'll want to be informed along the way, and they'll want to be held truly accountable for their actions. This will require four things from you as the owner of the strategy:

- ☐ Inspiration
- ☐ Role clarity
- ☐ Communication
- ☐ Empowerment

If you can master these four things, you'll be able to lead your team into action. So let's explore each one in a bit more detail.

First: inspiration. I've dedicated an entire chapter just to that subject. If your strategy is inspired, then you will be able to translate that inspiration to your team as well.

Inspiration—Check

- ☑ Inspiration
- ☐ Role clarity
- ☐ Communication
- ☐ Empowerment

Next: role clarity. This is why you spent so much time orchestrating your strategic score. Again, I've dedicated an entire chapter just to preparing you for this requirement. If you've completed this step, you will be able to bring clarity to your implementation team.

Role clarity—Check

- ☑ Inspiration
- ☑ Role clarity
- ☐ Communication
- ☐ Empowerment

Next: communication. This will involve sharing the final strategic presentation with the implementation team, as well as updating this team with the results of your strategy as it is being carried out. Remember that your plan will be constantly moving, constantly evolving, and constantly changing. This will require a high frequency of communication from you, the strategic owner, as the plan evolves.

To help with this, you might wish to select representatives from your strategic team who can act as conduits between you and each of their respective functions. These individuals do not necessarily have to be the organizational leaders of their functions; instead, they can simply serve as the functional go-to leaders for the purposes of implementing your strategy.

Almost every orchestra utilizes principal players or *principals* to help drive the performance of each individual section of instrumentalists. Some orchestras feature as many as 100 individual musicians. With these numbers, the conductor can only effectively lead those individuals with the help of these principals who, among other tasks, assist the conductor in communicating between and among the respective instrumental groups. An orchestra really is not unlike a company, which is why I like this particular analogy so much.

Your strategic principals can help you manage an evolving strategy. After you identify who your principals are, you need to meet with them regularly, solicit their feedback, give them responsibility over creating and leading actions that will evolve from your strategy, and utilize their leadership skills to communicate any changes in your plan back to the teams who will be tasked with implementing those changes. Orchestras perform together week after week. But they never stop meeting and rehearsing between performances to ensure that their programs continue to evolve. Your strategy is just as dynamic. Never stop evolving it, and never stop letting people know that you did.

Communication—Check

☑ Inspiration

☑ Role clarity

☑ Communication

☐ Empowerment

The last item is going to take a little more examination, which I believe can best be accomplished through a story.

After moving into a new home, I needed to buy window treatments. So I measured my windows, went down to a local home improvement store, picked out the blinds that I wanted to purchase, and went to place the order. I wanted a turnkey solution and was told, by a very polite store associate, that this was certainly an option but that such an arrangement would require that *they* come out to measure my windows before placing the order.

"How long will that take?" I inquired. "A couple of weeks at most" was the reply. So I signed up and waited for the call, even though I already had my measurements in hand.

Weeks went by. No call. So I called the store back to see what was going on. That's when someone told me that the store had been having some problems with the installation company. When I signed up for this, the store and the installer appeared to be one and the same. But now that there was a problem, the installer was apparently a completely separate entity. Still, with fast follow-up assured, I gave all parties involved the benefit of the doubt and decided to continue on.

More weeks went by, with more installation problems and more phone calls to and from any number of different people at the store who really couldn't help me. The installation company simply was not doing the job I needed it to do, and all of the different associates, supervisors, and managers that I was dealing with at the store apparently couldn't do a thing about it. The reason, I was told, was because the choosing of installers was handled at a different level in the company. So the decisions that directly affected my buying experience were too far removed from the people who were supposed to be tasked with solving my problems.

Needless to say, with each call or visit back to the store, I was growing more frustrated, and, although I'm ashamed to admit it, I thought that screaming at someone might just make me feel better. But picking on any of the people with whom I was dealing would constitute nothing short of bullying on my part, because there was really nothing that any of these individuals could do to help me with my issues. They all worked for a company that apparently said all of the right things in its strategy—providing a great customer experience, providing excellent service, and so on. But none of these employees had actually been *empowered* to fully carry out that strategy. And so the strategy could not possibly be implemented—at least not in this particular situation.

On the way home from one of my more frustrating visits, I stopped by a local Chinese restaurant for a meal with my family. My son ordered the Chicken Lo Mein, and part way through the meal he said that it tasted a little funny. Unfortunately, when you live in an environment where service providers aren't empowered to solve your problems, you eventually become conditioned to stop complaining altogether. Fresh off our window treatment fiasco, both my wife and my son had this exact initial reaction to the Chicken Lo Mein: "Just forget about it," they both said. But I had a lot of scores to settle that day, and I wasn't about to let this one pass. So I called the waiter over and politely told him what was going on. The plate was half eaten, mind you (my son has a healthy appetite, even for "funky" chicken, it seems). No matter. Without a question, without so much as a sniff of the plate, the waiter whisked the dish away and asked if he could get my son something else. Then within two minutes the manager came over and took the entire item off our bill.

This waiter was empowered to take the food back without any questions asked, and the manager backed it up without a thought. Smaller companies may have an easier time doing this because the chief decision maker is always close at hand. But what happens when that Chinese restaurant becomes a chain and the decision maker for that chain isn't always immediately accessible? The key will be for that decision maker to inspire his or her employees around the overall strategy of the company, ensure that everyone knows what part they can and should play in implementing the strategy, clearly communicate the strategy so that the employees can effectively carry it out, and empower each employee to take actions that will align with the overall strategic intent.

Check, Check, Check, and Check
- ☑ Inspiration
- ☑ Role clarity
- ☑ Communication
- ☑ Empowerment

This is how to successfully perform: four simple items that must be lived, not just spoken. If you do that, your team will perform, not for you, but for a strategy that they all truly believe in and *want* to carry out. This is the only way you will be able to achieve your strategic results.

One final thing about performing: there will always be a need for someone, at some point in time, to make the final call. Returning to our music analogy, one of the key roles of a record producer is to keep the band members from wanting to hurt one another as the album is being recorded! Creative people have creative differences, many of which are based on ego, personal preference, or one's own experiences.

It is the producer's job to reconcile all of these opinions and make the final creative call as to which direction to take. If you want to do this effectively, it will be important to clearly know your vision, stay firmly connected with your customers' needs, keep the big picture of your strategy constantly at the top of your mind, listen to feedback with an open mind, process all of that information almost instantaneously, and know when to step in to make the final call. In essence, the strategic producer will always have the final creative say. So when you are in the producer's role don't be afraid to step in when that final say is needed. Your investors expect it, your team will expect it, and your strategy is sure to require that level of involvement at one point or another.

Now your performance is under way. Everyone is excited, everyone is engaged, and before long, your performance will take on a life of its own—so much so, in fact, that you might even begin to lose sight of why you were performing in the first place. If this sounds inconceivable, just think about how many things your company currently does because that's "just the way you do them." Long-term plans tend to suffer from long-term amnesia, which is why you must stay constantly focused on why you developed your plan in the first place. And you do this by constantly, consistently, and diligently measuring your results against your original, sometimes evolving objectives.

MEASURING RESULTS

One of the key roles you will have as a strategic producer is to measure the success of your plan as it is being implemented. Assuming that you are following your own strategic score and are working with your principals, each of whom will help to lead her or his respective section of the orchestra, it will now be your job to conduct this orchestra by both keeping everyone focused on the score and driving the score with both leadership and feedback.

The role of strategic conductor, then, is the next hat you will need to wear in the strategic implementation process.

Conductors lead their teams by standing front and center, where all members of the orchestra can see them, and using their batons as a beacon upon which all members of the orchestra can keep their eyes focused. This provides necessary direction and helps join everyone together around the pursuit of a common goal. In business, your baton will be the *profit and loss statement (P&L).*

In my experience, the P&L (also called the *income statement*) is the financial tool that all business managers feel they *should* know; consequently, far too few ever admit if they don't know it, which is why I want to review it within the context of our process. At its core, the P&L is an extremely simple tool. To understand what it's all about, picture yourself running a small business, selling something like pencils. You know that you have to buy the pencils for a certain cost. And you want to sell the pencils for a price that will allow you to make some type of profit. Easy enough. So:

$$\text{Price} - \text{Cost} = \text{Profit}$$

If you multiply your unit price by the number of units you sell, you get the total dollars that you will be taking in as a result of selling your pencils. This becomes your *revenue*. If you do the same thing with your costs, you call this your *cost of goods sold (COGS)*. The difference between these two things is usually referred to as your *gross profit*. So now you have:

$$\text{Revenue} - \text{COGS} = \text{Gross Profit}$$

Your gross profit can be expressed either in terms of absolute dollars or as a percentage of your revenue, in which case it is usually referred to as a *gross margin*. Either way, this number does not yet represent what you will actually put in your pocket because, more than likely, there are still other expenses that need to be incurred in order to run your business. Perhaps you have travel expenses, marketing expenses, costs associated with running a small office, or the cost of other employees that you've hired. All of these expenses must be factored in before you can determine the true profit that your business will make. Typically these expenses are not directly related to the cost of the product you are selling, and therefore they are typically referred to as *operating expenses*.

Subtracting these expenses will now give you what is referred to as your *operating income* or *operating profit*, which can also be expressed either as an absolute dollar amount or as a percentage of your revenues (in which case it would typically be referred to as your *operating margin*). So now our formulas become:

$$\text{Revenue} - \text{COGS} = \text{Gross Profit}$$
$$\text{Gross Profit} - \text{Operating Expenses} = \text{Operating Income}$$

TABLE 8.1

Simplified P&L

Revenue	A
Cost of Goods Sold	B
Gross Profit	A – B = C
Operating Expenses	D
Operating Income	C – D = E

If we put this into tabular form, it looks something like Table 8.1.

Of course, if everything were this simple, nobody would ever have to admit that they don't fully understand the P&L! Unfortunately, most businesses are a lot more complex than our initial example would imply, and so the P&Ls for those businesses tend to be somewhat more complicated as well.

What you need to know is that the P&L will always boil down to these same five basic elements: revenue, cost of goods, gross profit, operating expenses, and operating income. The problem is that the more things you want to track, the more convoluted each of these line items will become. For example, there are many different ways to look at revenue. You can track gross sales, discounts, rebates, returns, or any other number of other revenue-related intricacies that might apply to your particular business. At the end of it all will be the net dollar amount that your company will collect from the sale of its products, often referred to as *net sales* or *net revenues*. But your P&L may show quite a few different revenue-related line items before you get down to that number.

Similarly, your cost of goods can be broken down into any number of different categories. For starters, you can track your variable costs separately from your fixed costs. *Variable costs* are defined as any cost that varies in proportion to the amount you sell, while *fixed costs* generally do not vary in direct proportion with how much you sell. You can also break down your product costs based on how they are being incurred. For example, if you are manufacturing your own product, you might want to track your labor, materials, and any related manufacturing overhead costs all as separate line items—the idea being that you may wish to understand and therefore manage each of these costs separately.

Operating expenses also have many different categories that can be tracked, many of which must be allocated across multiple product lines, making this section of the P&L much more applicable at a business unit level than at a product line level.

There are many other complexities that can be discussed in relation to the P&L, including the different terminologies that can be used to express any one of these five line items, as well as the many other types of margins that can be calculated using any of the numerous subcategories that typically occur between these five lines. Then there is the discussion about which costs should be counted as part of your COGS or which should be counted toward operating expenses. There is also the discussion around interest and taxes, which are accounted for after operating income, resulting in a company's *net income* or *net profit.* And, if we want to get really complicated, we can talk about *earnings before interest and taxes,* or *EBIT* for short (which is typically the same as operating income except that it may include some amount of nonoperating earnings as well), or *earnings before interest, taxes, depreciation, and amortization,* or *EBITDA* for short (which requires that you understand how certain assets have been depreciated or how certain expenses have been amortized within the P&L so that they can be removed and separately analyzed). This latter discussion will also require a firm understanding of how the P&L works together with another commonly used financial tool: the balance sheet, which keeps track of the actual assets and liabilities that a company has at any given time.

Although a deep discussion of these important complexities is outside of the context of this book, it is important that you learn as much as possible about all of the financial tools that are available to help you track the performance of your strategy. To assist you with this task, I have provided several excellent references in the back of this book, and I also encourage you to consult with whatever accounting and financial resources are available to you within your company or business, many of whom should also be a part of your strategic implementation team.

Even with all of these nuances, and the many more that I am not covering here, the P&L is generally a simple tool to both use and understand, as long as you are reading it *vertically* (that is, top to bottom). Used in this way, the P&L will help you gauge the relative short-term health of your business, meaning that a positive net profit in any given period should, at some point in the future, translate into cash for your business.

With that said, this is really only a small part of what a P&L is used for. More often than not, the P&L is used not only as an indicator of the current performance of your business but also as a tool to track that performance against some known baseline. That baseline can be in the form of a previous performance period, or a forecast that was completed for the current period you are measuring. In either scenario, in order to use the P&L in this way, you will need to know how to read the P&L both vertically and *horizontally* as well.

When I talk about reading the P&L horizontally, I am simply referring to adding two extra columns: one for your baseline and one for the variance between the baseline and the actual results. Essentially you need to compare your actual performance to some reference point in order to determine whether or not your objectives are being met. I have worked in businesses in which a 10 percent operating margin was considered to be world-class performance, whereas others would have been escorting people out the door with those numbers. The truth is, you can only gauge your company's performance based on your own expectations. That applies whether you are comparing to your own internal forecast, your business case, your strategic plan, your previous performance, your competitors' performance, or, as is most often the case, a combination of all these reference points. The idea here is that the absolute value of your performance is only relevant when looked at in comparison to the absolute value that you projected or that you previously achieved.

Table 8.2 is an example of what this horizontal P&L might look like using an internal forecast as the baseline comparison. To illustrate how to use this form of the P&L, we'll need to look at a quick example.

TABLE 8.2

Simplified P&L with Baseline Comparison

	Forecast	Actual	Variance
Revenue	A1	A2	A2 – A1
Cost of Goods Sold	B1	B2	B2 – B1
Gross Profit	C1	C2	C2 – C1
Operating Expenses	D1	D2	D2 – D1
Operating Income	E1	E2	E2 – E1

Let's say that your revenues for any given period are below your forecast—that is, $A2 - A1$ is a negative number. Let's also say that your COGS for that same period is above your forecast—that is, $B2 - B1$ is a positive number. So your sales were lower and your costs were higher than anticipated. To understand what may have happened in this case, you need to expand the revenue lines to see how many units were actually sold versus how many you thought you would sell. You can then derive the price to see if your price was higher or lower than you anticipated. Finally, you can derive your cost per unit using the same math. Once you have this information, you will have more clues as to what may have happened. These are just a few of the possible scenarios:

1. You raised your prices based on higher costs, and as a result you sold less.
2. You sold a different mix of products than you anticipated.
3. You sold to a different mix of customers than you anticipated.

By itself, a P&L will not tell you which, if any, of these scenarios actually occurred. What it will give you, however, are indicators that will help you narrow down the most probable causes. This, in turn, will allow you to target the specific metrics that can be used to validate the actual root cause of whatever variance you are seeing, thereby allowing you to take the necessary corrective actions (or build on your key successes).

The good news is that each business will, after some period of time, begin to show repeating patterns; that will allow you, in the role of the strategy owner, to identify the most likely causes of most any variance almost at a glance. This is where the magic of understanding the P&L horizontally will really come into play.

Using this information, you can keep your strategic team aligned by involving them in both the planning and tracking process. Your strategic principals will then feel some level of accountability in helping to forecast the business performance, and they will feel equal levels of accountability for achieving the results that they themselves helped to forecast. In this way, there is no greater tool to help drive teams toward common strategic objectives than the P&L.

I mentioned earlier that the P&L, by itself, rarely tells the entire story of what's happening within a business. It will give you ready clues as to where you need to dig deeper, but you will still require another level of key metrics that can help you to measure your performance against a set of fairly specific strategic objectives.

Enter the *balanced scorecard*.

The concept of the balanced scorecard was first brought to light in two *Harvard Business Review* articles written between 1992 and 1993 by Robert S. Kaplan and his associate David P. Norton. This was followed by a book by the same authors, written in 1996, entitled *The Balanced Scorecard: Translating Strategy into Action*—which is an appropriate reference for this stage of our process.

In its simplest form, the balanced scorecard encourages companies to measure their business performance using metrics that align with their strategies. That sounds simple enough. The twist, however, is that these metrics do not all have to be financially based. In fact, the basic design calls for measurements in each of four main categories as follows:

- Financial
- Customer
- Internal business process
- Learning and growth[1]

The idea is to take your strategic vision and resulting strategic objectives and tie these objectives to a manageable number of measurements that can be used to solidify your plan, track the effectiveness of your strategy, communicate the results back to your team, and drive your teams into action based on whatever results you are getting. The possibilities for measurements within each of these categories are nearly endless, and there are other categories that can and have been conceived since. The point is to have some set of tools and metrics that you can use to both further understand the underlying performance trends of your business and track the effectiveness of your strategy over the long term,

It is worth noting that this balanced scorecard concept, along with almost all of the previously established tools, processes, and frameworks that I have referenced throughout this book, continue to be evolved, refocused, and reapplied according to what works, what doesn't, and what each individual company needs. This, in my opinion, is just as it should be. One concept builds from another. One thought serves as the foundation for the next. This is as it is in business, just as it is in music, just as it is in life.

I believe this is quite possibly the most important lesson that you can take away from the entire strategic process that I have presented to you. Rather than try to follow every step exactly the way that I have written it, you can use my thoughts to inspire your own, just as I have used the thoughts of many others before me to inspire mine. The strategic process is a creative one, and creative processes will always continue to evolve.

Once your strategy goes into production, you will continue upon a nearly endless cycle of preparing, planning, producing, and measuring, using the past, present, and future to forge a path that can only be built upon Analysis, Recollection, Intuition, and Artistry. The steps will get you to this stage; your proficiencies will keep the cycle going, growing, and alive.

Figure 8.1 captures the strategic life cycle that you will continue to draw from and build upon throughout the production stage.

As your strategy is being implemented, it is important that you continue to measure your results against your plan and that you continue to reenvision your plan based on what you achieve and

FIGURE 8.1

The Strategic Life Cycle

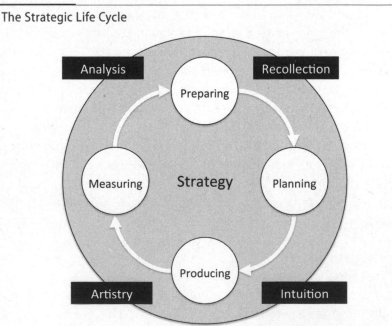

what you learn. This will lead to other strategies that address evolving business needs before they become urgent and evolving market needs before they are addressed by someone else. The best musical artists in the world are constantly reinventing themselves in response to their audience's likes, preferences, and needs. Their strategies are always evolving, and their fame and fortune are continuously sustainable as a result. Compare that to the countless number of one-hit wonders, who put out one good song before fading into obscurity. Those careers are usually short-lived, which is the same fate your business will suffer if you do not look after your strategic life cycle.

ENDGAME

At this point in our analogy, we've taken a feeling, translated it into a melody, arranged the melody into a song, orchestrated the song to achieve maximum impact, and then produced that song into something that is recorded, performed, and rewarded. So here's my measurement of whether or not a song has met its objectives:

When music reaches me the way the composer or songwriter intended it to, I get chills. That's the ultimate measurement for me. Once that happens, I want to keep feeling that way over and over again. I'll listen to the song many times; I'll buy an overpriced ticket to go see the song performed live; and I'll even shell out $60 for a concert T-shirt that probably cost no more than a few dollars to produce. Chills are a powerful reaction; they indicate that something has touched me beyond my rational mind. If one of my songs has accomplished that for someone else, there can be no better measurement of success.

When your strategy hits the mark, it will inspire those same chills. And those chills will translate into financial results, customer results, process results, and even learning results. Because when you hit the mark, everything else follows.

That's what I want you, your teams, and your customers to feel. Yes, your strategy should cause physical chills because it was *that* good. That's what will separate a strategic plan from a strategic composition, and that's what will separate the science from the art.

And when it all comes together, you'll know you've experienced the true art of creative strategy generation.

Finding Your Creativity

You've written the songs, you've decided who will play what parts, and you've laid out how those parts should be played. Is there really any room for creativity during the production stage? Absolutely! Here are some tips to help you find yours:

- When musicians enter the studio to record a new track, the same song played 50 different times can literally sound 50 different ways, even though all the same notes are being played. The difference between the good and bad takes is in how connected the musicians felt to what they were playing, and how connected they felt to one another while they were playing it. It is the producer's job to pick up on those connections and, if possible, inspire them to happen. As the strategic producer, you can do this by drawing upon your Artistry, where passion and expression join together to help you create something that's unique, exciting, and impactful.

- There is a creative energy that happens when people get together to brainstorm ideas and seek out positive solutions to challenging situations. If the results of your strategy are not meeting expectations, brainstorming will go much farther toward solving the problem than finger pointing. Every finger of blame that you point represents a missed collaborative connection and, with it, a missed potential creative solution. Instead of reaching out your finger to point at people, reach it out to connect with them.

- The band KISS wrote some great songs. But where they really differentiated themselves was in their performance. KISS concerts were unlike anything anyone had ever seen. Why? Because the band members expressed themselves in a way that nobody had done before them. Through that expression, they were able to connect with their audiences and give people something they needed and couldn't get from anywhere else. This helped make KISS one of the most successful rock bands in history. The point is: you don't have to execute your strategy like everyone else. Companies won't always do business the way they're doing it today. Someone will come along and redefine it—and that someone could very well be you.

CHAPTER 9

CODA

Now that we have stepped through the Creative Strategy Generation process using music composition as the analogy, I think it is important to reinforce a few key points. The idea behind composing great strategies is to utilize a creative process rather than an academic or imitative one. In Part 1 of this book, I introduced you to the four proficiencies (Analysis, Recollection, Intuition, and Artistry) that you must build in order to generate creative strategies. In Part 2, I showed you how to use those proficiencies to compose strategies using a creative process similar to that of writing music. And although music happens to be my passion, and one that many people can relate to, it is by no means the only creative process that can be metaphorically explored.

The mnemonic ARIA that I used to capture the four strategic proficiencies actually has a very interesting subtext that applies to nearly any creative endeavor. In music, the term *aria* is typically defined as a "solo song with instrumental accompaniment."[1] Now that we have stepped through the entire process, it is easy to see how this term so perfectly encapsulates the role that your proficiencies should play. Analysis, Recollection, Intuition, and Artistry are solo skills that you need to possess in order to compose and lead a creative strategic plan. As you apply your process, however, accompaniment will also be required in order to bring those skills to life. In this way, your creative process will involve bringing more and more resources together around your proficiencies to help you produce a unique and special output. This can involve bringing in outside insights, tools, training, people, or any other type of collaborative resources that can help you grow your ideas into full-fledged works of art. A solo with accompaniment: I can't think of a better way to describe the entire strategic process.

The idea, then, isn't to write your strategies exactly the way I write songs. That's just one way to look at it. Part 2 of this book is simply a metaphor for applying your own collaborative creative process to the solo proficiencies that you developed and explored in Part 1. No matter the creative analogy, the seven steps will always be the same:

1. **Preparation.** Your training, skills, research, and observation
2. **Inspiration.** What you hope to achieve and what is driving you
3. **Genre.** Your target audience
4. **Ideation.** The core of what you want to express
5. **Arrangement.** Building a story to help you express your ideas
6. **Orchestration.** Bringing together resources to help you tell your story
7. **Production.** Producing a final work of art

Whether you are a composer, an artist, a screenwriter, a theatrical producer, or a business strategist, these are the same seven steps that will be required to produce your creative work of art. And make no mistake about it: the very best business strategies are indeed creative works of art.

Feel free to find your own metaphor based on whatever creative endeavor you happen to be passionate about. Then use that metaphor to help you generate your own creative strategy by applying the same steps. Whatever analogy you choose, you need to find your passion not only in the end result but also in the entire process from concept to delivery. When you do that, you'll be composing timeless strategies that other people will be writing about for years to come. That's when you'll have found the key to creative strategy generation.

PART 3

TOOLS

INTRODUCTION

In this final section, I will provide you with additional tools and resources that will help support and supplement the creative strategic process that I've laid out throughout this book. These tools will be presented in three parts:

1. **Quick Reference Guide.** This is a quick summary of each of the seven steps of the process, with an overview of the key tools that have been provided to support each step.

2. **Strategic Presentation Guideline.** Here I provide a guideline for preparing the strategic presentation that was discussed during the Arrangement step. This is a 12-"slide" outline that you can use to help prepare your own presentation following the strategic storytelling arc.

3. **Tidbits of Wisdom.** These are specific quotes from each chapter that should serve as a quick reminder of some of the key messages from the book.

I also encourage you to visit the website **http://composingstrategy .com** for more tools, templates, and examples, as well as information on how to contact me if you want to learn, share, or discover more about this wonderful art of creative strategy generation!

Thank you for reading, and enjoy your strategic journey!

APPENDIX A

QUICK REFERENCE GUIDE

What follows is a summary of the Creative Strategy Generation process that is outlined in this book. This can be used as a quick reference guide for how to build your strategy from preparation through production, following the model shown in Figure A.1.

FIGURE A.1

Creative Strategy Generation Model

ANALYSIS	RECOLLECTION	INTUITION	ARTISTRY
Present	Past	Future	Path
Company/Capabilities	Influences	Vision	Strategy
Competitors	History	Goals	Story
Customers	Performance	Objectives	Resources
Industry	Experience	Target Market	Execution

← INPUTS →		← OUTPUTS →	
PREPARATION	PREPARATION	INSPIRATION	IDEATION
		GENRE	ARRANGEMENT
			ORCHESTRATION
			PRODUCTION
I	II	III	IV

PREPARATION

Step 1: Completing Your Baseline Analysis

Complete your baseline analysis (see Figure A.2) with an eye toward the past, present, and future. Capture as much information as you can around the internal factors (company/capabilities) and the external factors (competitors, customer, industry) that will affect your overall plan. Also be sure to capture the motivation for your strategy, which you will later translate into your vision, goals, and objectives.

FIGURE A.2

Baseline Analysis

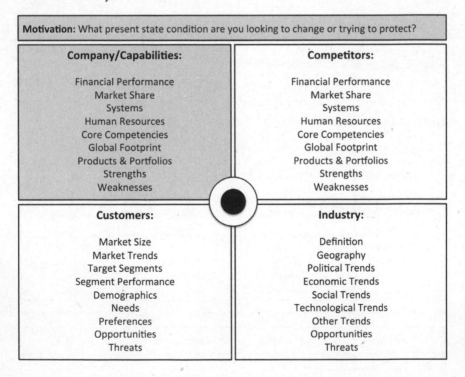

INSPIRATION

Step 2a: Performing Your SWOT Analysis

Using the information from your baseline analysis, complete a SWOT analysis (see Figure A.3), being sure to end with the opportunities, which are what your strategies will ultimately be designed to address. You should think of your SWOT analysis in terms of both internal and external factors, so that it will correlate closely with your baseline analysis. Additionally, you should focus your strengths and weaknesses analysis on the present day, while looking toward the future for opportunities and threats. This will ensure a smoother bridge from your baseline analysis to your strategic plan.

FIGURE A.3

SWOT Analysis

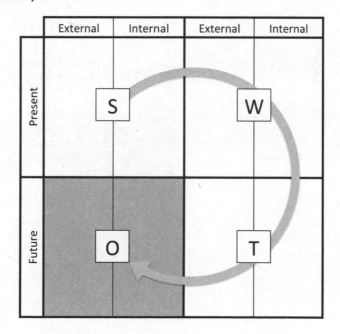

Step 2b: Developing Your Vision, Goals, and Objectives

Starting with the motivation for your strategy that you identified through your baseline analysis, and using the insights that you gained through your SWOT analysis, establish the vision, goals, and objectives for your strategy (see Figure A.4). Be sure to create an inspired vision that is focused on both the needs of your company as well as the needs of your customers. You will use your vision, goals, and objectives to filter the opportunities from your SWOT analysis and decide on which ones you ultimately want to pursue in your strategy.

FIGURE A.4

Vision-Goals-Objectives Pyramid

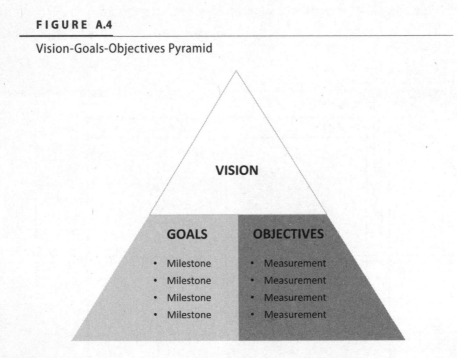

GENRE

Step 3: Understanding Your Target Market

Using your filtered market opportunities, carefully choose and understand the markets you will pursue in your strategy, and capture the needs of those markets by creating a Team Card for each (see Figure A.5). This will help to keep you focused on the needs of your customers as you begin to develop your strategy. Be sure to run any new insights you uncover during this step back through your SWOT analysis, reframing your vision, goals, and objectives if necessary.

FIGURE A.5

Team Card

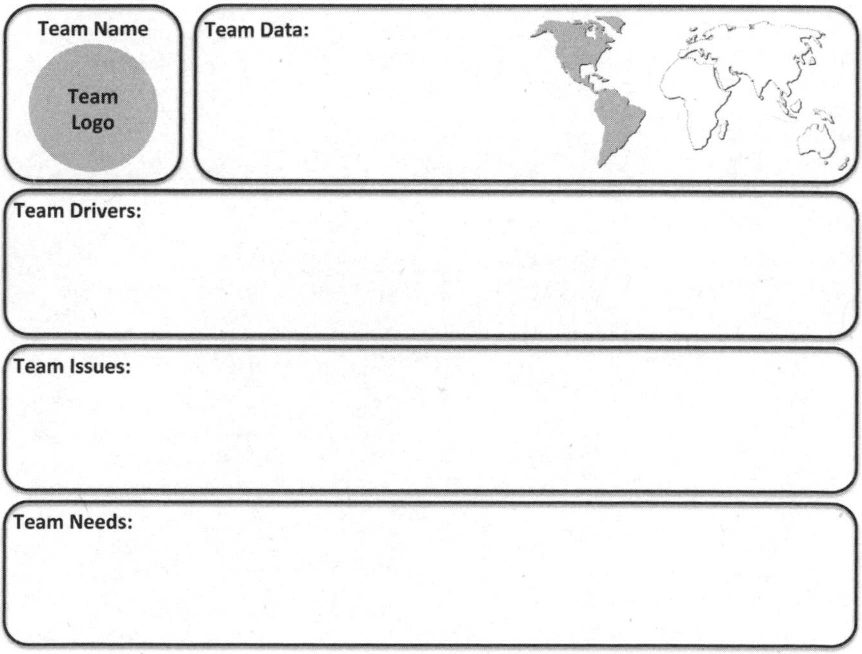

IDEATION

Step 4a: Composing Your Strategic Melodies

Using your filtered market and product opportunities as a guide, develop your high-level strategic melodies by focusing through three strategic perspectives: customer, company, and competitor (see Figure A.6). This will provide a methodology to bridge from the *what* of your vision, goals, and objectives, to the *how* of your strategies. More specifically, your strategic melodies will address how you intend to pursue the market and product opportunities that you have chosen.

FIGURE A.6

Strategic Perspectives

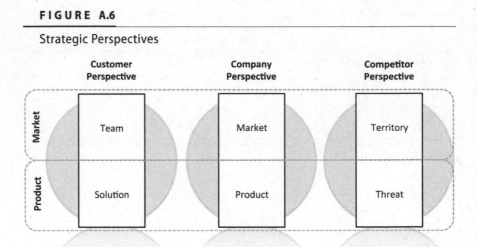

Step 4b: Creating Your Go-to-Market Plan

Once you have composed your overarching strategies, you can develop your Go-to-Market Plan, providing high-level strategic guidance for each of the four marketing mix elements of product, price, promotion, and place (see Figure A.7). This plan will serve to guide your strategic actions during the implementation stage of your strategy.

FIGURE A.7

Composing Your Strategies and Go-to-Market Plan

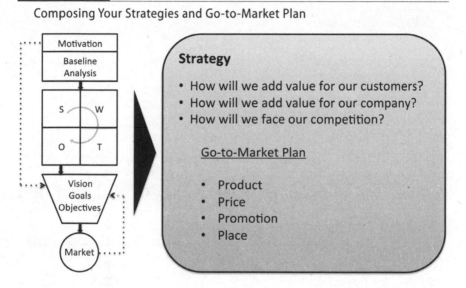

ARRANGEMENT

Step 5: Developing Your Strategic Story

Next, you will want to put your strategy in a form that can be easily communicated and understood. You will do this by completing your story, assembling all of your story elements, and enhancing your story with the right level of tone, energy, and harmony to successfully drive the implementation (see Figure A.8).

FIGURE A.8

Strategic Arrangement

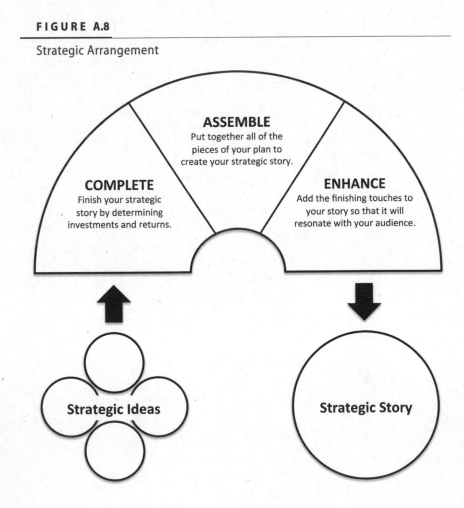

ORCHESTRATION

Step 6a: Laying Out Your Orchestra

In order to get your strategy ready for implementation, it will be important to identify and guide the resources that will be needed to carry out your plan. You will do this by assigning each implementation function to one of four roles—leader, driver, supporter, or accentuator—and then mapping these functions visually so that their relative roles can be easily identified (see Figure A.9).

FIGURE A.9

Strategic Orchestra Map

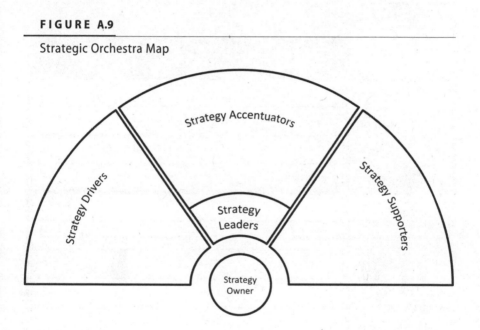

Step 6b: Creating Your Strategic Score

Once you have identified functional roles and responsibilities, you will then be tasking those teams with helping to develop and carry out actions that align with your Go-to-Market Plan. The key actions can be captured on a strategic score (see Figure A.10), which will continually help to guide your strategy throughout the implementation stage.

FIGURE A.10

The Strategic Score

		YEAR 1	YEAR 2	YEAR 3
Product	Product			
	Engineering		Actions	
	Operations			
	Service			
Price	Product			
	Marketing		Actions	
	Sales			
	Support			
Promotion	Product			
	Marketing		Actions	
	Sales			
	Support			
Place	Product			
	Marketing		Actions	
	Sales			
	Support			

PRODUCTION

Step 7: Implementing Your Strategy and Measuring Results

Your strategic implementation will have a life cycle, much like the life cycle of your product itself. As such, it will be necessary to treat your strategy as an ever-evolving entity that will be dynamically modified as the implementation progresses. This life cycle will consist of the four high-level activities of preparing, planning, producing, and measuring, dynamically supported by your four proficiencies of Analysis, Recollection, Intuition, and Artistry (see Figure A.11). And so, the process comes full circle, both literally and figuratively.

FIGURE A.11

The Strategic Life Cycle

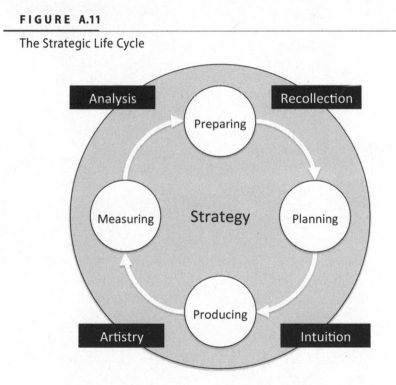

B

THE STRATEGIC PRESENTATION

Your strategic presentation can take any form you like, as long as it follows the strategic arc that we discussed in Chapter 6 and as shown in Figure B.1.

FIGURE B.1

The Strategic Arc

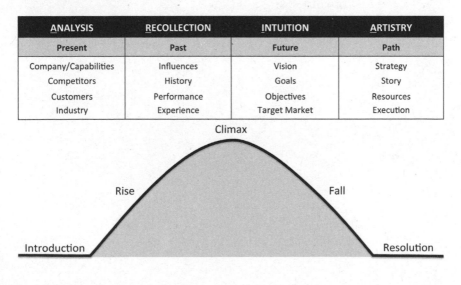

ANALYSIS	RECOLLECTION	INTUITION	ARTISTRY
Present	Past	Future	Path
Company/Capabilities	Influences	Vision	Strategy
Competitors	History	Goals	Story
Customers	Performance	Objectives	Resources
Industry	Experience	Target Market	Execution

Climax

Rise   Fall

Introduction   Resolution

The following guide gives a general idea of how your strategic presentation should flow. Although I am presenting this guide in the form of specific "slides," I encourage you to use these as an outline rather than a template. For example, you may want to expand upon some of the slides that I am suggesting, or you may choose to eliminate some slides altogether. You might also consider telling your story using a completely different medium and forgoing the use of any slides at all. Similarly, you should experiment with the order and flow of your presentation so your story is told in a way that reflects your particular situation.

Against that backdrop, here are three tips that I encourage you to follow no matter which type of presentation you choose:

1. Make your presentation highly visual, striking just the right balance between images and words. Your slides, if you choose to use them at all, should serve to illustrate your story, not tell it word for word.

2. Present your information at an uncomfortably high level. In reality, you will need to show a relatively small amount of data to support your strategic story.

3. Do not begin your story with the ending. There is no place for an executive summary in your strategic presentation. Save your required investments and projected financial results for the end of your story.

What follows are the guidelines for your strategic presentation.

Product/Portfolio Snapshot

- Introduce Your Product/Portfolio

HINTS
- Don't assume that your audience knows your products.
- Show your audience not only what your products are, but also how they are used.
- Use visuals to illustrate key points.
- Introduce your positioning and value proposition.
- Don't spend too much time explaining every detail of your product!

Current Financial Picture

- Past and Present Financial Performance
  - Revenue
  - Profitability
  - Market Share

HINTS
- Talk about how your performance compares to overall company expectations.
- Indicate performance by region (if applicable).
- Be sure to define the market that your share applies to.
- You should be able to explain any significant trends.
- Show only the information that will be relevant to your story—don't overdo it!

Customers

- Target Market Segment(s)
- Market Forecast(s)
- User Profiles
- Customer Needs
- Market Opportunities
- Market Threats

HINTS
- Summarize customer needs at a high level and in terms that people can relate to.
- Include applicable geographic, demographic, and market size data.
- If you use user stories or personas in your presentation, be sure to show how these individual viewpoints represent entire segments.
- Be sure to cite any data sources you may have used to determine market forecasts.

Industry

- Industry Trends
  - Political
  - Economic
  - Social
  - Technological
- Industry Opportunities
- Industry Threats

HINTS
- Utilize your PEST analysis.
- Remember to talk to both where the industry is now and where you think it is going in the future.
- Talk about how industry trends might affect customer needs.
- Introduce industry opportunities and threats at a high level.

Competition

- Competitive Landscape
- Competitor Market Shares
- Competitor Strengths
- Competitor Weaknesses

HINTS
- Remember to address both where the competition is now and where you think it is going in the future.
- Provide a snapshot of competitor market share trends.
- Talk about how current competitive trends might affect customer needs.
- Think about how competitive strengths and weaknesses compare to your own.

Company Analysis

- Company Strengths
- Company Weaknesses
- Product Strengths
- Product Weaknesses
- Comparison to Competitive Strengths and Weaknesses

HINTS
- Analyze your systems, processes, human resources, and organizational capabilities.
- Share any relevant company/product history that may be applicable to your story.
- Try to view your company through the eyes of your customers.
- Remember to compare your strengths and weaknesses to your competitors.
- BE HONEST in your assessment.

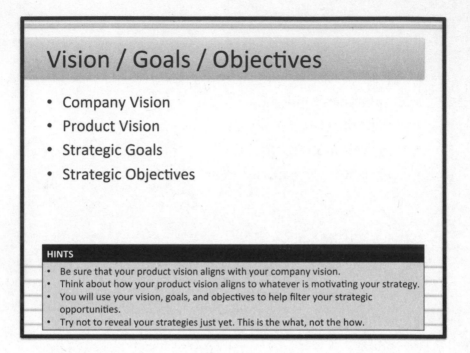

Vision / Goals / Objectives

- Company Vision
- Product Vision
- Strategic Goals
- Strategic Objectives

HINTS
- Be sure that your product vision aligns with your company vision.
- Think about how your product vision aligns to whatever is motivating your strategy.
- You will use your vision, goals, and objectives to help filter your strategic opportunities.
- Try not to reveal your strategies just yet. This is the what, not the how.

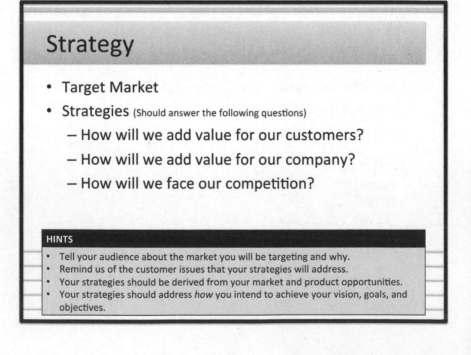

Strategy

- Target Market
- Strategies (Should answer the following questions)
    - How will we add value for our customers?
    - How will we add value for our company?
    - How will we face our competition?

HINTS
- Tell your audience about the market you will be targeting and why.
- Remind us of the customer issues that your strategies will address.
- Your strategies should be derived from your market and product opportunities.
- Your strategies should address *how* you intend to achieve your vision, goals, and objectives.

Go-to-Market Plan

- Product Strategy
- Price Strategy
- Promotion Strategy
- Place Strategy

HINTS
- Do not to get too detailed here; providing an overall direction for each P should suffice.
- Try to anticipate the reactions of competitors and customers to each of your market actions.
- Feel free to use a different marketing mix model if it better suits your plan.

Investment & Resources

- Required Resources
  - Human Resources
  - Equipment & Systems
  - Promotional Expenses
- Required Investments
  - Capital Expenditures
  - Ongoing Expenses

HINTS
- Challenge yourself to think about if your company is truly equipped to execute the strategy and, if not, what additional investments will be required.
- This is a high-level estimate; don't be afraid to make assumptions and state what those assumptions are.
- This is not a business case. Do not get too detailed in this presentation.

Results

- Long-Term Financial Results
  - Revenue
  - Profitability
  - Ongoing Expenses / Depreciation
- Long-Term Market Share Results
- Customer Benefit

HINTS
- Think in terms of a three- to five-year horizon.
- Be sure to tie your results back to your strategic objectives.
- Remember to break your revenue growth into price, share, and market components.
- State any assumptions on pricing or costs that will affect your margins over time.

Summary

- Restate the Strategy
- Restate the Expected Results
  - Customer Benefit
  - Company Benefit
  - Competitor Reaction
- Ask for the Order!

HINTS
- Summarize at the end of your presentation, NOT at the beginning.
- Restate your story in just a few sentences, preferably with a visual that will leave a lasting impression on your audience.
- Your audience should leave feeling EXCITED about your strategic plan!
- If there is something you need, don't forget to ask for it!

APPENDIX C

TIDBITS OF WISDOM

Introduction

"I cannot teach you how to be creative. What I can do is teach you how to tap into the creativity that you are innately born with but perhaps didn't know you had."

Chapter 1: ARIA

"The key to being an artist is that you have to care enough about something to want to express it, and then you have to translate what you care about in a way that people want to experience it."

Chapter 2: Preparation

"A truly great leader will tell his or her troops not only *what* they are fighting for but also *why* they are fighting."

Chapter 3: Inspiration

"You can only change the world if you are willing to change your own world with it."

Chapter 4: Genre

"Few companies want to view themselves as putting their own needs above the needs of their customers, even though this in reality may be exactly the situation they are in."

Chapter 5: Ideation

"Your strategy should provide the context for your actions."

Chapter 6: Arrangement

"Your deep knowledge of any topic can most effectively be demonstrated through your ability to break down that knowledge in a way that everyone can easily understand and absorb."

Chapter 7: Orchestration

"Collaboration isn't always easy, but it is almost always more rewarding than doing something by yourself—as long as you seek to truly understand the people you're collaborating with."

Chapter 8: Production

"One concept builds from another. One thought serves as the foundation for the next. This is as it is in business, just as it is in music, just as it is in life."

Chapter 9: Coda

"The very best business strategies are indeed creative works of art."

NOTES

Chapter 1

1. Marilyn Berger, "Irving Berlin, Nation's Songwriter, Dies," *New York Times*, September 23, 1989, http://www.nytimes.com/1989/09/23/obituaries/irving-berlin-nation-s-songwriter-dies.html.
2. *Guinness World Records 2015* (Guinness World Records Limited, 2014), Kindle Edition, 166.
3. Lore Thaler, Stephen R. Arnott, and Melvyn A. Goodale, "Neural Correlates of Natural Human Echolocation in Early and Late Blind Echolocation Experts," *PLoS ONE*, 2011, 6(5):e20162. doi:10.1371/journal.pone.0020162.
4. "U.S. Workers More Satisfied? Just Barely," The Conference Board Press Release, June 18, 2014, http://www.conference-board.org/press/pressdetail.cfm?pressid=5214.

Chapter 2

1. "Strategy," *Online Etymology Dictionary*, http://www.etymonline.com/index.php?term=strategy, accessed January 14, 2015.
2. *The Complete Works of Pausanias*, trans. W. H. S. Jones (Delphi Classics, 2014), Kindle Edition, 10.24.1.
3. Wayne Coffey, *The Boys of Winter: The Untold Story of a Coach, a Dream, and the 1980 U.S. Olympic Hockey Team* (New York: Broadway Books, 2005), Kindle Edition.
4. Julianne Glatz, "Canning Food, from Napoleon to Now," *Illinois Times*, June 3, 2010, http://illinoistimes.com/article-7361-canning-food,-from-napoleon-to-now.html.
5. Francis J. Aguilar, *Scanning the Business Environment* (New York: Macmillan, 1967).
6. A. H. Maslow, "A Theory of Human Motivation," *Psychological Review*, Vol. 50, No. 4, July 1943.
7. Michael E. Porter, *Competitive Strategy* (New York: Free Press, 1980).
8. H. Igor Ansoff, "Strategies for Diversification," *Harvard Business Review*, Vol. 35, Issue 5, Sep–Oct 1957, pp. 113–124.
9. Kenichi Ohmae, *The Mind of the Strategist* (New York: McGraw-Hill, 1982).
10. W. Chan Kim and Renée Mauborgne, *Blue Ocean Strategy* (Boston: Harvard Business School Press, 2005).

Chapter 3

1. "Inspiration," Online Etymology Dictionary, http://www.etymonline.com/index.php?term=inspiration, accessed January 15, 2015.
2. Albert S. Humphrey, "SWOT Analysis for Management Consulting," *SRI Alumni Association Newsletter*, December 2005.
3. Ibid.
4. Heinz Weihrich, "The TOWS Matrix: A Tool for Situational Analysis," *Long Range Planning*, January 1982, 15(2): 54–66, doi: 10.1016/0024-6301(82)90120-0.
5. G. T. Doran, "There's a S.M.A.R.T. Way to Write Management's Goals and Objectives," *Management Review*, November 1981, Vol. 70, No. 11, 35–36.

Chapter 4

1. "Every Noise at Once," Everynoise.com, http://everynoise.com/engenre map.html, accessed January 15, 2015.
2. Philip Kotler, and Gary Armstrong, *Principles of Marketing*, 15th ed. (Boston: Pearson, 2014), Kindle Edition, 193–199.
3. Alan Cooper, *The Inmates Are Running the Asylum* (Indianapolis: SAMS, 2004), Kindle Edition.
4. Roy F. Baumeister and Mark R. Leary, "The Need to Belong: Desire for Interpersonal Attachments as a Fundamental Human Motivation," *Psychological Bulletin*, 1995, Vol. 117, No. 3, 497–529.
5. Deloitte Center for Health Solutions, *The U.S. Health Care Market: A Strategic View of Consumer Segmentation* (Deloitte Development LLC, 2012).
6. Theodore Levitt, *The Marketing Imagination* (New York: The Free Press, 1986).

Chapter 5

1. Kenichi Ohmae, *The Mind of the Strategist* (New York: McGraw-Hill, 1982).
2. Arthur A. Thompson Jr., A. J. Strickland III, and John E. Gamble, *Crafting and Executing Strategy: The Quest for Competitive Advantage*, 14th ed. (New York: McGraw-Hill, 2005), 5.
3. Gandolofo Dominici, "From Marketing Mix to E-Marketing Mix: A Literature Overview and Classification," *CCSE International Journal of Business and Management*, September 2009, Vol. 4, No 9.
4. Neil H. Borden, "The Concept of the Marketing Mix," *Journal of Advertising Research*, June 1964, Vol. 4, No. 2.
5. "Apple Launches iPad," Apple Inc. Press Release, January 27, 2010, http://www.apple.com/pr/library/2010/01/27Apple-Launches-iPad.html.

6. Ibid.
7. Philip Kotler and Gary Armstrong, *Principles of Marketing*, 15th ed. (Boston: Pearson, 2014), Kindle Edition, 228.
8. Rosser Reeves, *Reality in Advertising* (New York: Knopf, 1961).
9. Al Ries and Jack Trout, *Positioning: The Battle for Your Mind* (New York: McGraw-Hill, 2001), Kindle Edition.
10. Tom Connellan, *Inside the Magic Kingdom: Seven Keys to Disney's Success* (Atlanta: Bard Press, 1997), Chapter 3.

Chapter 6

1. Alfred D. Chandler Jr., *Strategy and Structure: Chapters in the History of the American Industrial Enterprise* (Cambridge, MA: MIT Press, 1962, 1990), Kindle Edition.
2. Aristotle, *Poetics*, trans. S. H. Butcher (Public Domain), Kindle Edition, VII.
3. Ibid., VI.
4. Dr. Gustav Freytag, *Technique of the Drama: An Exposition of Dramatic Composition and Art*, trans. Elias J. MacEwan (Chicago: Scott Foresman and Company, 1900), Kindle Edition.
5. *Up*, directed by Pete Docter and Bob Peterson (Walt Disney Pictures, 2009).
6. Daniel Liu Bowling, Janani Sundararajan, Shui'er Han, and Dale Purves, "Expression of Emotion in Eastern and Western Music Mirrors Vocalization," *PLoS ONE*, 2012, 7(3):e31942. doi:10.1371/journal.pone.0031942.
7. Albert Mehrabian, *Silent Messages* (Belmont, CA: Wadsworth, 1971).

Chapter 7

1. "Responsibility Assignment Matrix," *Wikipedia*, last modified December 13, 2014, http://en.wikipedia.org/wiki/Responsibility_assignment_matrix.

Chapter 8

1. Robert S. Kaplan and David P. Norton, *The Balanced Scorecard: Translating Strategy into Action* (Boston: Harvard Business Review Press, 1996).

Chapter 9

1. "Aria," Encyclopædia Britannica, Encyclopædia Britannica Online, Encyclopædia Britannica Inc., accessed March 15, 2015, http://www.britannica.com/EBchecked/topic/34102/aria.

RESOURCES

The following books are all a part of my personal library. Some were used as points of reference for *Creative Strategy Generation*, while others have served as sources of inspiration and influence for my own practices, processes, and creativity over the years.

Business

Aguilar, Francis Joseph. *Scanning the Business Environment*. New York: Macmillan, 1967.

Ansoff, H. Igor. *Corporate Strategy*. New York: McGraw-Hill, 1965.

Berman, Karen, and Joe Knight, with John Case. *Financial Intelligence*. Boston: Harvard Business Review Press, 2013.

Chandler, Alfred D., Jr. *Strategy and Structure: Chapters in the History of the American Industrial Enterprise*. Cambridge, MA: The MIT Press, 1962.

Christensen, Clayton M. *The Innovator's Dilemma*. Boston: Harvard Business Review Press, 1997.

Collins, Jim. *Good to Great*. New York: Harper Business, 2001.

Cooper, Alan. *The Inmates Are Running the Asylum*. Indianapolis: SAMS, 2004.

Day, George S., and Christine Moorman. *Strategy from the Outside In*. New York: McGraw-Hill, 2010.

Dixit, Avinash K., and Barry J. Nalebuff. *Thinking Strategically*. New York: W.W. Norton & Company, 1991.

Donovan, Jeremy. *How to Deliver a TED Talk*. New York: McGraw-Hill, 2014.

Dranove, David, and Sonia Marciano. *Kellogg on Strategy*. Hoboken, NJ: John Wiley & Sons, 2005.

Duarte, Nancy. *Resonate*. Hoboken, NJ: John Wiley & Sons, 2010.

Duggan, William. *Strategic Intuition*. New York: Columbia University Press, 2007.

Freedman, Lawrence. *Strategy: A History*. Oxford, UK: Oxford University Press, 2013.

Gerzema, John, and Ed Lebar. *The Brand Bubble*. San Francisco, CA: Jossey-Bass, 2008.

Haines, Steven. *Managing Product Management*. New York: McGraw-Hill, 2012.

Haines, Steven. *The Product Manager's Desk Reference*, 2nd ed. New York: McGraw-Hill, 2014.

Haines, Steven. *The Product Manager's Survival Guide*. New York: McGraw-Hill, 2013.

Hayzlett, Jeffrey, with Jim Eber. *Running the Gauntlet*. New York: McGraw-Hill, 2012.

Horwath, Rich. *Deep Dive*. Austin, TX: Greenleaf Book Group Press, 2009.

Ittelson, Thomas. *Financial Statements*. Franklin Lakes, NJ: Career Press, 1998.

Johnson, Mark W. *Seizing the White Space*. Boston: Harvard Business Press, 2010.

Kaplan, Robert S., and David P. Norton. *The Balanced Scorecard: Translating Strategy into Action*. Boston: Harvard Business Review Press, 1996.

Kiechel, Walter, III. *The Lords of Strategy*. Boston: Harvard Business Press, 2010.

Kim, W. Chan, and Renée Mauborgne. *Blue Ocean Strategy*. Boston: Harvard Business School Press, 2005.

Kotler, Philip, and Gary Armstrong. *Principles of Marketing*, 15th ed. Boston: Pearson, 2014.

Lafley, A. G., and Roger L. Martin. *Playing to Win: How Strategy Really Works*. Boston: Harvard Business Review Press, 2013.

Levitt, Theodore. *The Marketing Imagination*. New York: The Free Press, 1986.

McGrath, Michael E. *Product Strategy for High-Technology Companies*, 2nd ed. New York: McGraw-Hill, 2001.

McKeown, Max. *The Strategy Book*. Harlow, England: Pearson, 2012.

Mehrabian, Albert. *Silent Messages*. Belmont, CA: Wadsworth, 1971.

Mintzberg, Henry. *The Rise and Fall of Strategic Planning*. New York: The Free Press, 1994.

Mintzberg, Henry, Bruce Ahlstrand, and Joseph Lampel. *Strategy Safari*. New York: The Free Press, 1998.

Montgomery, Cynthia A. *The Strategist*. New York: Harper Business, 2012.

Moore, Geoffrey A. *Crossing the Chasm*. New York: HarperCollins, 1991.

Moore, J. I. *Writers on Strategy and Strategic Management*, 2nd ed. London: Penguin Books, 2001.

Murray, Chris. *The Marketing Gurus*. New York: Penguin Group, 2006.

Nierenberg, Roger. *Maestro*. New York: Portfolio, 2009.

Ohmae, Kenichi. *The Mind of the Strategist*. New York: McGraw-Hill, 1982.

Olsen, Erica. *Strategic Planning Kit for Dummies*, 2nd ed. Hoboken, NJ: John Wiley & Sons, 2012.

Pink, Daniel H. *A Whole New Mind*. New York: Riverhead Books, 2005.

Pope, Atlee Valentine, and George F. Brown Jr. *CoDestiny*. Austin, TX: Greenleaf Book Group Press, 2011.

Porter, Michael E. *Competitive Advantage*. New York: The Free Press, 1985.

Porter, Michael E. *Competitive Strategy*. New York: The Free Press, 1980.

Ries, Al, and Jack Trout, *Positioning: The Battle for Your Mind*. New York: McGraw-Hill, 2001.

Robert, Michel. *The Power of Strategic Thinking*. New York: McGraw-Hill, 2000.

Rumelt, Richard P. *Good Strategy, Bad Strategy*. New York: Crown Business, 2011.

Simmons, Gene. *Me, Inc.* New York: Dey Street Books, 2014.

Thompson, Arthur A., Jr., A. J. Strickland III, and John E. Gamble. *Crafting and Executing Strategy: The Quest for Competitive Advantage*, 14th ed. New York: McGraw-Hill, 2005.

Treacy, Michael, and Fred Wiersema. *The Discipline of Market Leaders.* Cambridge, MA: Perseus Books, 1995.

Underhill, Paco. *Why We Buy.* New York: Simon & Schuster, 2009.

Weissman, Jerry. *Presenting to Win.* Upper Saddle River, NJ: FT Press, 2006.

West, G. Page III. *Strategic Management*, 2nd ed. Winston-Salem, NC: Riderwood Publishing, 2013.

Music and Creativity

Adler, Samuel. *The Study of Orchestration*, 3rd ed. New York: W.W. Norton & Company, 2002.

Braheny, John. *The Craft and Business of Songwriting.* Cincinnati, OH: Writer's Digest Books, 1988.

Citron, Stephen. *Songwriting: A Complete Guide to the Craft.* New York: Limelight Editions, 1998.

Cohen, Allen, and Steven L. Rosenhaus. *Writing Musical Theater.* New York: Palgrave Macmillan, 2006.

Cooke, Mervyn. *A History of Film Music.* Cambridge, UK: Cambridge University Press, 2008.

Freytag, Dr. Gustav. *Technique of the Drama: An Exposition of Dramatic Composition and Art*, trans. Elias J. MacEwan. Chicago: Scott Foresman and Company, 1900.

Horowitz, Mark Eden. *Sondheim on Music.* Lanham, MD: The Scarecrow Press, 2003.

Kennan, Kent, and Donald Grantham. *The Technique of Orchestration*, 6th ed. Upper Saddle River, NJ: Prentice Hall, 2002.

Pejrolo, Andrea, and Richard DeRosa. *Acoustic and MIDI Orchestration for the Contemporary Composer.* Burlington, MA: Focal Press, 2007.

Perry, Megan. *How to Be a Record Producer in the Digital Era.* New York: Billboard Books, 2008.

Rachel, Daniel. *The Art of Noise: Conversations with Great Songwriters.* New York: St. Martin's Griffin, 2013.

Robinson, Ken. *Out of Our Minds: Learning to Be Creative*, 2nd ed. West Sussex, UK: Capstone Publishing, 2011.

Tucker, Susan. *The Secrets of Songwriting.* New York: Allworth Press, 2003.

Waterman, J. Douglas, ed. *Song: The World's Best Songwriters on Creating the Music That Moves Us.* Cincinnati, OH: Writer's Digest Books, 2007.

Webb, Jimmy. *Tunesmith: Inside the Art of Songwriting.* New York: Hyperion, 1998.

Zollo, Paul. *Songwriters on Songwriting*, 4th ed. Cincinnati, OH: Da Capo Press, 2003.

INDEX

ABOUT THE AUTHOR

Bob Caporale is the president of Sequent Learning Networks, a New York City–based training and advisory firm specializing in product management, product marketing, and strategic planning. Throughout his career, Bob has held leadership and executive roles in engineering, marketing, product management, and general management for multi-billion-dollar companies such as Pirelli and Thomas & Betts Corporation. He can be contacted for consulting and advisory work at **http://www.sequentlearning.com.**

Bob is also an accomplished keyboardist, composer, and songwriter. He has written and produced over 100 independently released songs, albums, and soundtracks and has also written a full-length musical that he hopes to find time to produce someday! Links to his music can be found at **http://www.bobcaporale.com.**